# Comic Maths

Brian Williamson

COMIC MATHS
ISBN 978-0-9561602-0-1

First Edition



Cover design by Kathryn Wilson, character concepts by Brian Williamson

Illustrations in the text by Brian Williamson apart from:-

Cannon, canon firing ice creams on front pages and Comic Maths word art
by Kathryn Wilson
John's 1 and 2 in comic number 4
by George Williamson
Improved larger footballs in Answers in The Back
by Alice Williamson



First published in 2009
Brian Williamson Publishing
Visit me at www.DrBrianWilliamson.com



A Cataloging-in-Publication (CIP) record of this book is held at the British Library and at the Library of Congress.

To Mum and Dad

# SPECIAL THANKS

to the hundreds of brilliant children who have worked with me on this book!

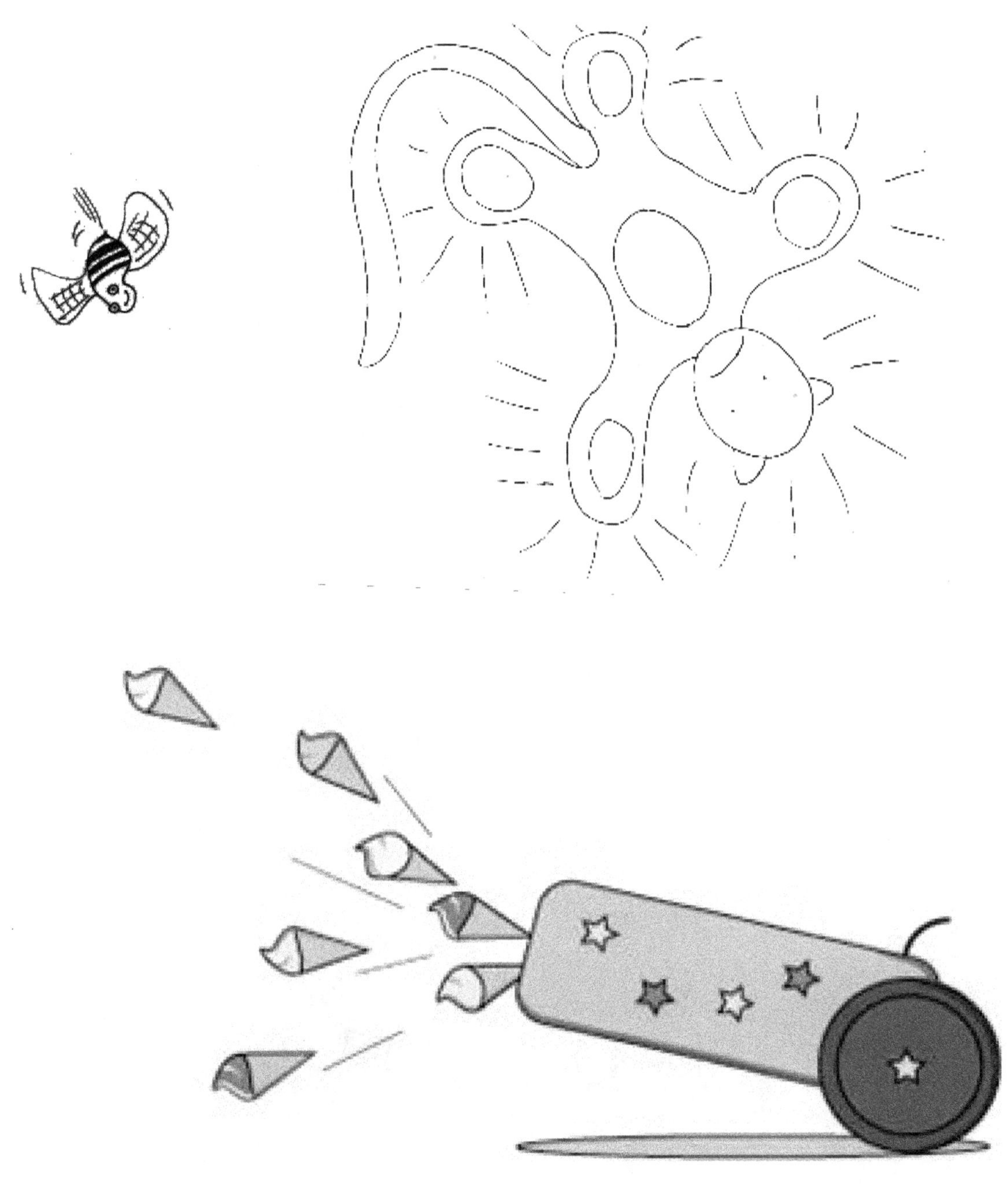

# Welcome to Comic Maths!

**From Sue, John and Anne Betty, Charlie the Monkey, Bill, John, Granddad, Anne's Mum, Kilo and Milli...**

and . . .

# BIG ROBERT

Age 19
who knows everything

and other friends.

Hi from Brian the author.

This book has been written for young English-speaking children everywhere! It concerns pre-number, number, pre-algebra, measure, geometry, handling data and chance. It aims to address aspects of learning such as confidence, exploration, imagination, making mistakes and motivation.

Comic Maths features Sue, John and Anne (best friends!), Granddad and Bill (wise old professors), Anne's mum (who likes to see what the children are doing), Betty (who is a really clever fun friend), Kilo, Milli and Charlie the Monkey, who all do their best to entertain us! Crazy Baby makes us think by saying those things that only babies can say! Big Robert (Age 19) knows more than most people and is just a bit bossy sometimes!! Guests like The Little People, Hedgehog, Flat face Round bottom and Buzzy Bee, appear throughout!

Towards the end of the book you will find the '*Comic Maths Colouring Book*', '*Extra Sums for Greedy People*', '*Notes for Grown-ups*', '*Answers in the Back*' and a '*Where to find it*' index.

Thanks are due to everyone, who has known this book is on its way, for their encouragement and patience. Thanks to all the children, some now grown-ups themselves, who have worked on maths with me. Thanks to Kathryn Wilson for bringing the cover to life, to Hillary from Lulu Support for her advice, to George and Alice for their support, and to my special mentor, Jane, for listening.

Comic Maths has been fun to make.
I hope that it will be fun for you as well!

Brian Williamson Ph.D.

21st June 2009

# The Chooser

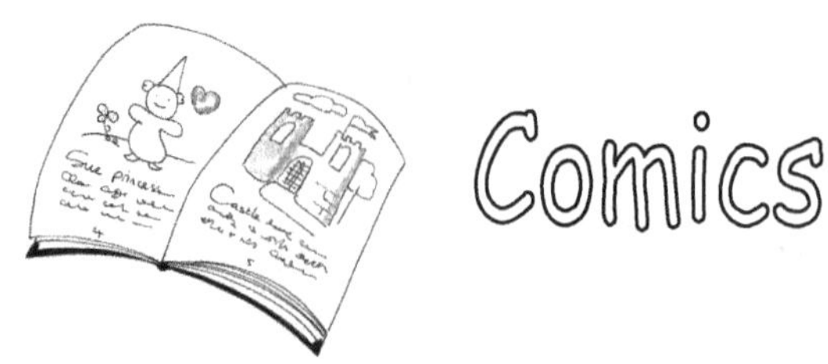

# Comics

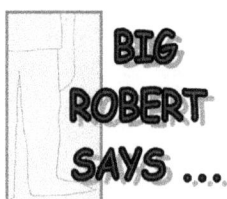

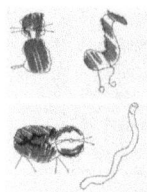

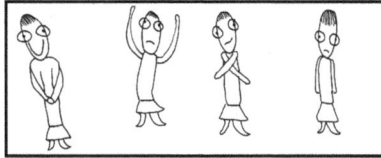

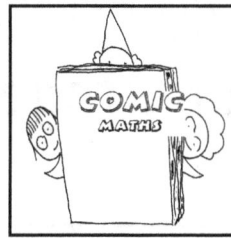

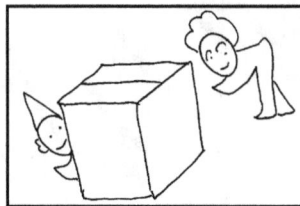

# Hi from the Comic Maths Family.

Children, monkeys, grasshoppers and aliens ... it's a big HI from the Comic Maths Family on stage for the very first time ever!!!!

The Comic Maths Family say Hi ...
Please clap!

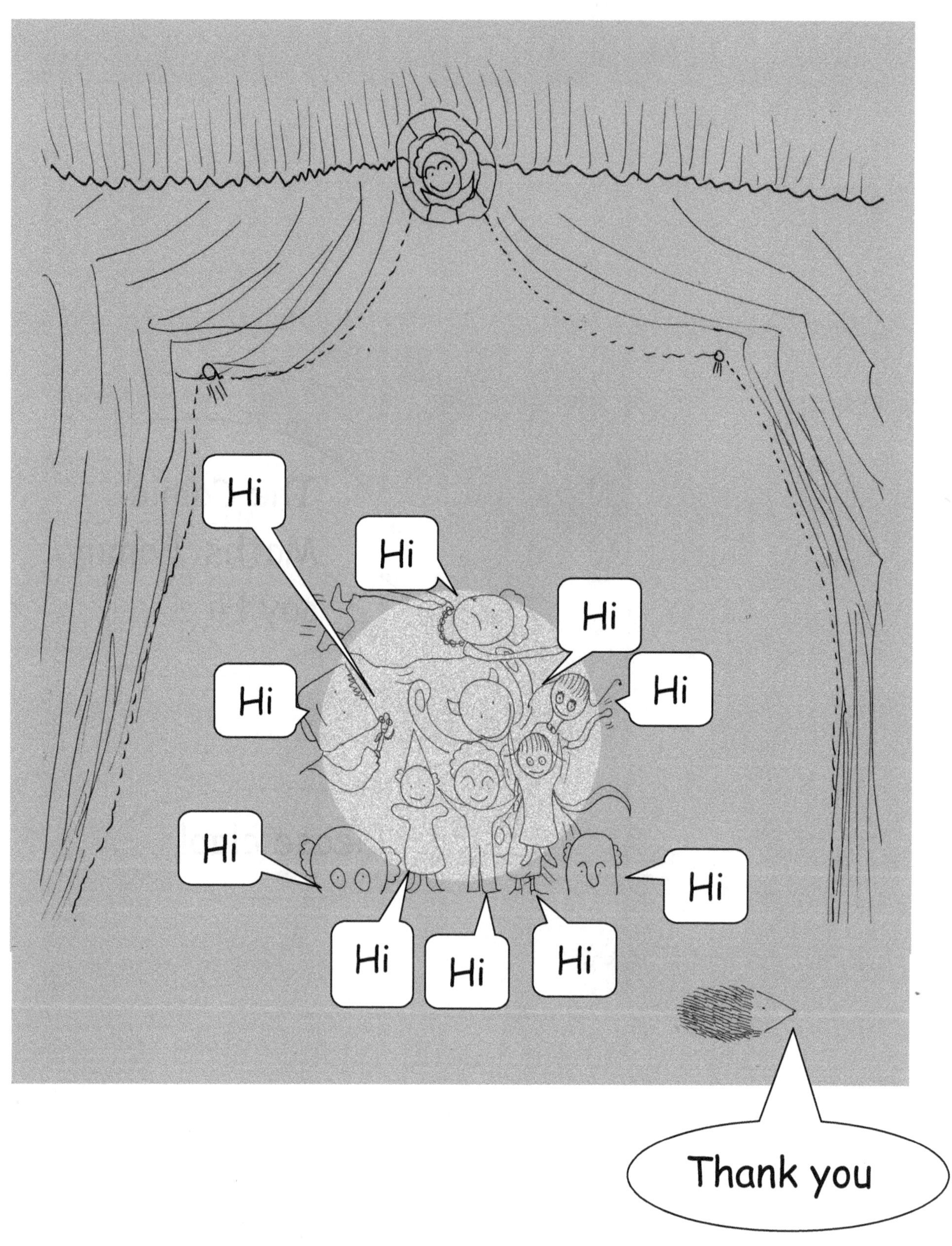
Hi
Hi
Hi
Hi
Hi
Hi
Hi
Hi
Hi
Hi
Thank you

... and for our
special guest star
BIG ROBERT
clap louder!!

Now ladies and gentlemen there will be a short BREAK ... and then a story about John.
Thank you

Go away John!!!!

A Story about John
John likes drawing
Drawing is the best thing ever!
Drawing footballs is the very very best!!!!
John likes football.
Football is best!
I could do that ALL day!!

Maths is bad and boring.
It is NOT drawing.
It is NOT football!!
Yes it is!
It is both!!
Is not both.
IS
Not Is
Not Is
Not Is
Not Is
Don't be children children!

**You can draw pictures to learn maths.
You can play games to learn maths.
They will see!! ...**

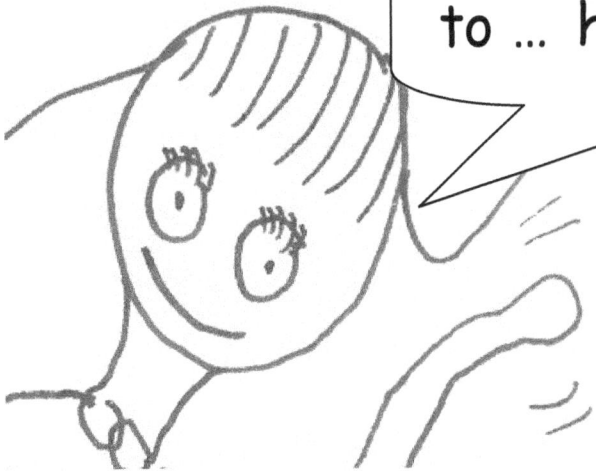

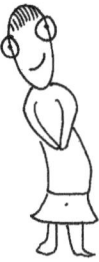

We can do sums in our heads.
I can write sums on my hat!
WHY would anyone do that?
OK John likes to draw.
We will make a comic maths book for him!!!
John likes to play games.
READY Do it!! DONE.
OK Sue, but who is going to ... help???????

I wonder.

Who will help make the comics?

ME!!

and me!

and me!

and me!

and me!

and me!

and me!

and me!

and me!

and me!

… and don't forget little old BIG ROBERT ME!!

# Everyone can help!

**John,**
You can help by playing football and drawing pictures.

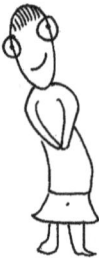

**Sue**,
You can help just by being a helpful person.

Always wear your party hat!

**Anne**,
I think that you should help by being clever all the time.

Your mum should learn her lessons from you!

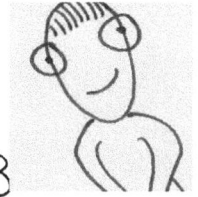

**Granddad,**

You know a lot of things about maths. We need your bright ideas.

Please keep on helping . . .

**Betty and Bill,**

Betty you are a clever and funny friend. Make us have fun!!!

Bill you are the best uncle. Help granddad and the children to work hard. Never give up!!

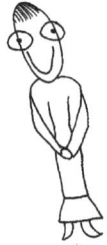

**Kilo,**
What would we do without you?

Give us strength. Help us to understand big numbers ...

. . . and stop banging your head!!

**Charlie!**
I wish that I could be a monkey like you and eat all those bananas. Milli the Monkey. Oh No!!!!

Big Robert,
Please stay around to answer difficult questions.
And me, Milli.
I will just be quiet and watch.
NO Milli.
You help us to understand little numbers!
kilo

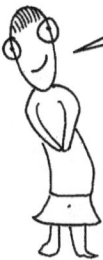

# You can help too . . .

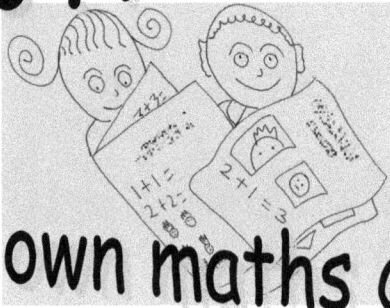

## make your own maths comics!

Sums are....

Draw John and Anne playing football. Draw Sue talking.

The Banana Dance!!

Draw granddad having an idea. Draw Charlie dancing.

Draw Milli being silly. Draw Kilo banging his head!

Make your own maths comics and give them to your friends!

Photocopy the next three pages.
Fill in the gaps with your own stories, games and ideas!

My Comic Story

| | |
|---|---|
| | |
| | |

## My Comic Maths Joke

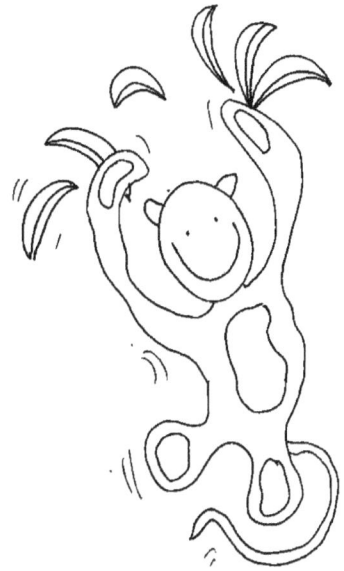

Do these sums!

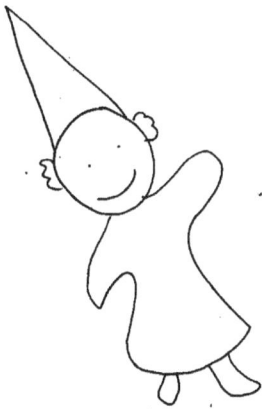

1.

2.

3.

4.

5.

## The hardest sum in the world!!!!

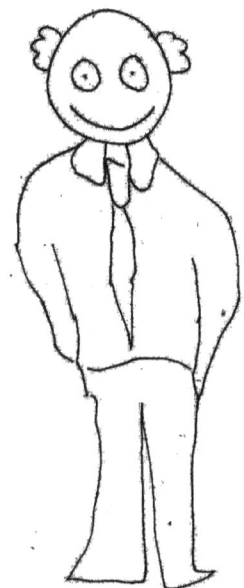

Play my Comic Maths made-up game.

# Hi from The Crazy Baby.

Anne, Sue and John found a baby.
This baby is different
Boo! Boo! Boo!
He **says** funny things!
Onions
... and **thinks** funny things!

... and does funny things!
CRAZY CRAZY BABY!

# A BIG Hi from BIG ROBERT.

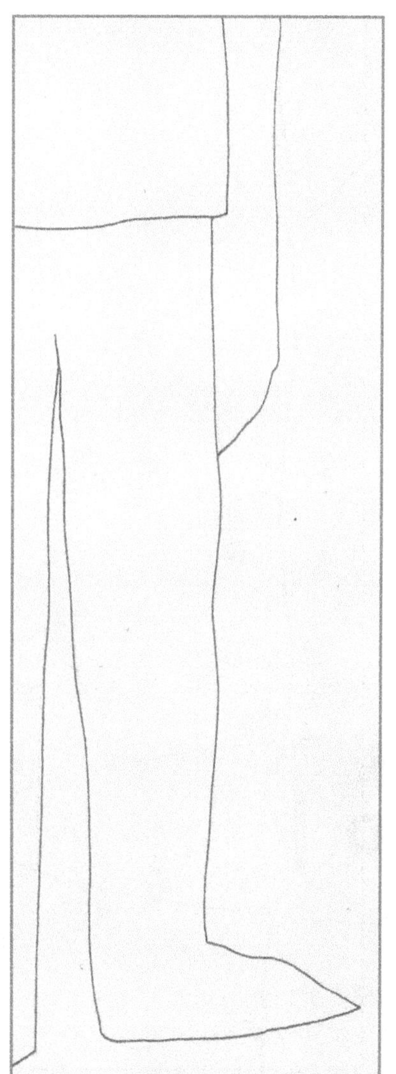

My name is

BIG ROBERT

. If you don't do what I say then I will ....

**matherize**

you!!!! (only joking)

Don't worry.

I got **matherized** once and it didn't hurt!

See you later!
ALLIGATOR!

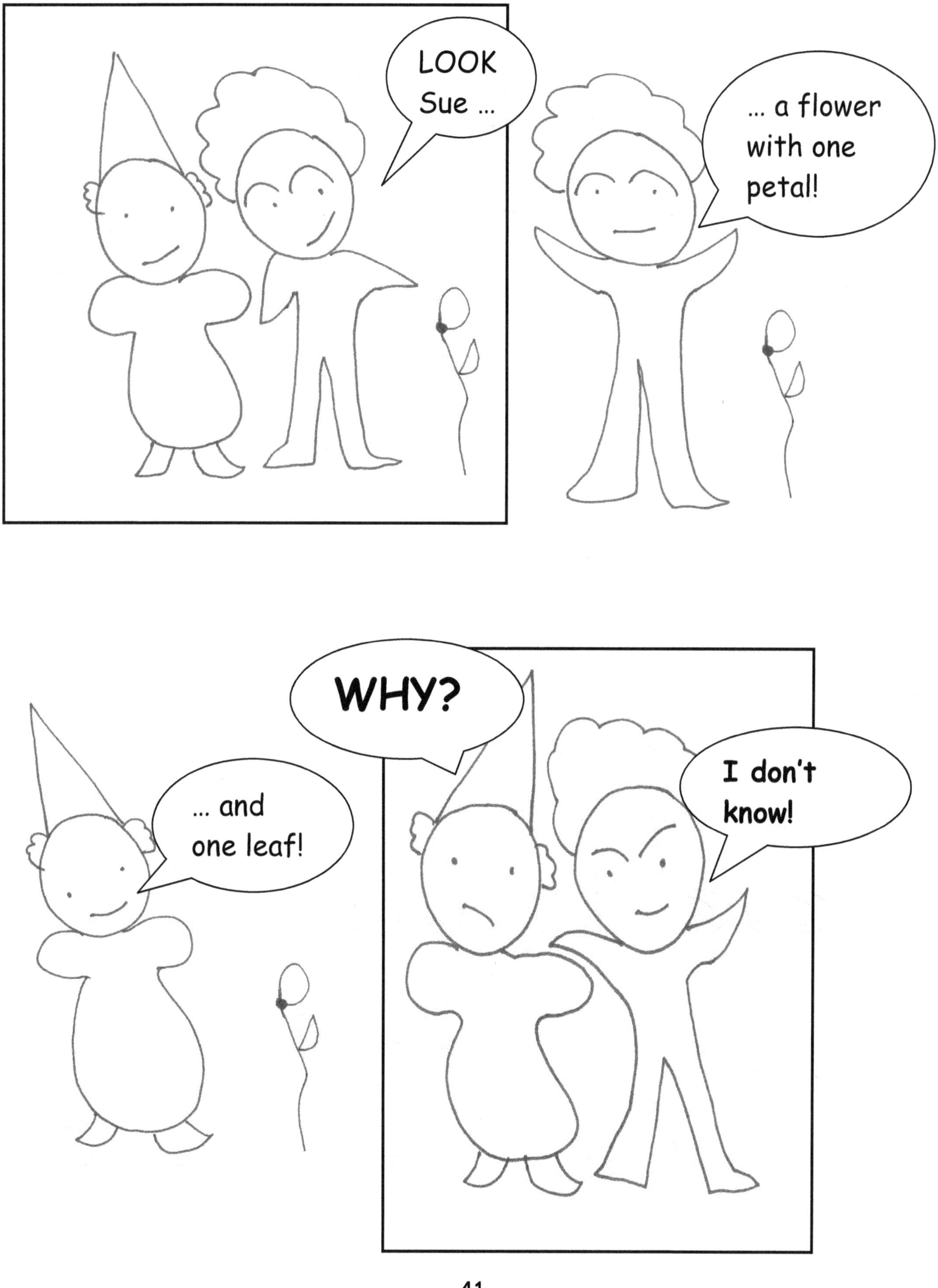

... and one leaf!

**WHY?**

**I don't know!**

1 2 3

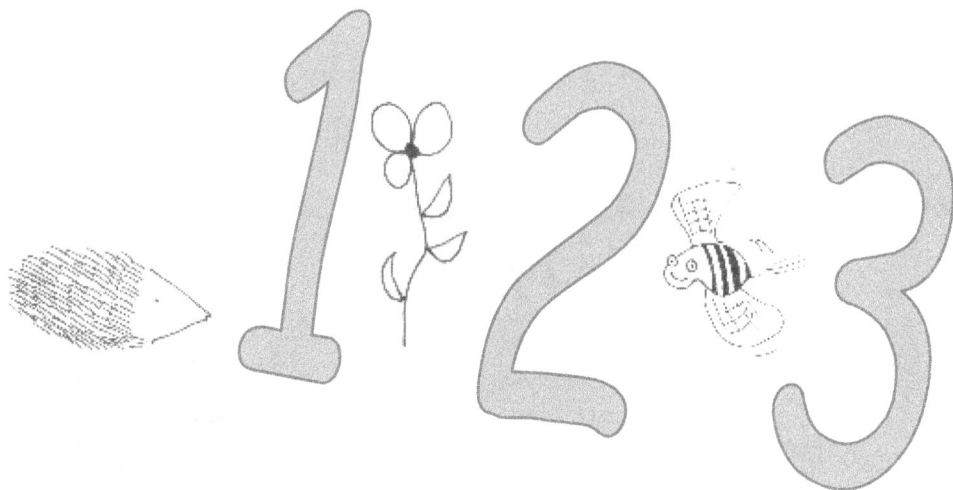

colour in these pictures

**COPY ME!**

2
two

1
3
three

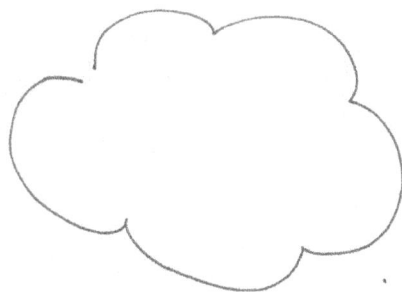

CRAZY BABY!
thinks about 3
three
It is a word
No it is a number.
One two three 1, 2, 3
3
3 elephants
3
3 suns
3 hiccups
I can have three. 3 fish. 3 chips. 3 chairs. 3 cats. 3 apples. 3 grandmas on toast. 3 friends. 3 houses. 3 trees. 3 flowers. 3 bowls of rice pudding. 3 birthdays a year . . .
STOP IT!!

John. Why do you always draw and paint things?
Because I am an ...
artist!!!

John drew some animals.

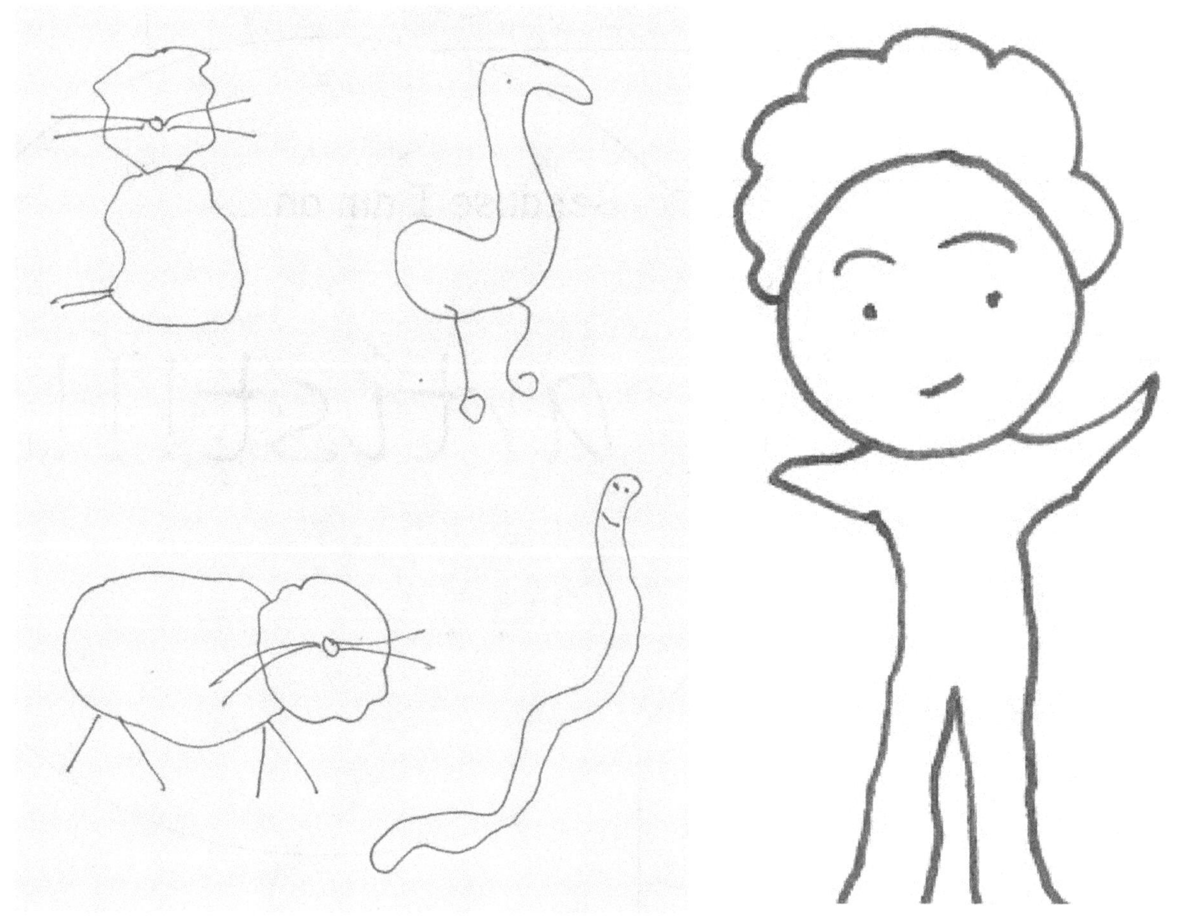

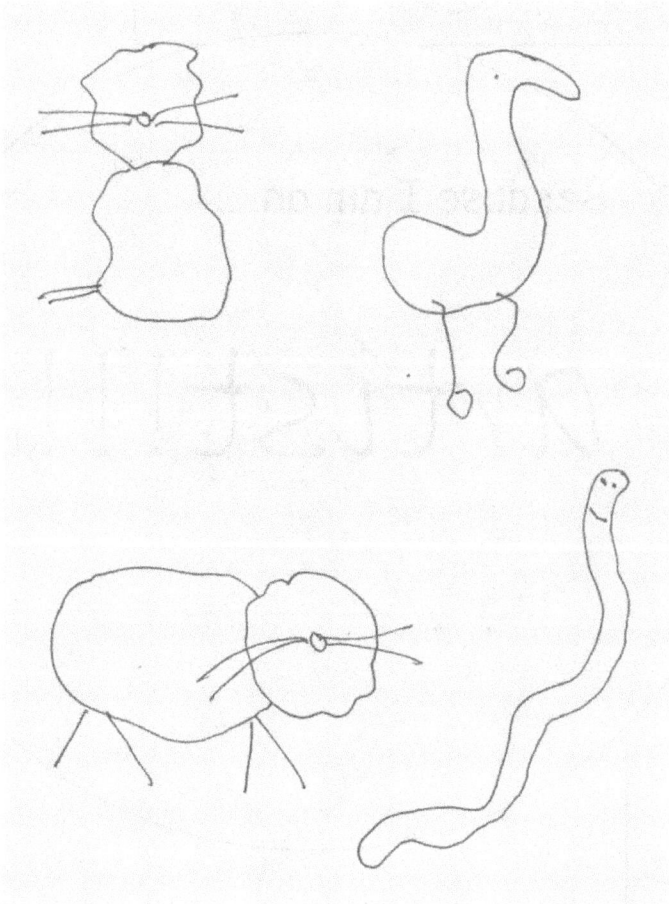

Sue coloured them in and counted.

1

2

3

4

There are 4 animals.

John drew some more animals.
Now you colour and count.

There are ___ animals.

John drew some aliens. Colour count these.

There are ___ aliens.

Thanks for telling me!

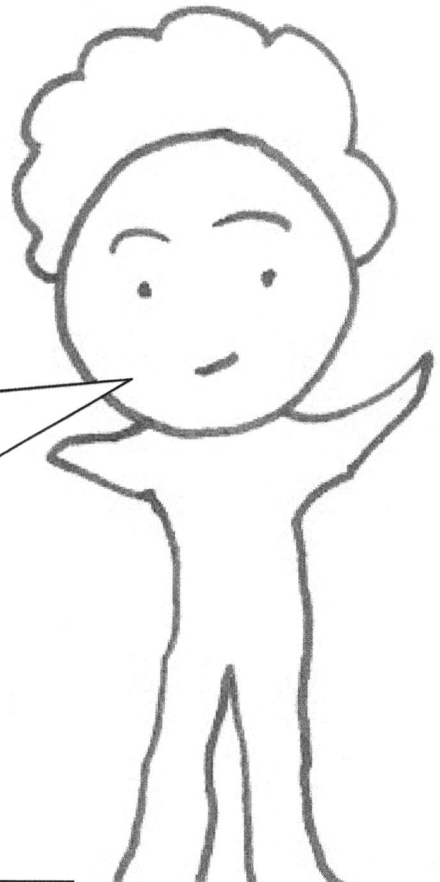

Colour and count the Comic Maths Family!

There are ____ of them.

**CRAZY BABY!** counts the aliens.

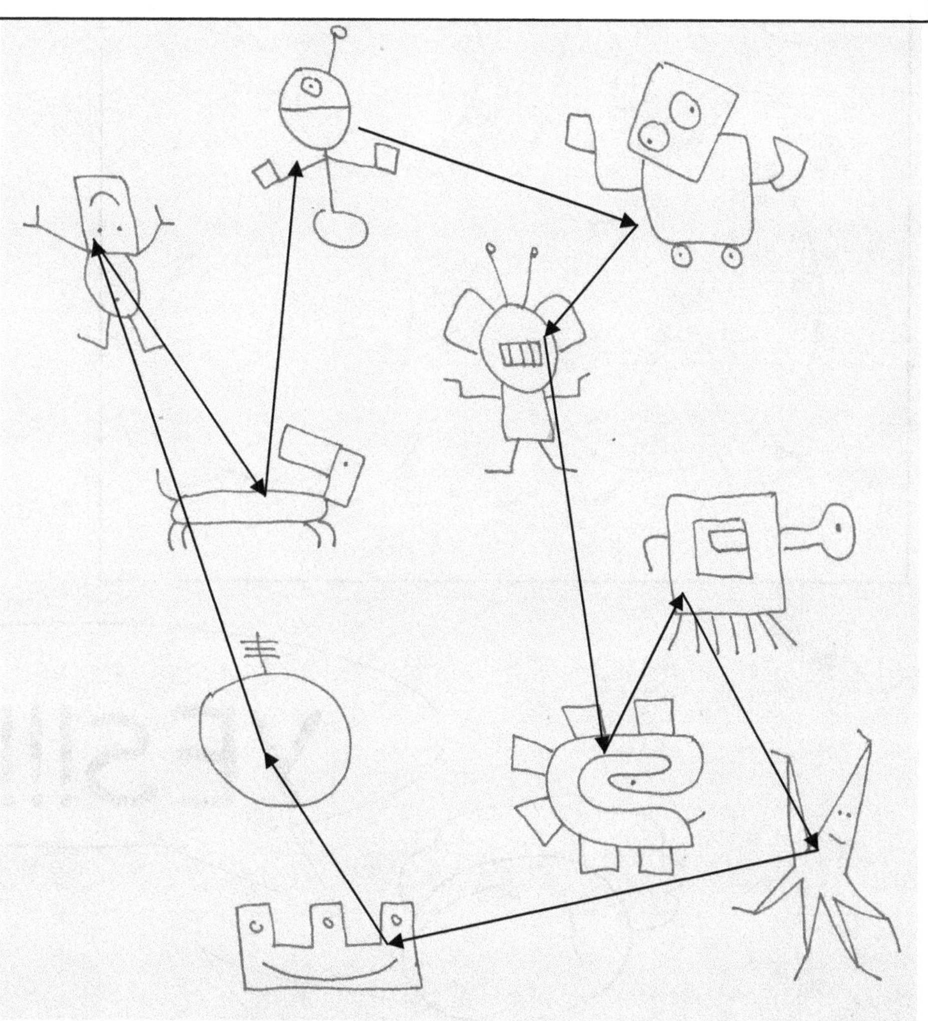

Which way did you count?

My way **CRAZY BABY!**

John ...
John ...

YES!!!!!!!!

Why do you play football?
Because I am a ...
FOOTBALLER!!

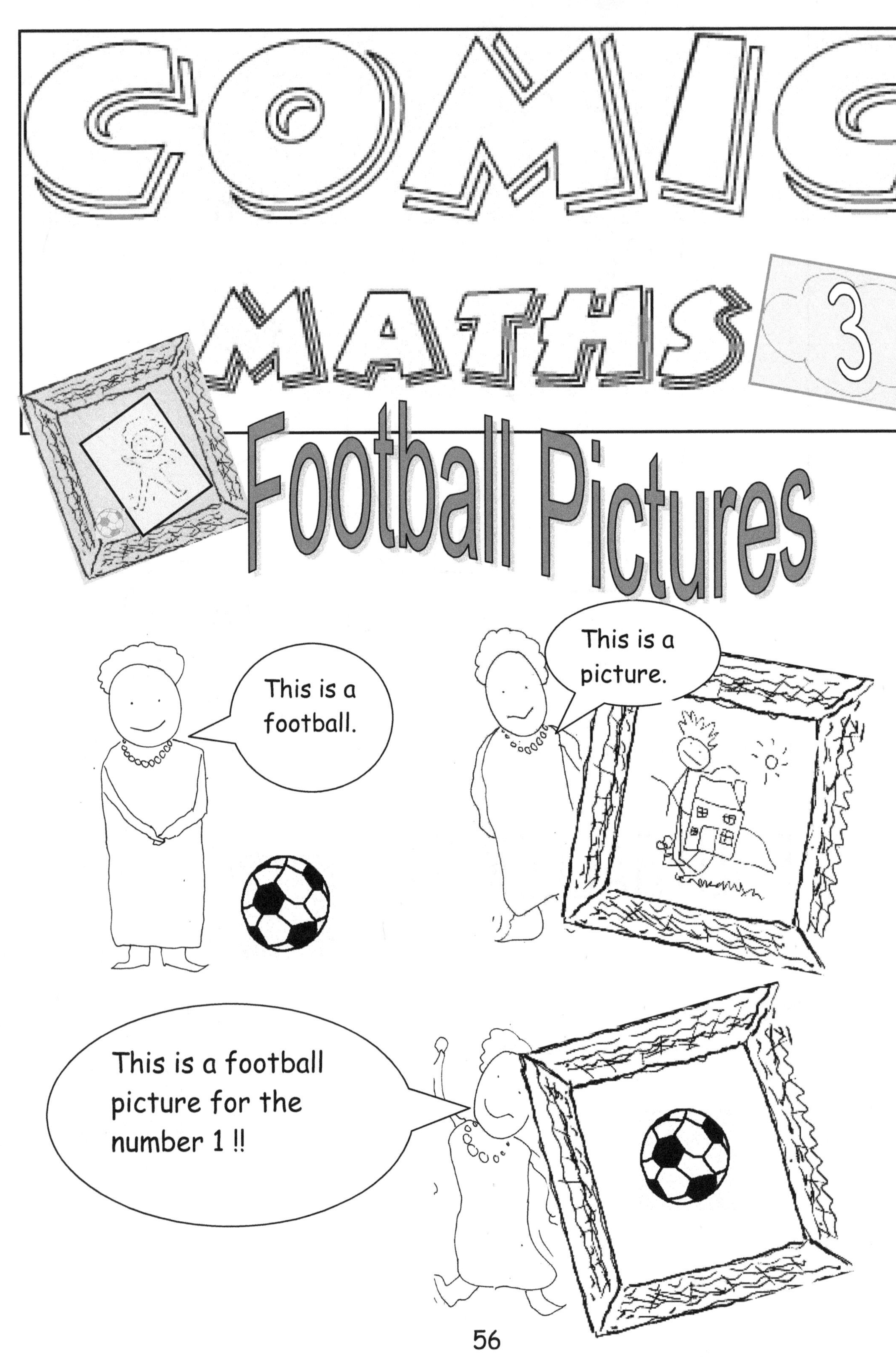
COMIC MATHS 3
Football Pictures
This is a football.
This is a picture.
This is a football picture for the number 1 !!

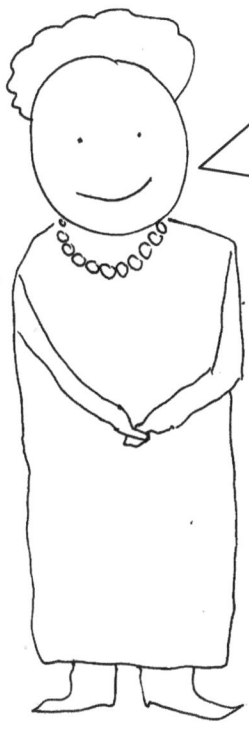

Draw more football pictures.

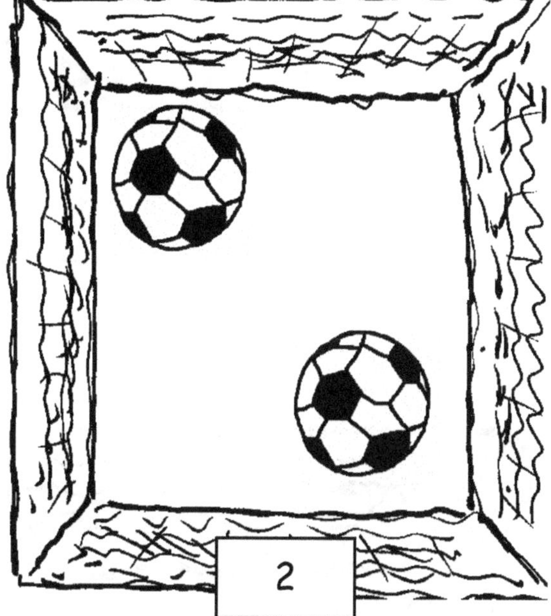
2

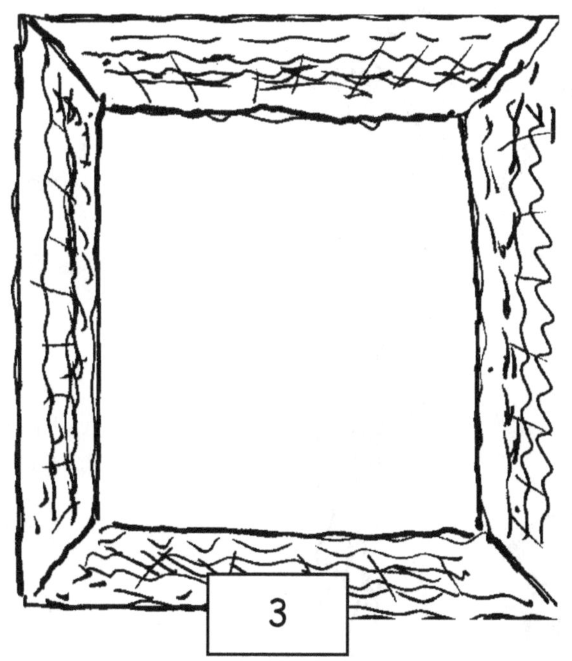
3

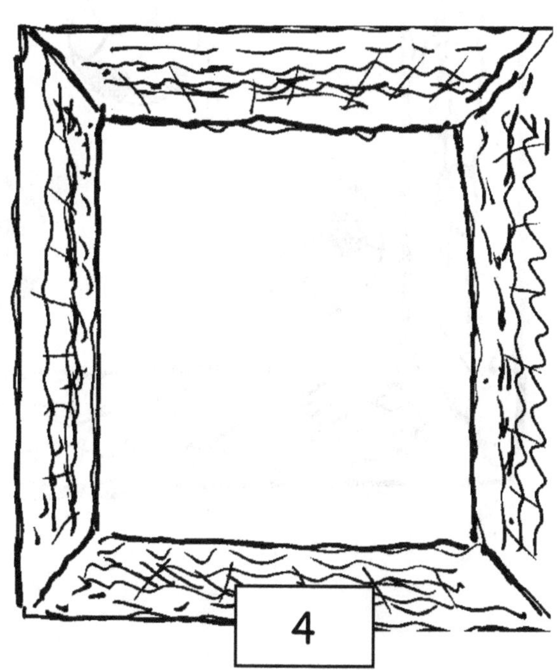
4

I like this football picture
because ...
4 footballs and 1 in the middle
makes 5.

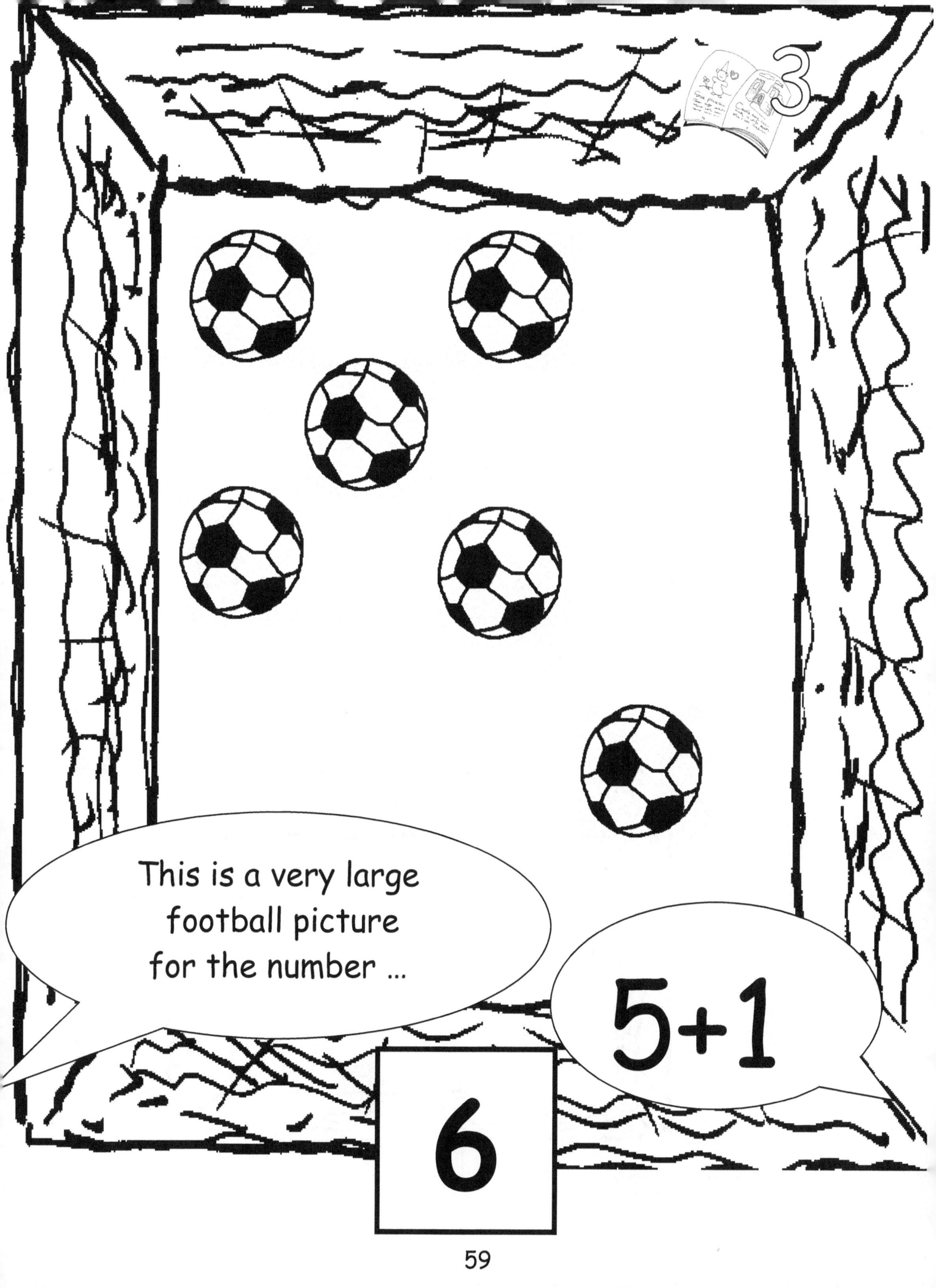
3
This is a very large
football picture
for the number ...
5+1
6

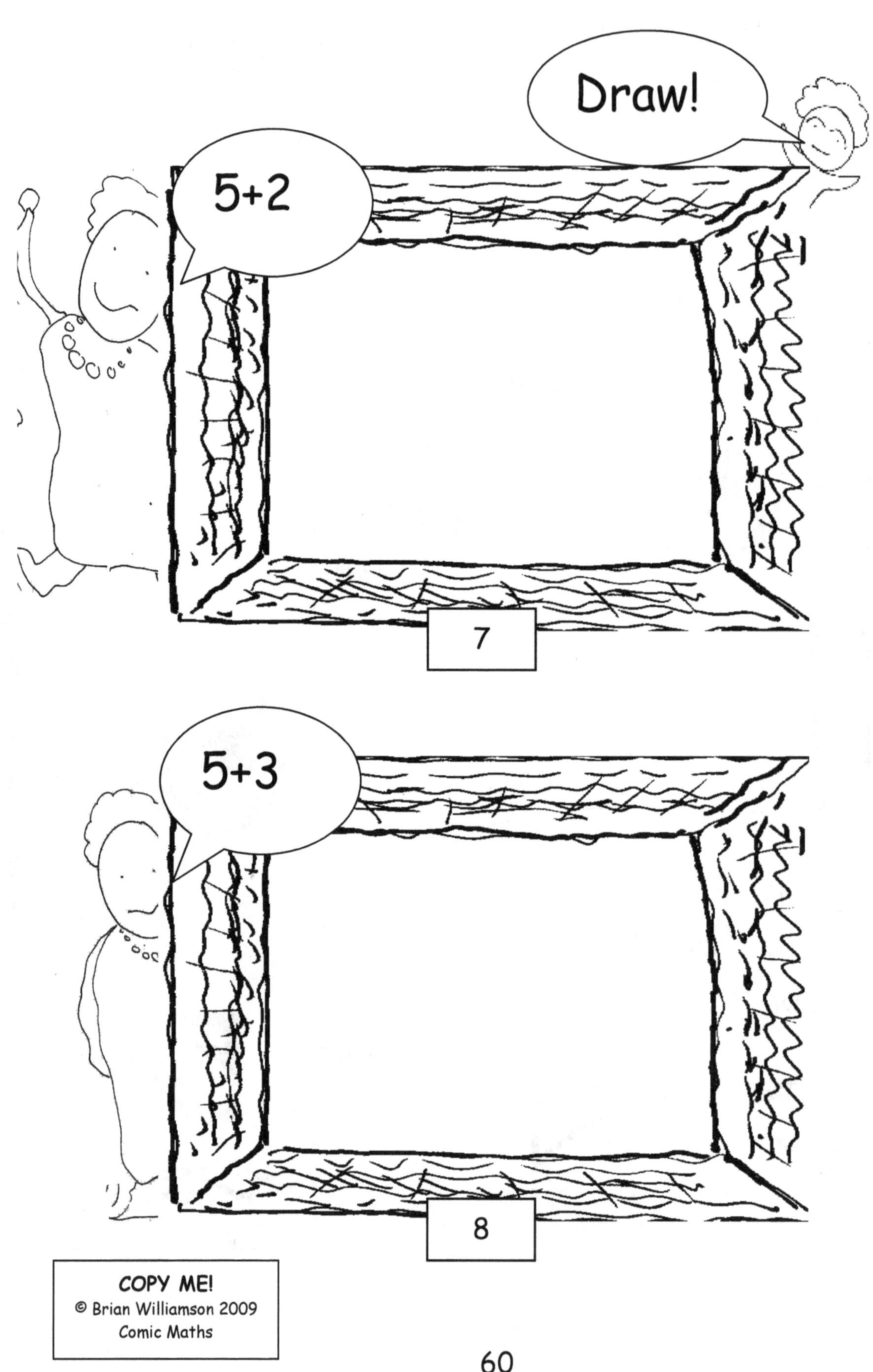
Draw!
5+2
7
5+3
8

3
Draw!
5+4
9
5+5
10

CRAZY BABY!
says 7 and 9
are like flowers
We grow the same way.
I feel like a flower!
What do you think 8 is like?
8 is like a ______________
COPY ME!
© Brian Williamson 2009
Comic Maths

John can draw anything.
NOT ANYTHING!!!

COMIC
MATHS
Play Writing
John can draw anything!!
He can!
He can make faces out of numbers.
Never
Look. Here are John's one and two.
Try to make some number faces of your own.

John drew a swan for Sue.

It looks like a two!

Anne drew an eight.

Anne eight!

John drew an eight a different way!

John is a SPACE ROCKET holding a pen!
Making rocket noises!! Making an eight!!

Eights are GREAT!!
You try
BE SAFE Ask a grown-up

# CRAZY BABY!

likes a picture

A picture of 8.

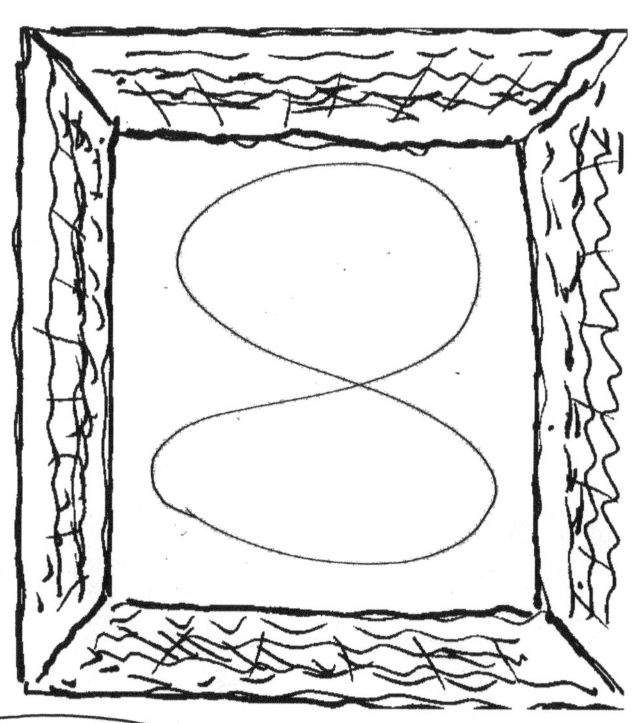

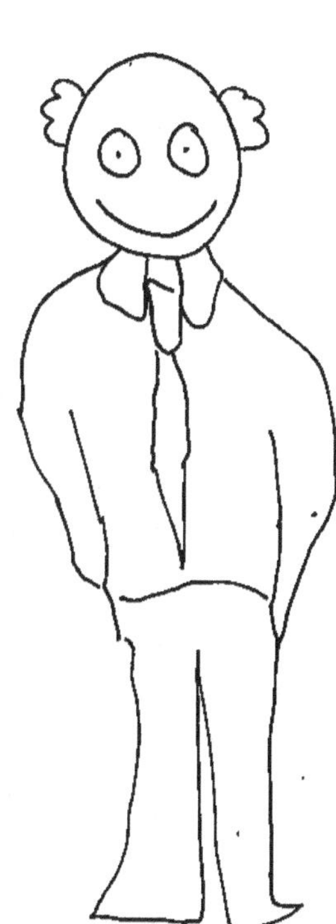

Beautiful!

# CRAZY BABY!

Is he crazy? ____

John, Sue and Anne meet Charlie the Monkey.

Do you always get your sums wrong?

Yes!!

# Charlie the Monkey the Mad Guesser!!!

How many footballs Charlie?
100
How many footballs Charlie?
2

Be Charlie.

# CRAZY BABY! learns is

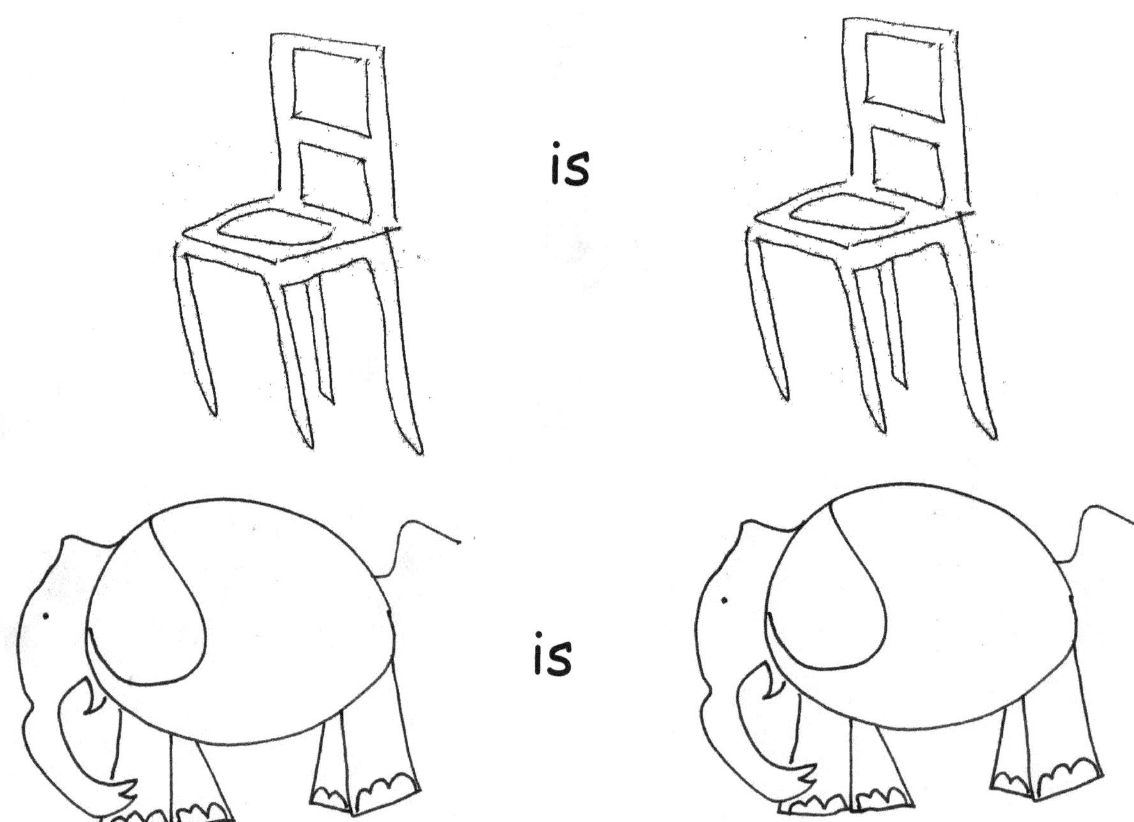


5 = 5

I know that!!!

John, Sue and Anne meet Betty the fortune teller.

Tomorrow Anne will have 6 eyes!!!!
CRAZY Betty!!

COMIC
MATHS 6
WHAT cOMES nEXT?????
I think that everyone would like to know
WHAT cOMES nEXT????? don't you?
Ask Charlie,
WHAT cOMES nEXT????
he's the mad guesser!

Draw the next monster . . .

Draw the next hedgehog

Draw the next fluffy cloud sheep . . .

Draw the next Anne's face . . .

?
Anne, how many eyes have you got?
5
HELP!!!!!

Anne can be so scary.
Tomorrow she will have 6 eyes!!

# CRAZY BABY!
makes a mess

Don't make a mess!!
Make it simple!!

Which is best? Mess or simple? ________

We are best friends.
I am the BEST friend!!!
NO!!

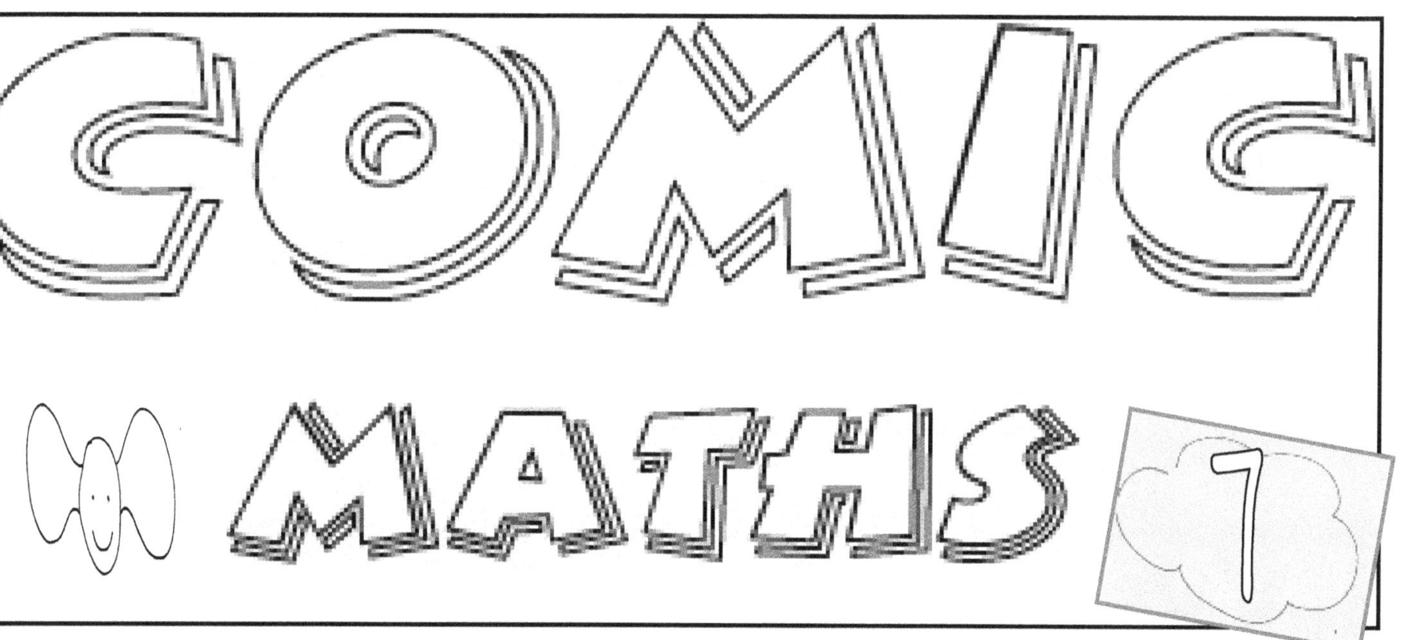


# My square is bigger than your square!

# My ears are bigger than your ears!

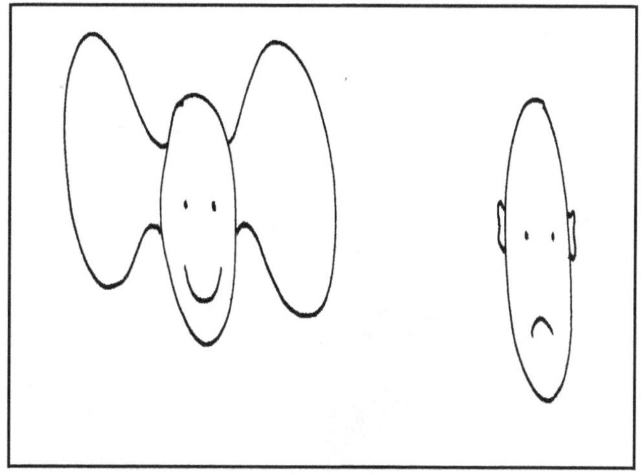

Colour in the person with the longest arms.

John is a cheat.

Colour in the heaviest person.

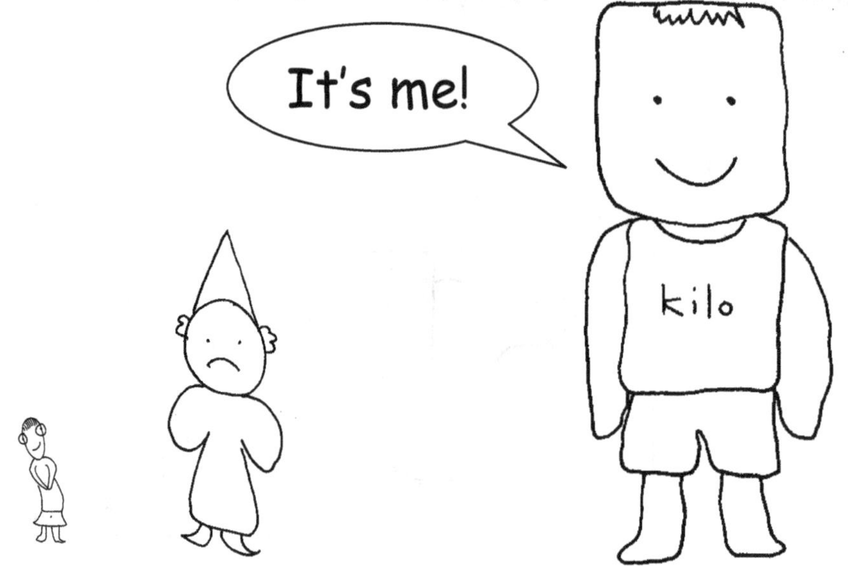
It's me!
kilo

Colour in the person with the biggest drink.

Colour in the person who has got the biggest square!

Play this game with your friends.

- Who can find the biggest ball?
- Who can find the biggest spoon?
- Who is the tallest?
- Who has the longest nose?

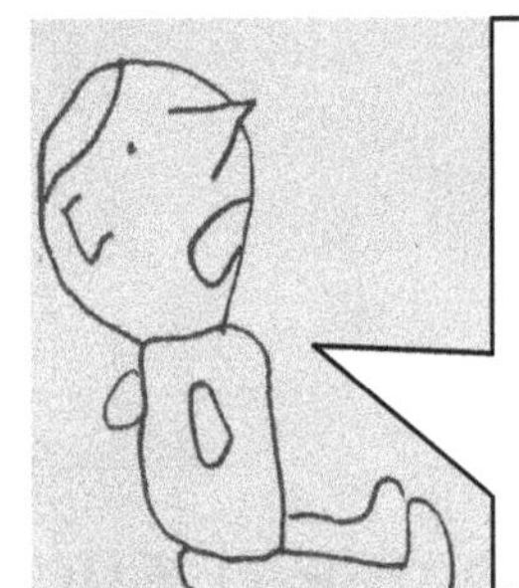

# CRAZY BABY!

meets monster number

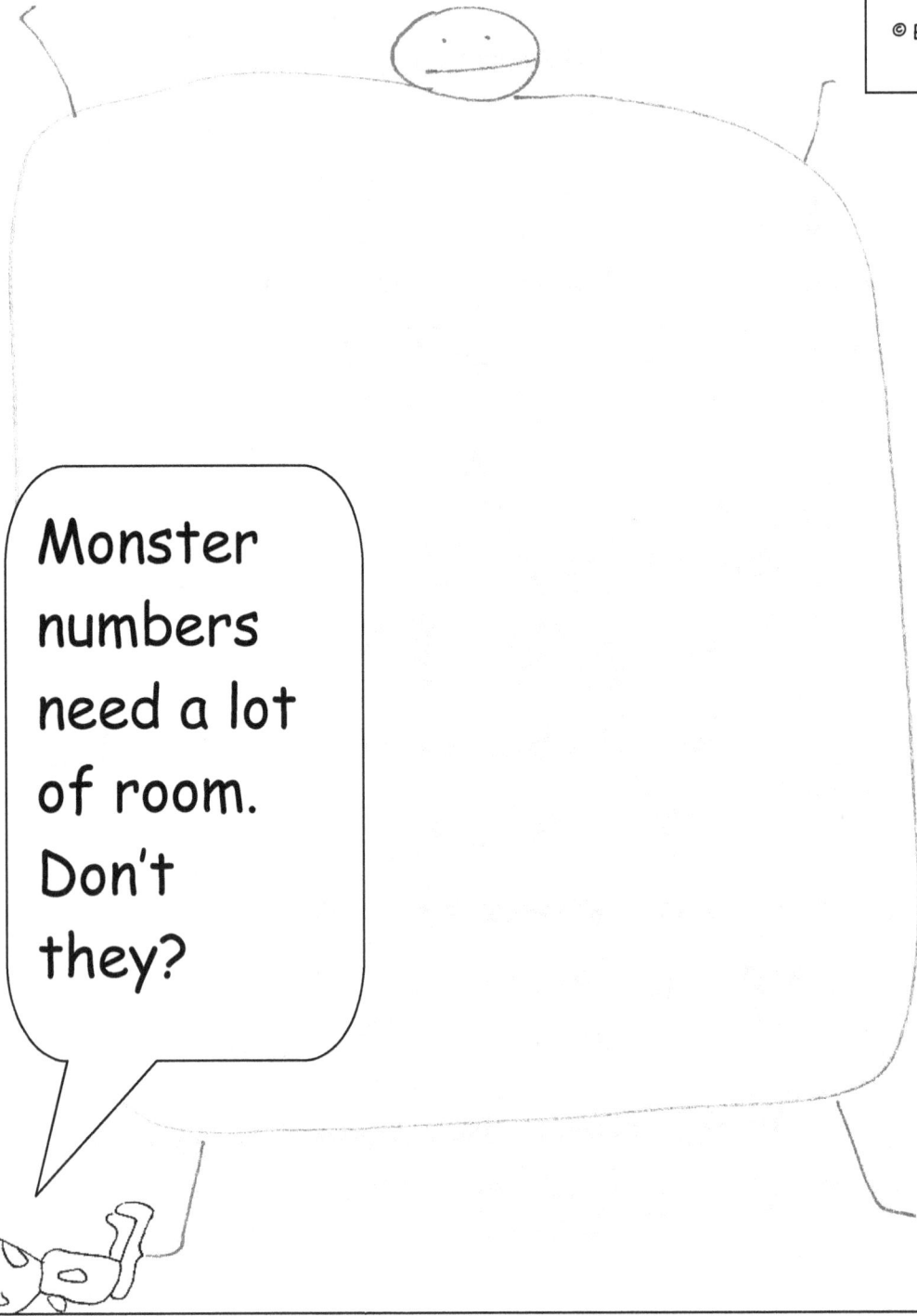

Monster numbers need a lot of room. Don't they?

What is the biggest number you know?

______________________________

Please may I take Anne to a party tonight?
No John. Her bedtime is 7 o'clock.

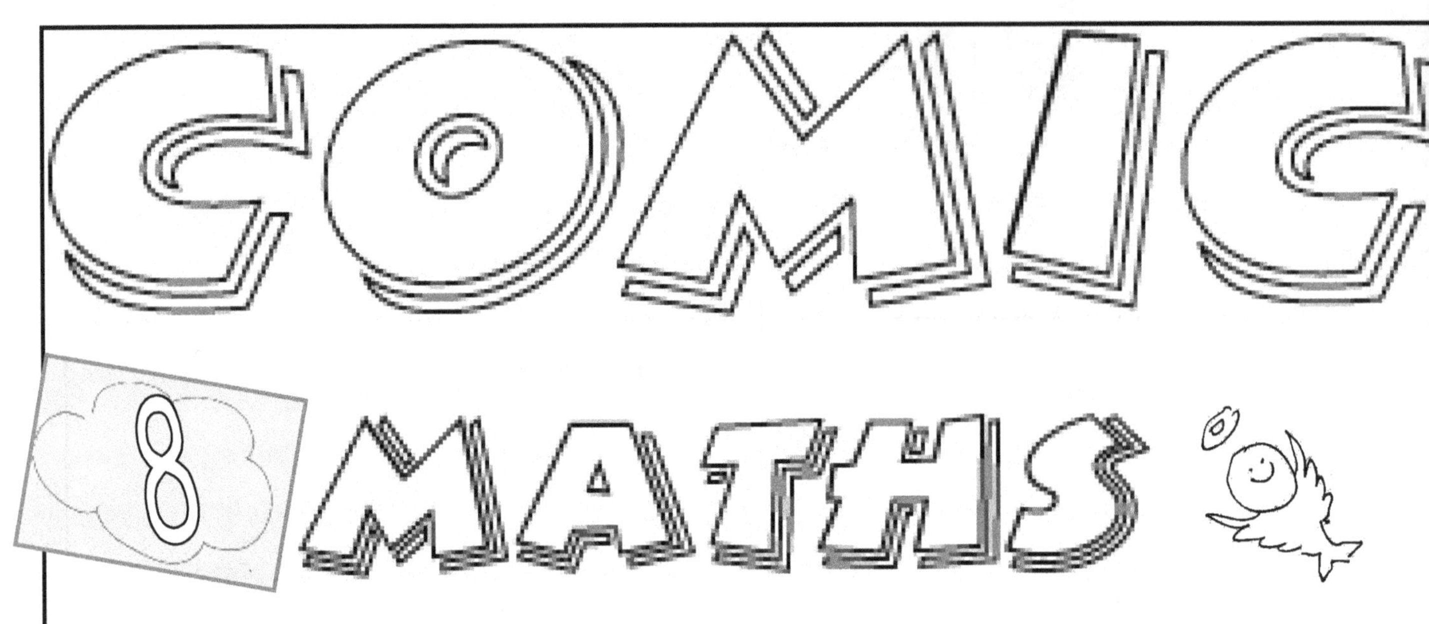

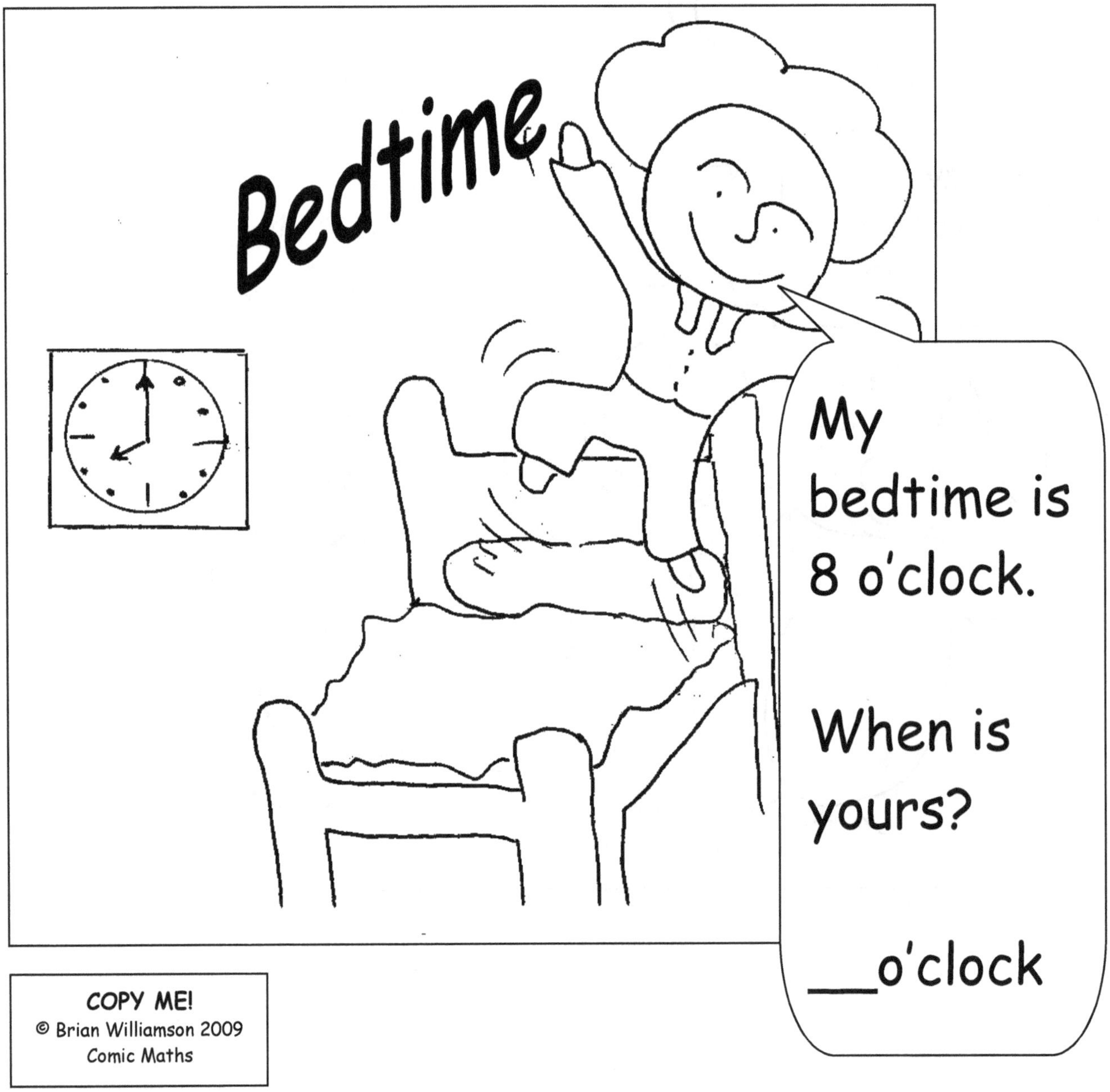

Bedtime

My bedtime is 8 o'clock.

When is yours?

___o'clock

Most days John . . .

Eats his breakfast 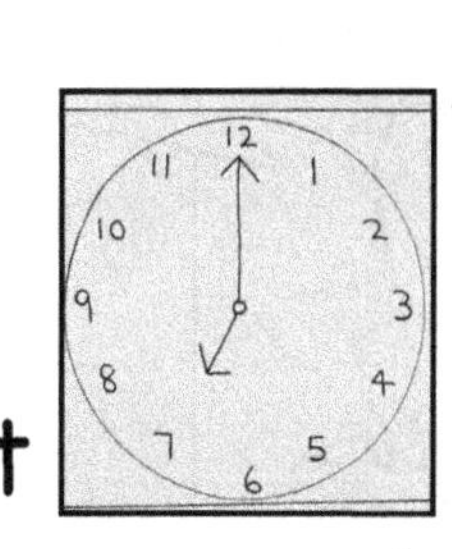
at 7 o'clock in the morning!.

Cleans his teeth
at 8 o'clock.

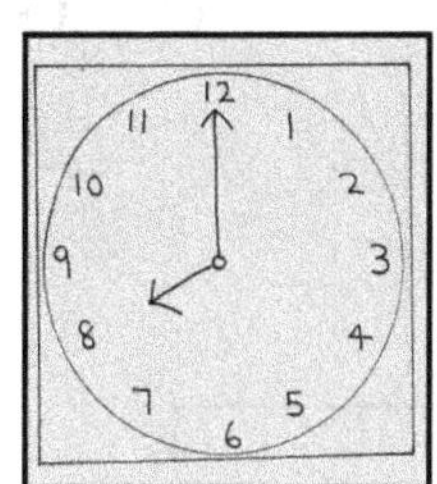

Plays maths with his
teacher at 10 o'clock.

Eats his lunch at
12 o'clock NOON!

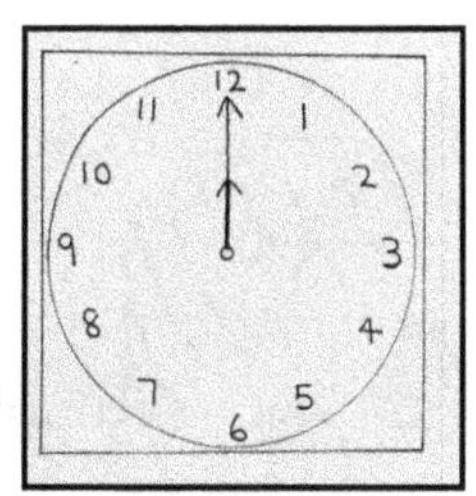

Plays outside at
3 o'clock.

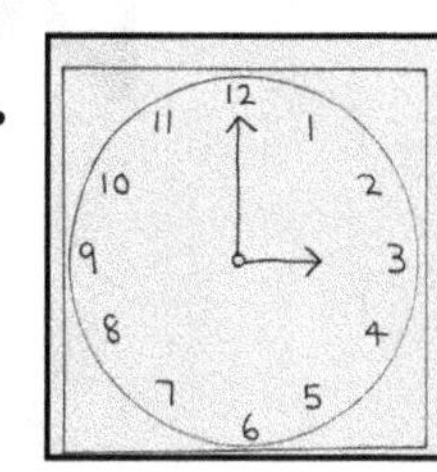

Don't like sausages.

Eats his tea at
5 o'clock.

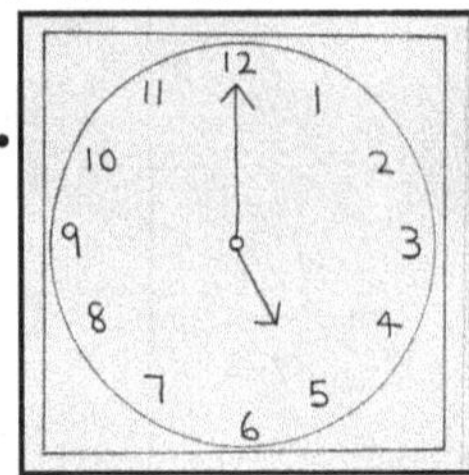

Cleans his teeth
at 6 o'clock.

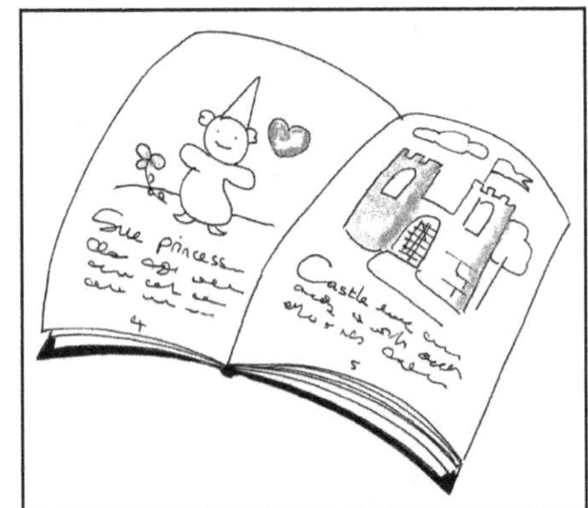

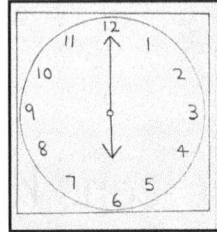

Reads a comic about castles
and Princess Sue at 7 o'clock.

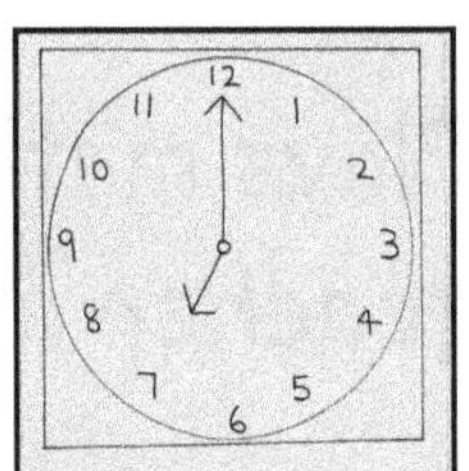

and at
8 o'clock it is ...

**and...**

8

at 12 o'clock **MIDNIGHT** John dreams of scratchy tigers, smiling angels and being at sea in a storm in his bed!

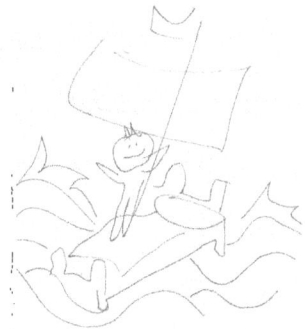

Make the clocks show the times John ...

# Did you know? One day John ...

played maths with his teacher at

**MIDNIGHT!**

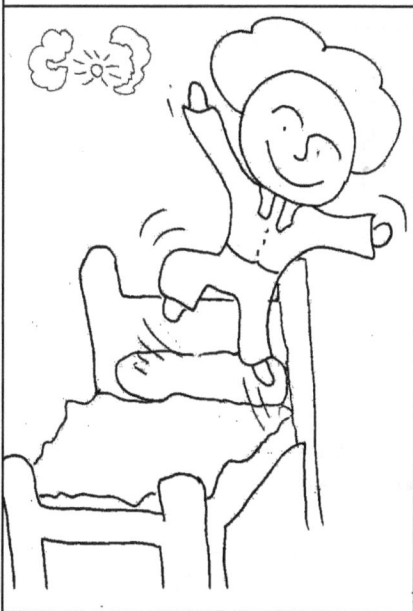

... and went to bed at 3 o'clock in the afternoon.

# Change John's day to make it as **CRAZY** as you like ...

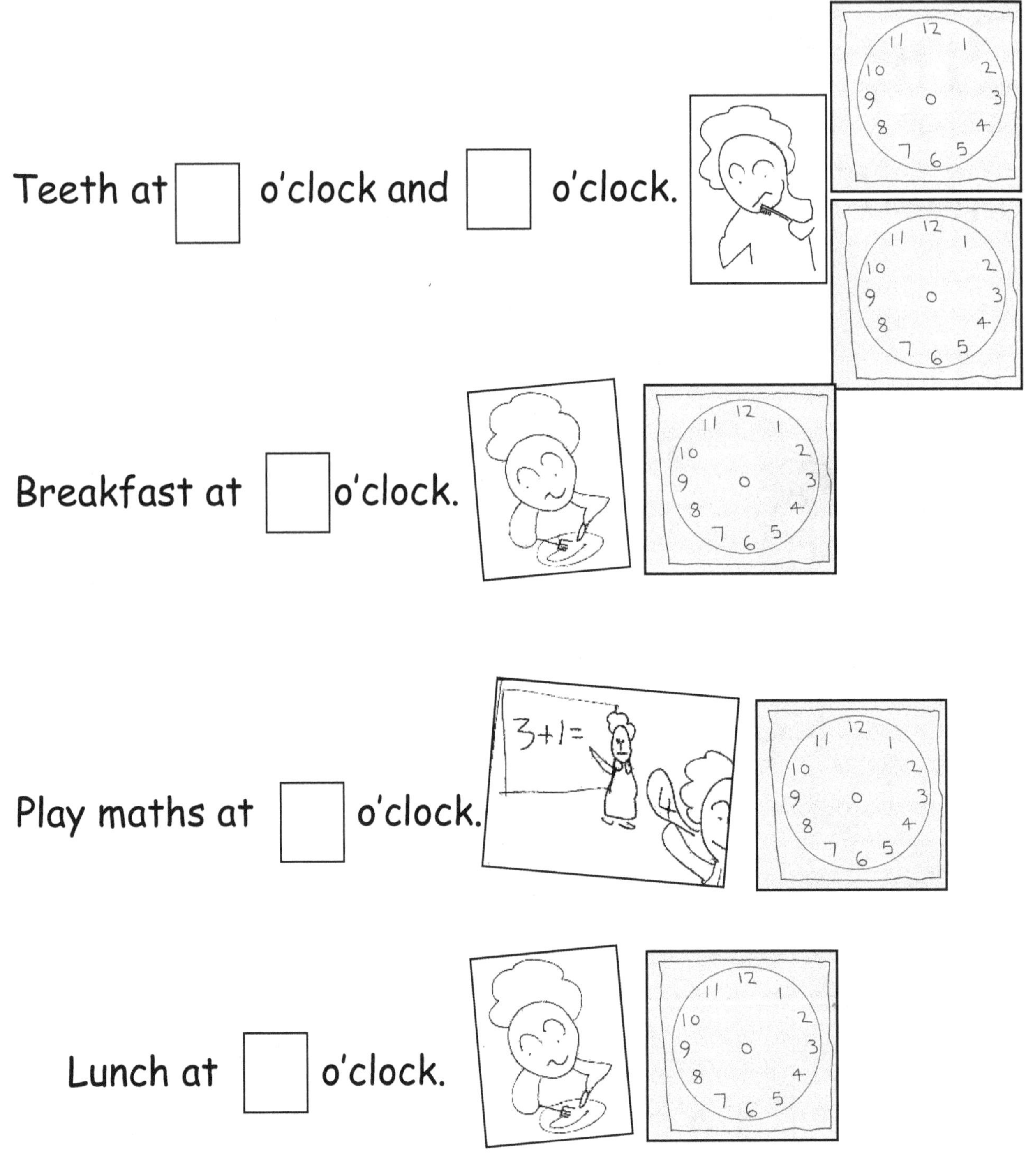

Teeth at ☐ o'clock and ☐ o'clock.
Breakfast at ☐ o'clock.
Play maths at ☐ o'clock.
3+1=
Lunch at ☐ o'clock.

Plays outside at ☐ o'clock.

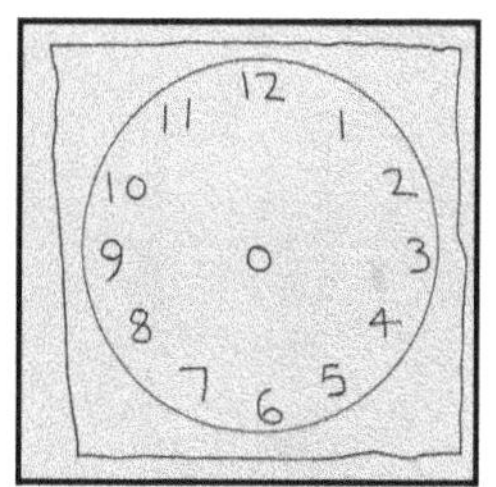

Eats his tea at ☐ o'clock.

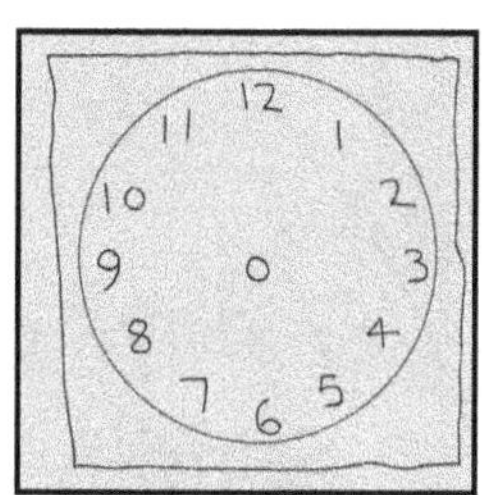

Reads a story about castles
and Princess Sue at ☐ o'clock.

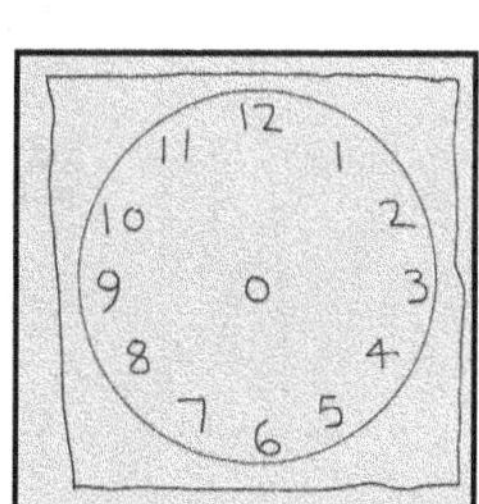

Bedtime at ☐ o'clock.

Dreams of scratchy tigers, smiling angels and being at sea in a storm in his bed at ☐ o'clock.

# CRAZY BABY!

thinks it's always Sunday

7 days after
Sunday is Sunday.
14 days after
Sunday is Sunday.
21 days after
Sunday is Sunday.
28 days after
Sunday is Sunday.
35 days after
Sunday is Sunday.

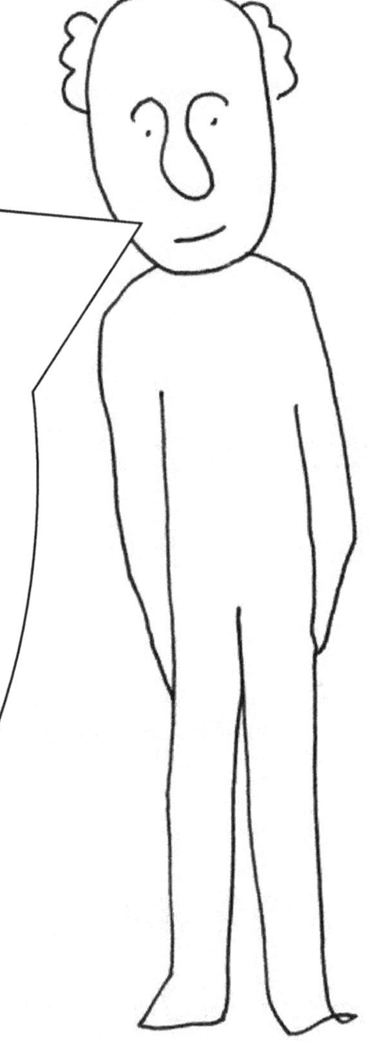

BILL, **why** is it **ALWAYS** Sunday?

John, Sue, Anne, Anne's Mum, Granddad and Milli are going on holiday ...
... to a beech!!!!!

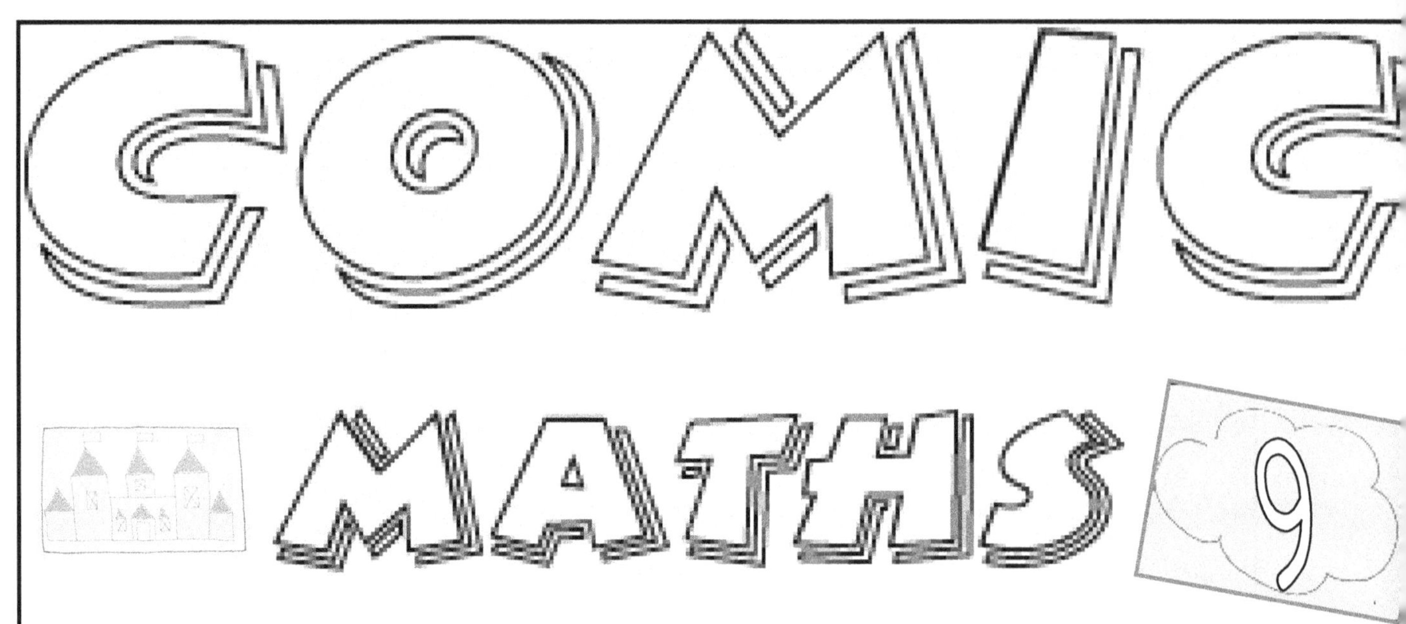


# CARDBOARD CASTLES

John, Anne, Mili and Granddad made a castle using cardboard boxes. They asked Anne's Mum to cut out holes for the windows.

John drew a picture of the best castle

John ...
the castle is
**flat!!!**

## Draw a better castle.

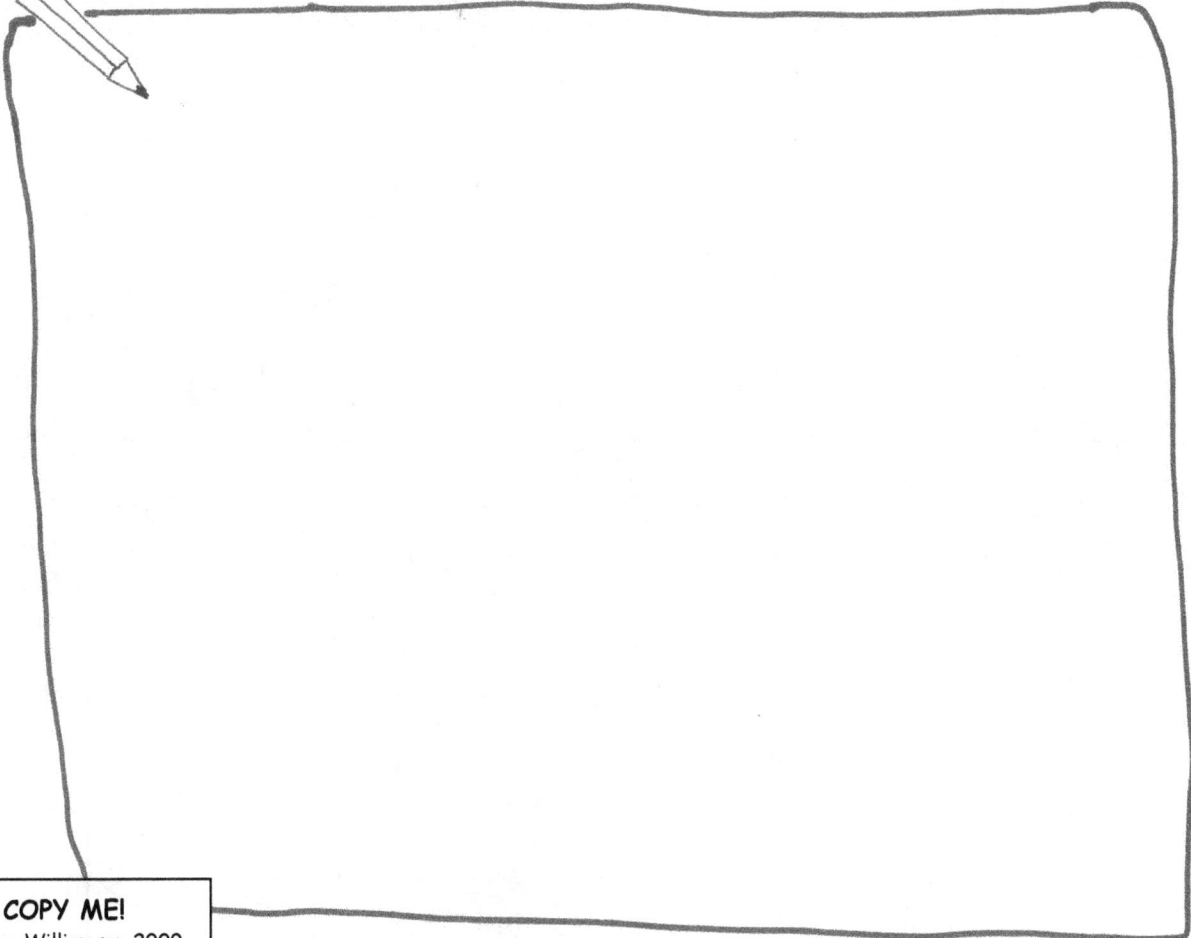

Sue had a fight with a cardboard box.
It nearly knocked her hat off!!

**You** try making a castle out of cardboard boxes!
Ask a grown-up to cut the windows out and **enjoy**!

# CRAZY BABY!

meets a Shape family

Mr. and Mrs. Square and their children . . .

.... Rectangle and Triangle.

Do you know someone who looks like a triangle? ______

Stop being silly John.

Stop being silly Anne's mum.

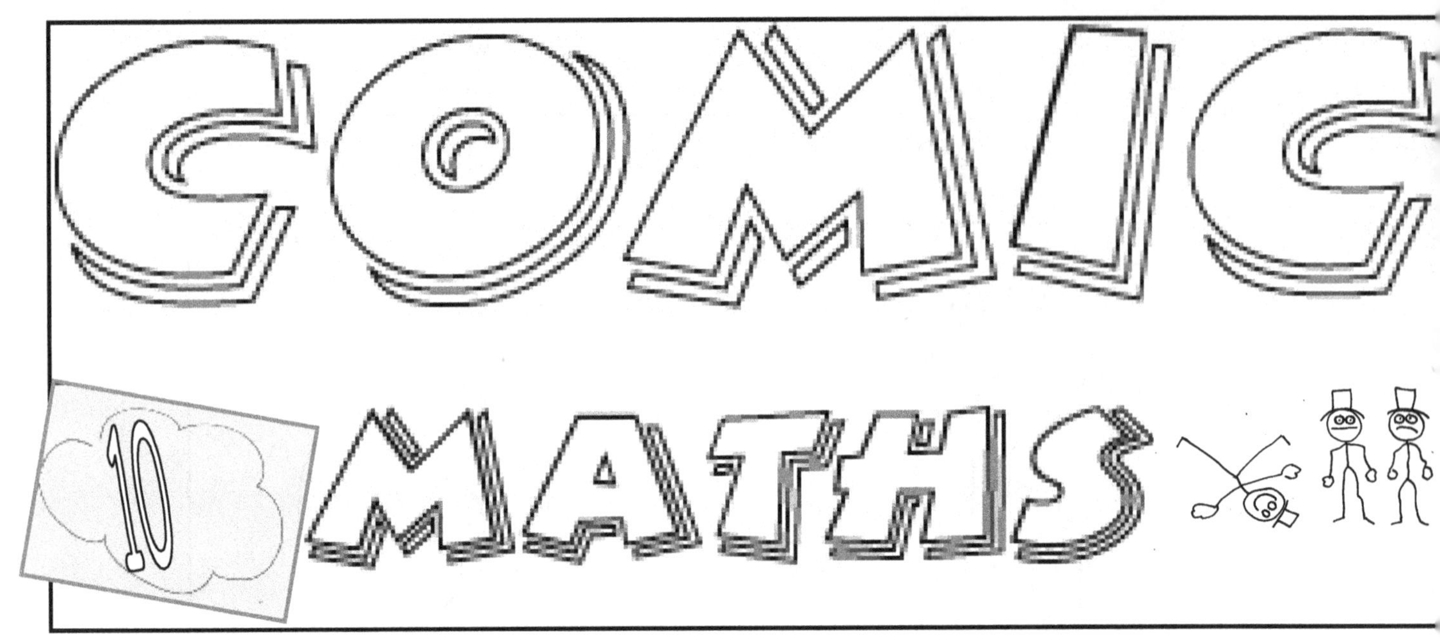

# Silly People!!!

Some people are silly.
Some people are not.

Who do you think is silly in these pictures?

Colour their faces **red** and count them.

How many?

| | |
|---|---|
| Silly | |
| Not Silly | |
| Everyone | |

How many?

| | |
|---|---|
| Silly | |
| Not Silly | |
| Everyone | |

| How many? | |
|---|---|
| Silly | |
| Not Silly | |
| Everyone | |

Tell a friend how you knew that a person was silly.

CRAZY BABY!
plays tens and units
1 ten
19
9 units
John tens
Sue units
Tree tens
Space ship units
__________ tens
_______ units

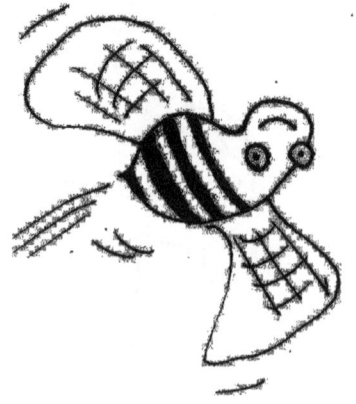

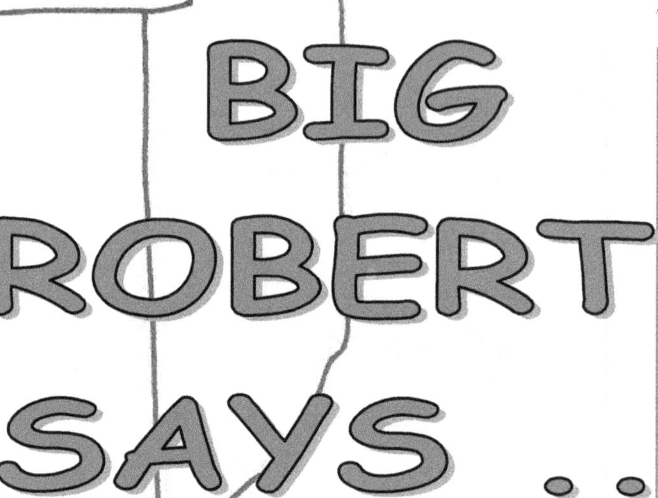


BIG
ROBERT is
the best!

# draw

one football
two feet
three hands
four heads
five legs
six arms
seven noses
eight eyes
nine ears
ten elephants

one sun
two moons
three teachers
four grandmas
five mums
six dads
seven flowers in a pot
eight brothers
nine sisters
ten aliens

Lots of paper and pencils needed!

# draw a hand

## like Granddad

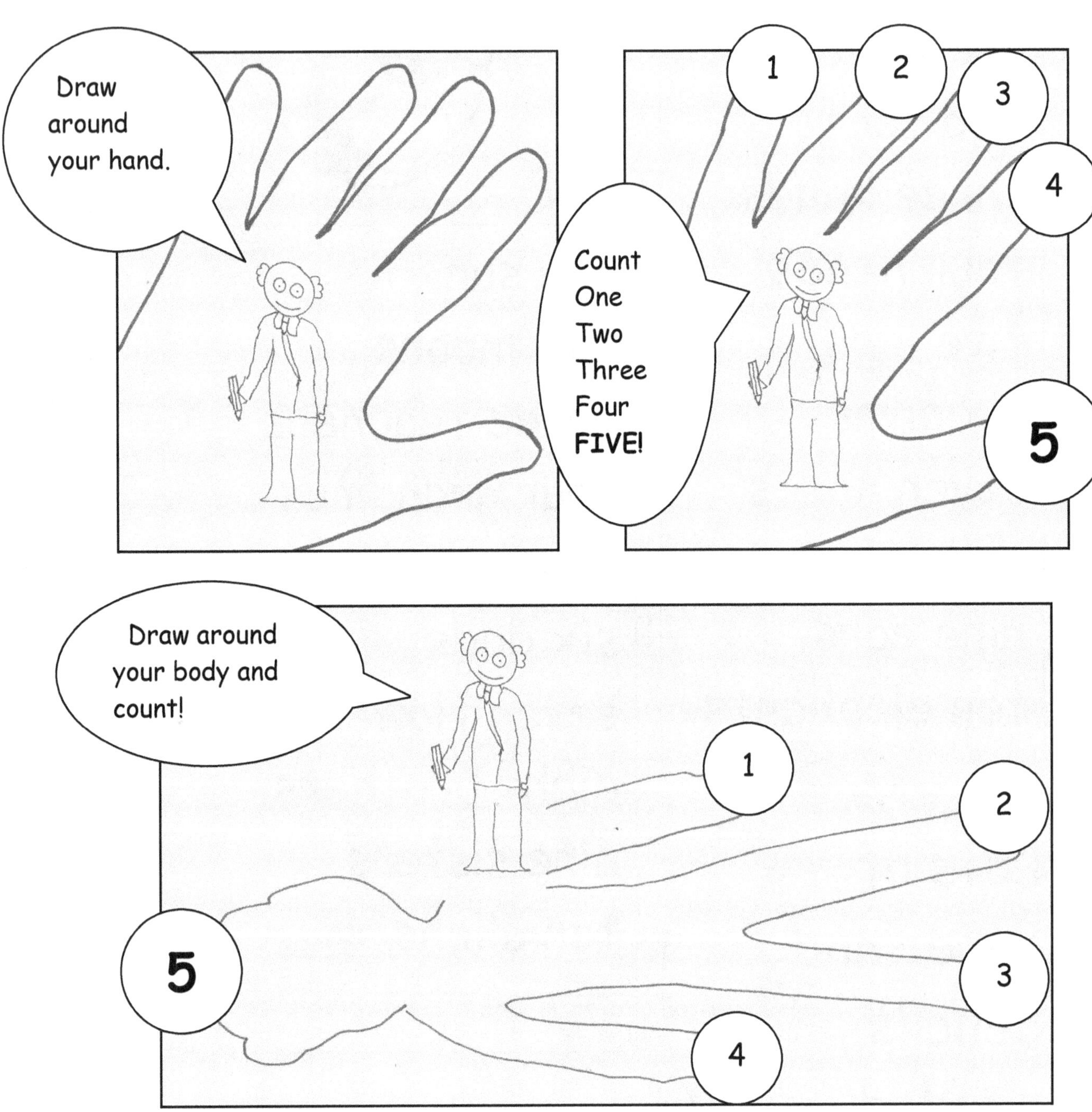

Draw around your hand.
1
2
3
4
5
Count One Two Three Four **FIVE!**
Draw around your body and count!
1
2
3
4
5

# Play ... BLAST OFF!!!

Run up to somebody and say

5 4 3 2 1

BLAST OFF!!!

Run up to somebody and say

20 19 18 17 16 15 14 13 12 11 10 9 8 7 6 5 4 3 2 1

BLAST OFF!!!

# Do dot to dot!!

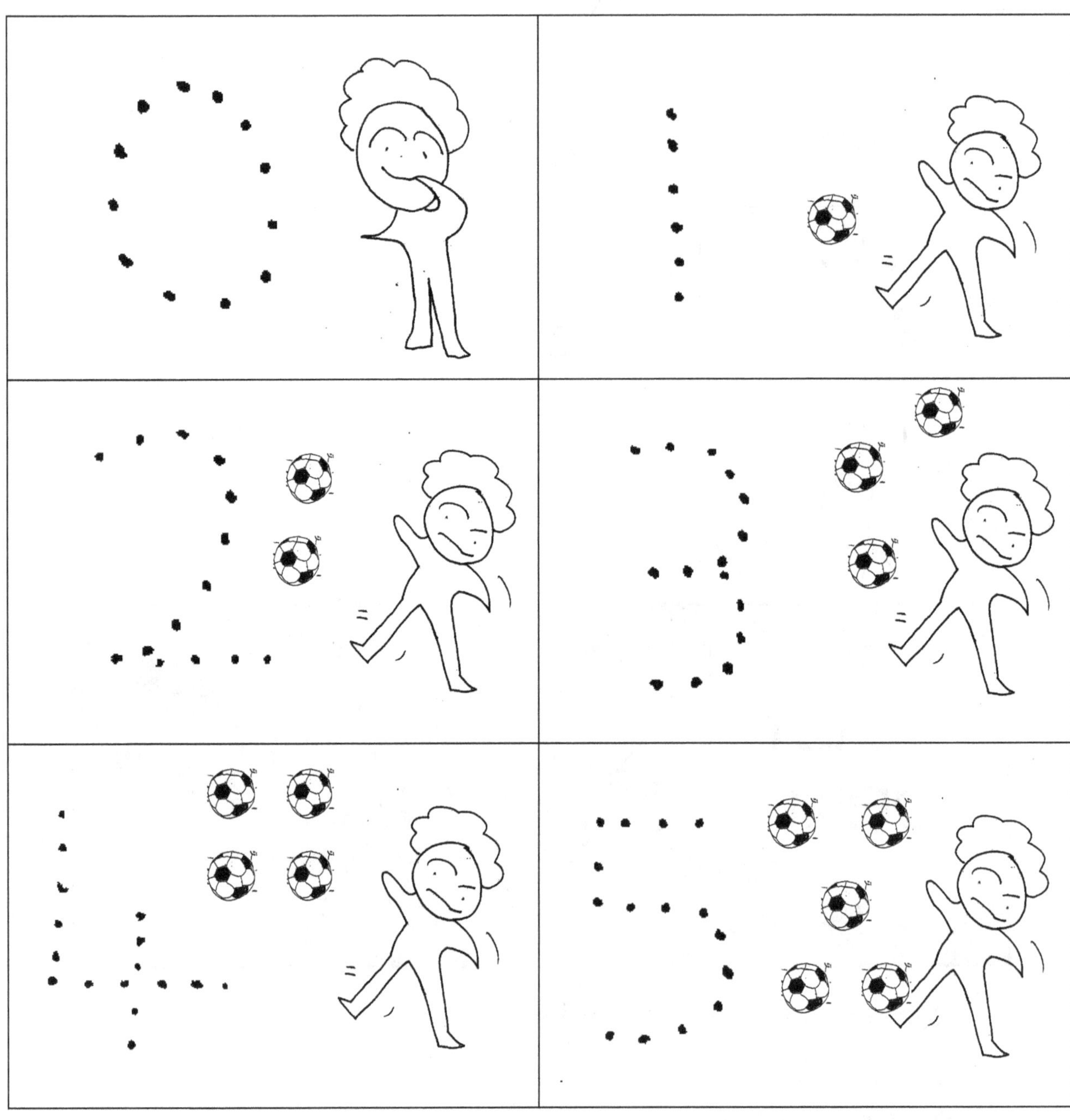

COPY ME!

Comic Maths

BIG
ROBERT
SAYS ...

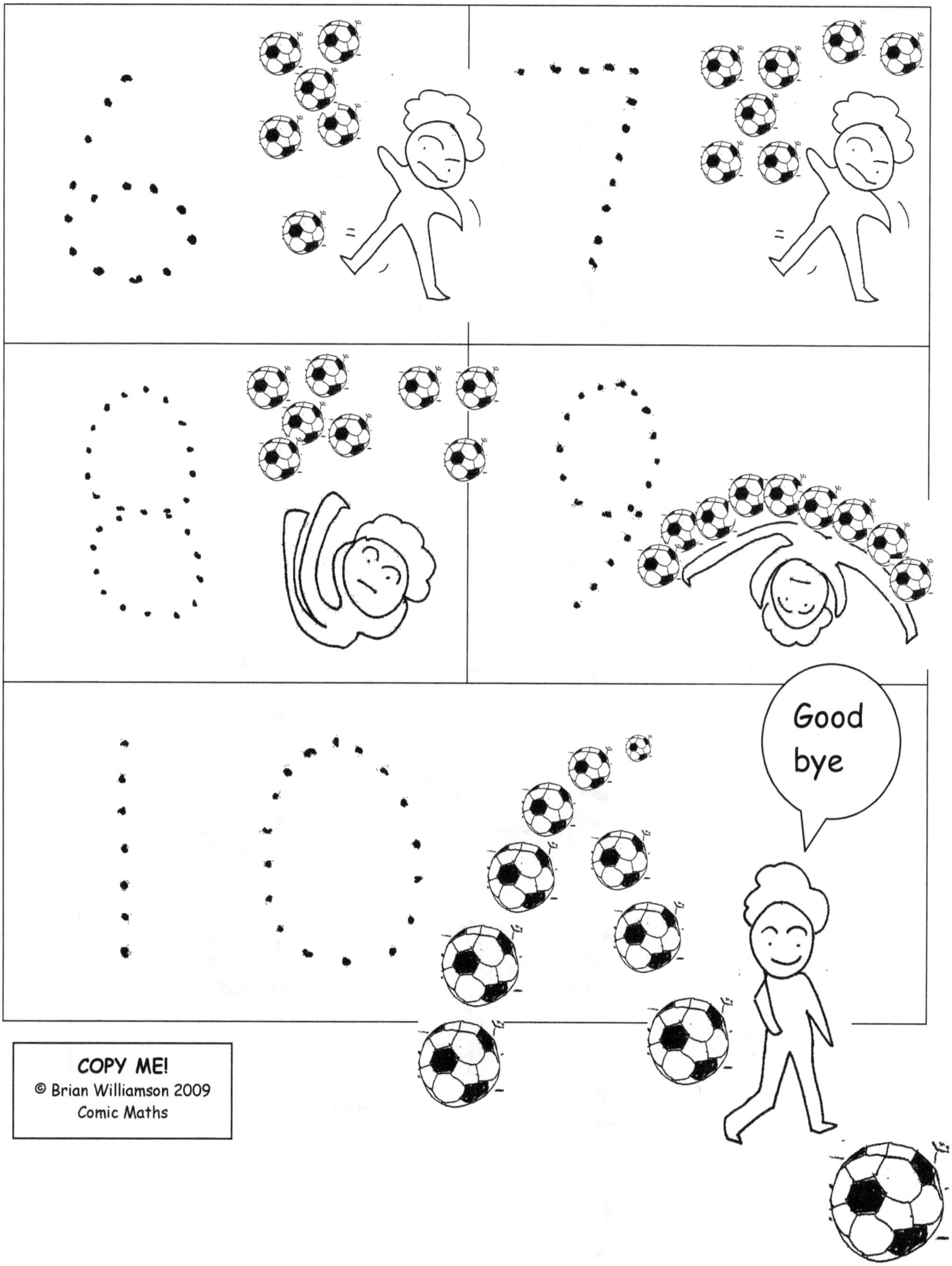

Good bye

find ✸

10 + ✸ = 10

9 + ✸ = 10

8 + ✸ = 10

7 + ✸ = 10

6 + ✸ = 10

5 + ✸ = 10

4 + ✸ = 10

3 + ✸ = 10

2 + ✸ = 10

1 + ✸ = 10

0 + ✸ = 10

SPOT

the 5's

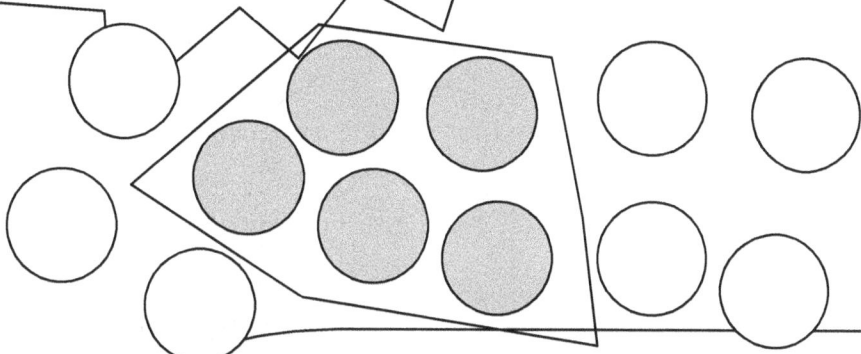

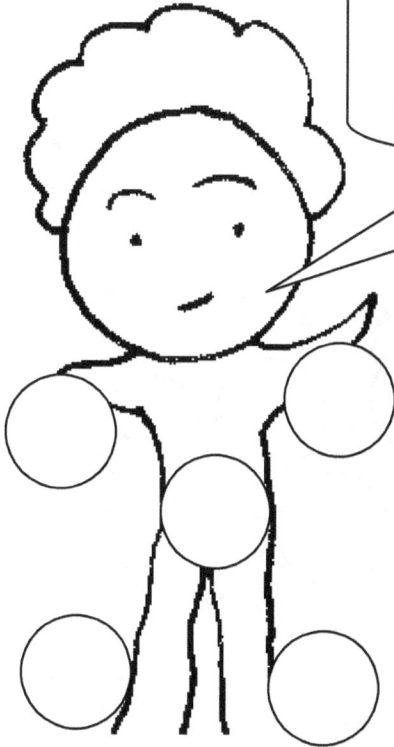

Put a line around every 5 you can find.

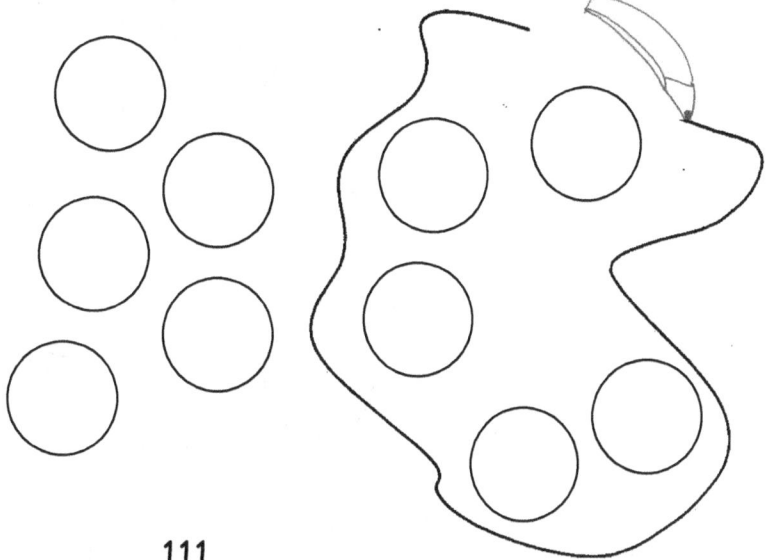

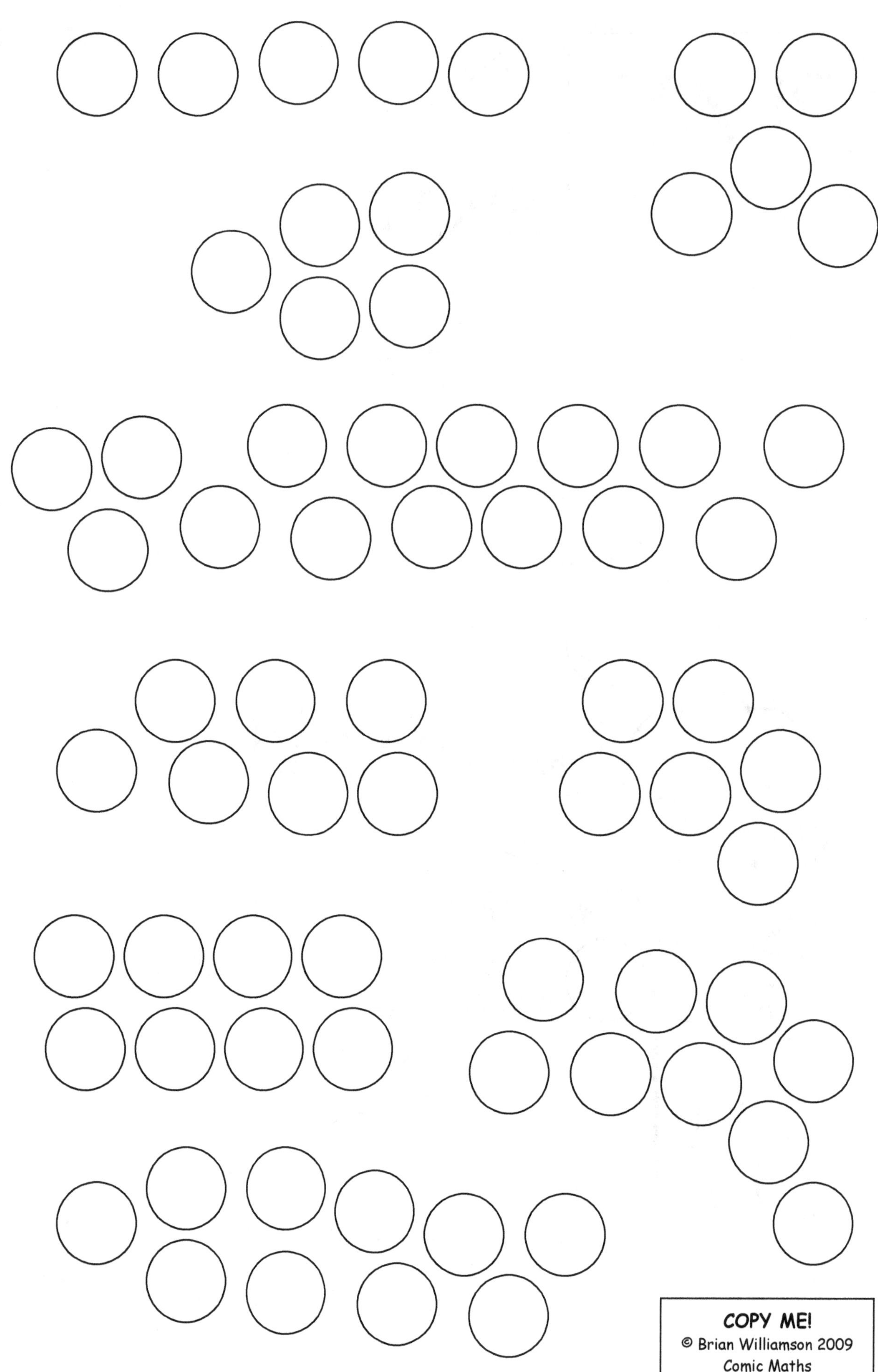

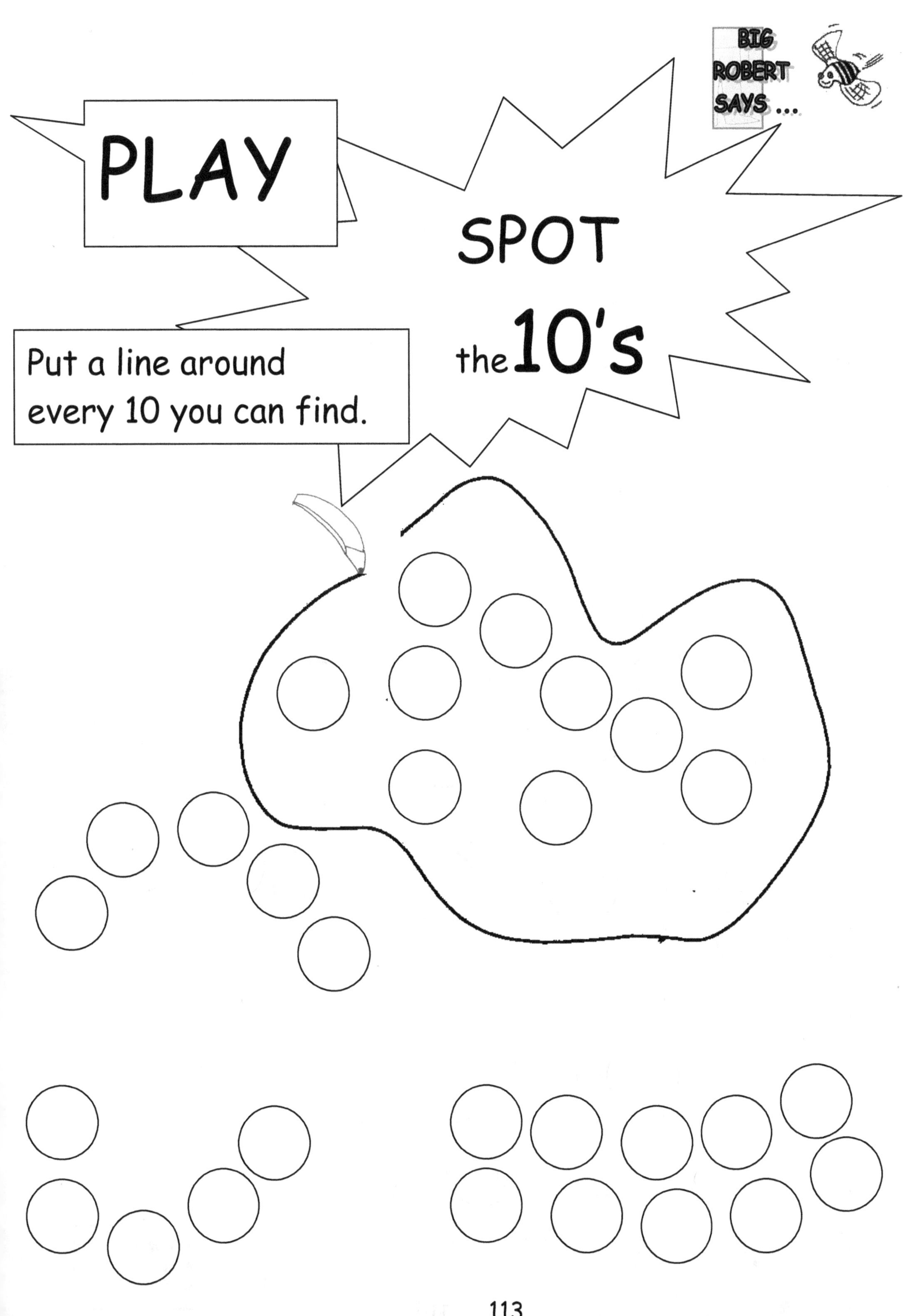
BIG ROBERT SAYS ...
PLAY
SPOT the 10's
Put a line around every 10 you can find.

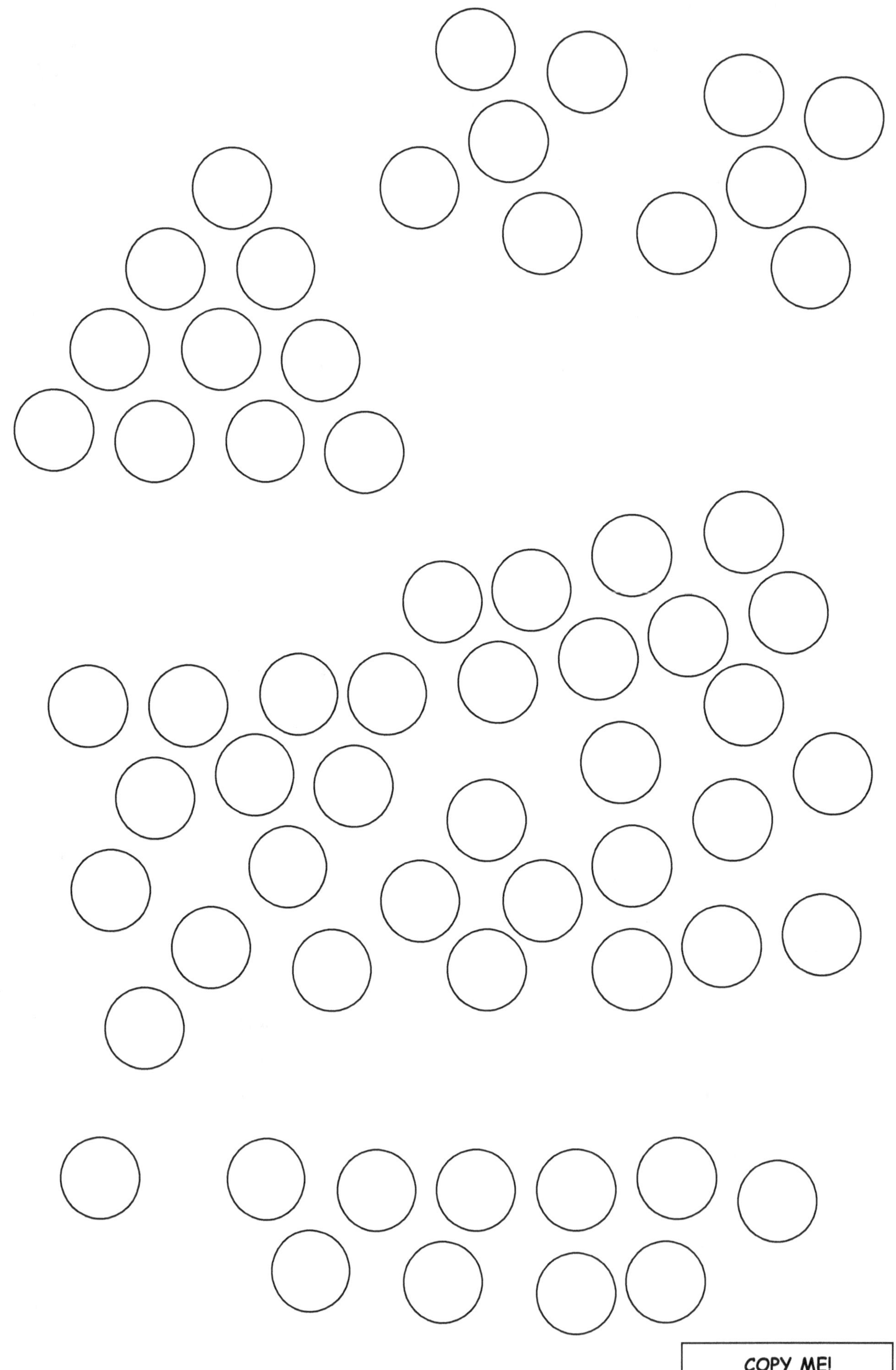

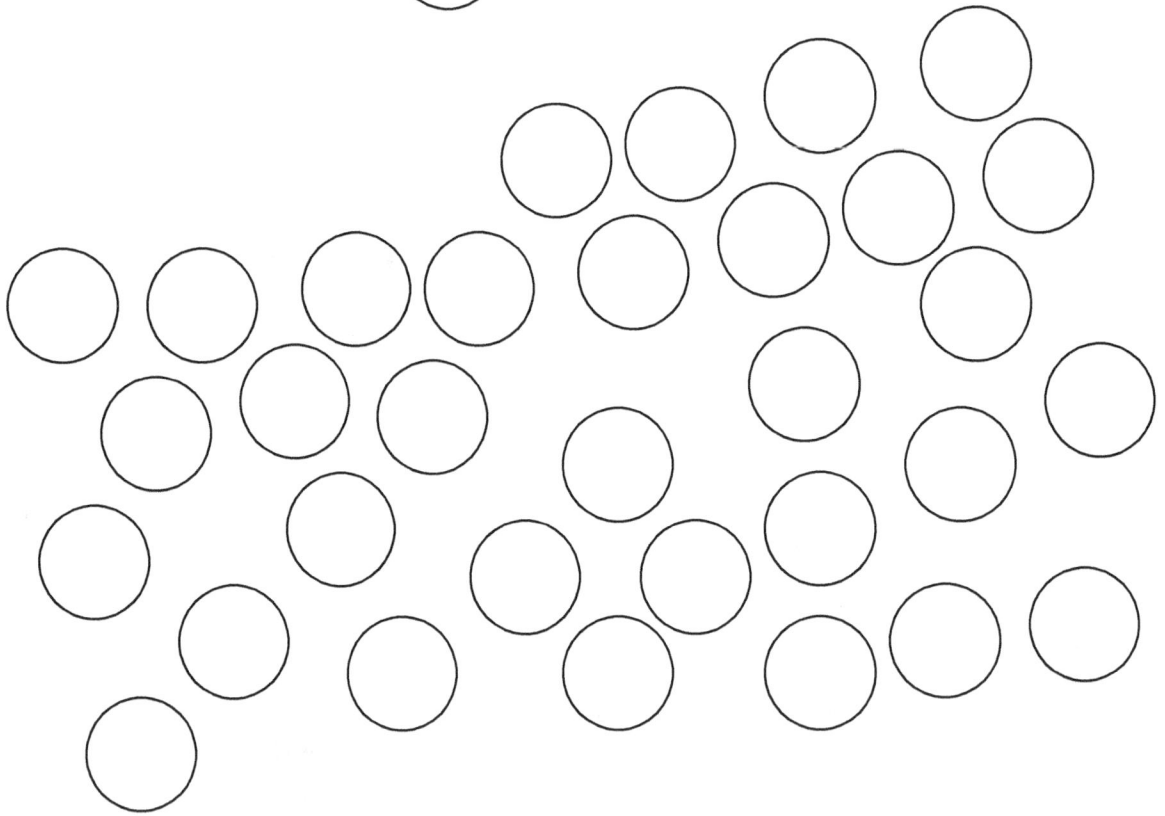

# Make up your own game.

Making up your own game can be good.

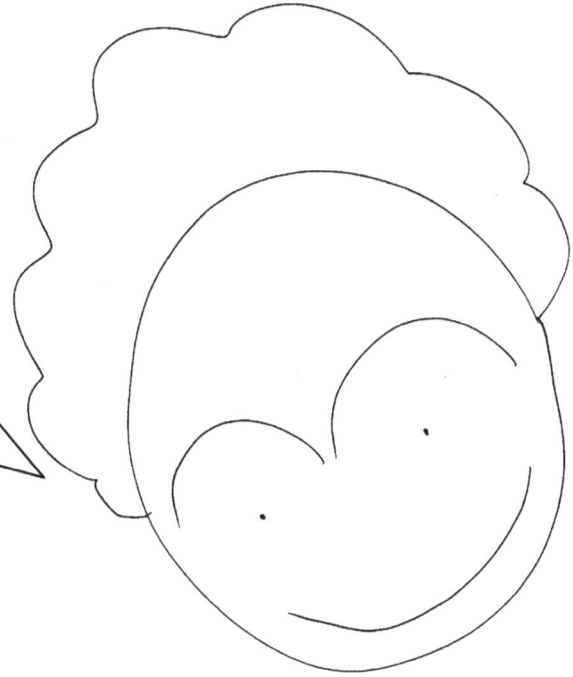

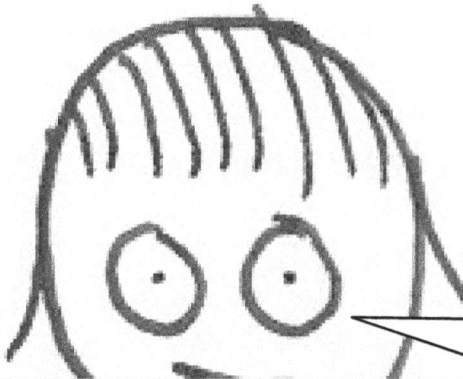

I made up these rules

| Rules |
|---|
| 1. Be three stones go back. |
| 2. Spill the paint pot ... jump! |
| 3. If you have six then you win. |

Make up your own game.

# Rules

1. ______________________________
2. ______________________________
3. ______________________________
4. ______________________________
5. ______________________________
6. ______________________________

______________________________

______________________________

Play your game with a grown-up.
REMEMBER you are the boss!

# I say. You say.

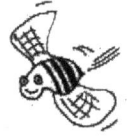

BIG ROBERT SAYS ...

I say 5.
You say 6.

I say 7.
You say 8.

I say 1.
You say 2.

I say 9.
You say __.

Change the rule!
I say 6.
You say 5.
5
I say 12.
You say 11.
I say 4.
You say ___.
I say ___.
You say 15.
15

Have a good
SCRIBBLE
on this page!!!

BIG ROBERT SAYS ...

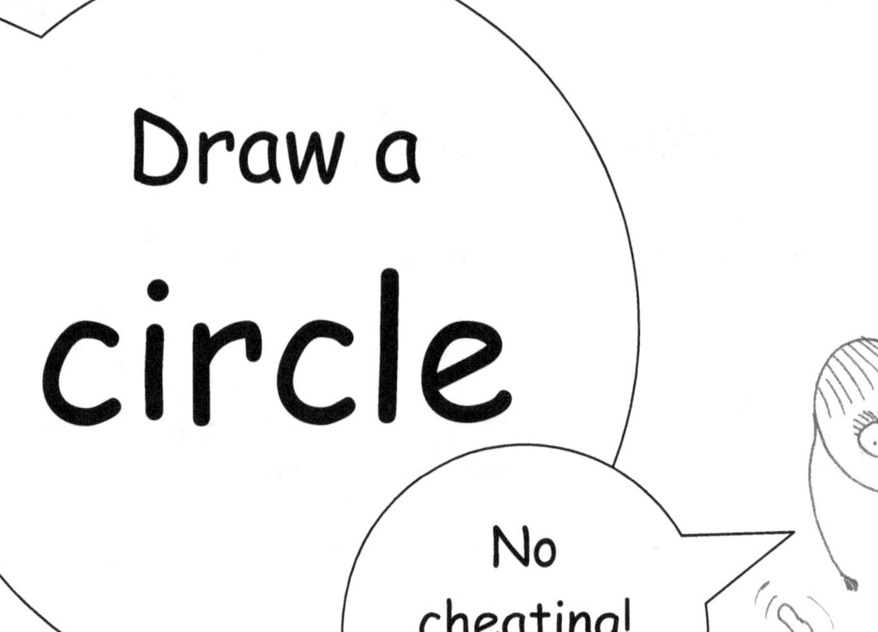
Draw a
circle
No
cheating!

Try again
and again
and again!

COPY ME!

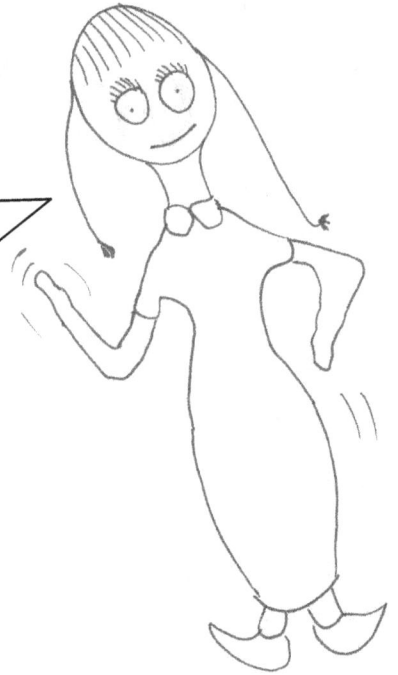

# Draw me a **something**

## Draw anything you like!

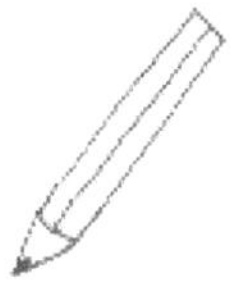

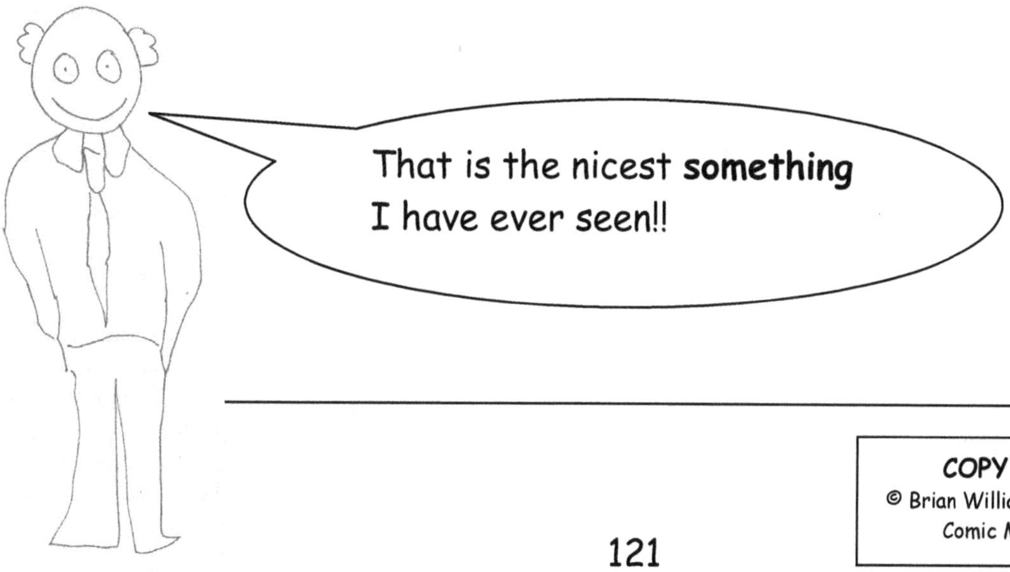

That is the nicest **something**
I have ever seen!!

Draw me 4 more **somethings**

COPY ME!

I wish I were 7
I wish I were 7
I AM 7

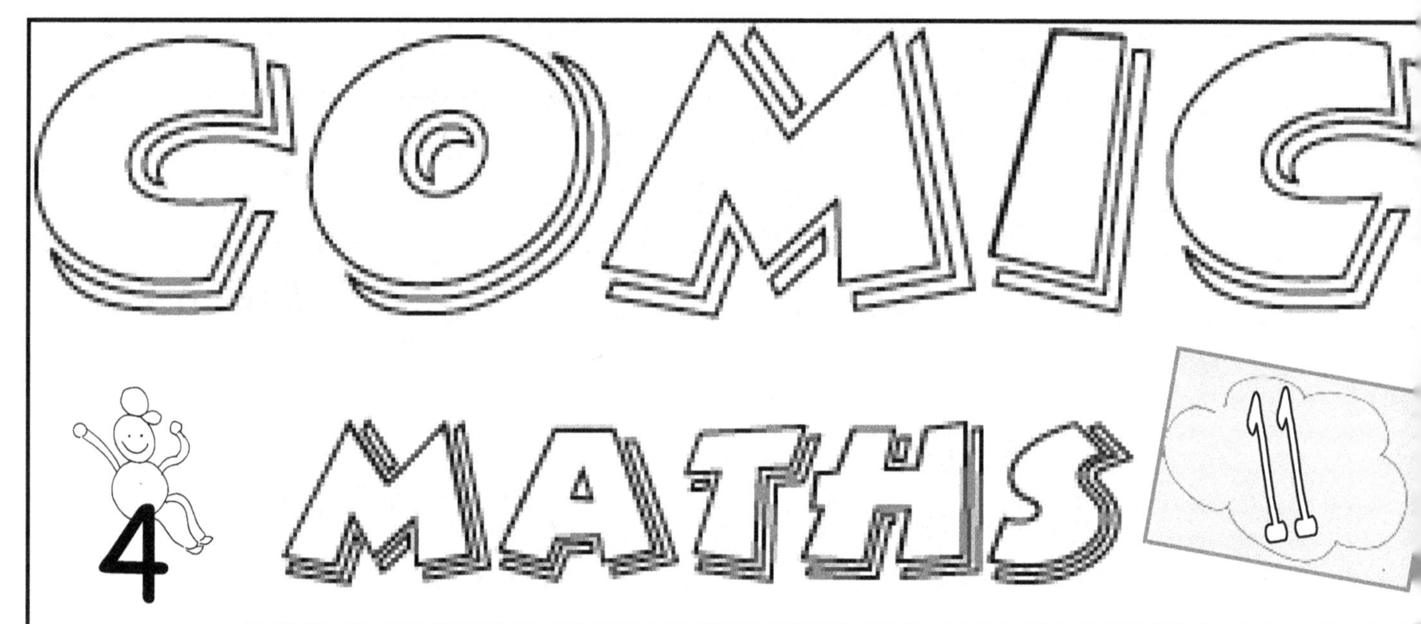


## Who's on the tops of the age of 4?

Betty is on tops of the age of 4.

Betty is older than 4.

Crazy Baby is on bottoms of the age of 4.

Crazy Baby is younger than 4.

Poor baby!

Charlie the Monkey is just 2.

Granddad is 80.

Betty is 49.

Bill is 66.

Anne's Mum is 33.

Sue is 5.

Anne is 7.

Milli is 0 and a little bit more.

John is 6.

Kilo is very very very old.

Colour in the youngest.

Colour in the oldest.

Colour in the youngest.

11
Who is on the tops of the age of 4?
8 names to find.
1 2 3 4
5 6 7 8


Who is on the tops of the age of 6?

6 names to find.

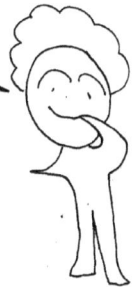

| 1 | 2 | 3 |
|---|---|---|
| 4 | 5 | 6 |

Who is on the tops of the age of 35?

Who is on the tops of the age of 70?

2 names to find
and one of them is mine!
1
2
kilo

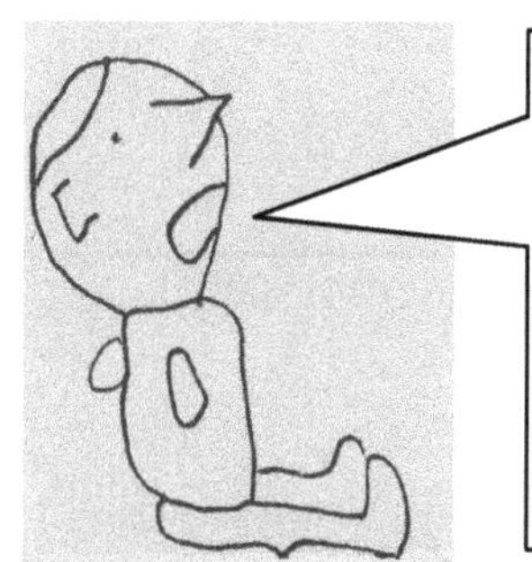

# CRAZY BABY!

Jumps to his birthday

1 day

2 days

3 days

4 days

19th

20th

21st

22nd

18th May

5 days

23rd May

5 days to my birthday!!

Find a calendar and jump to your birthday!!

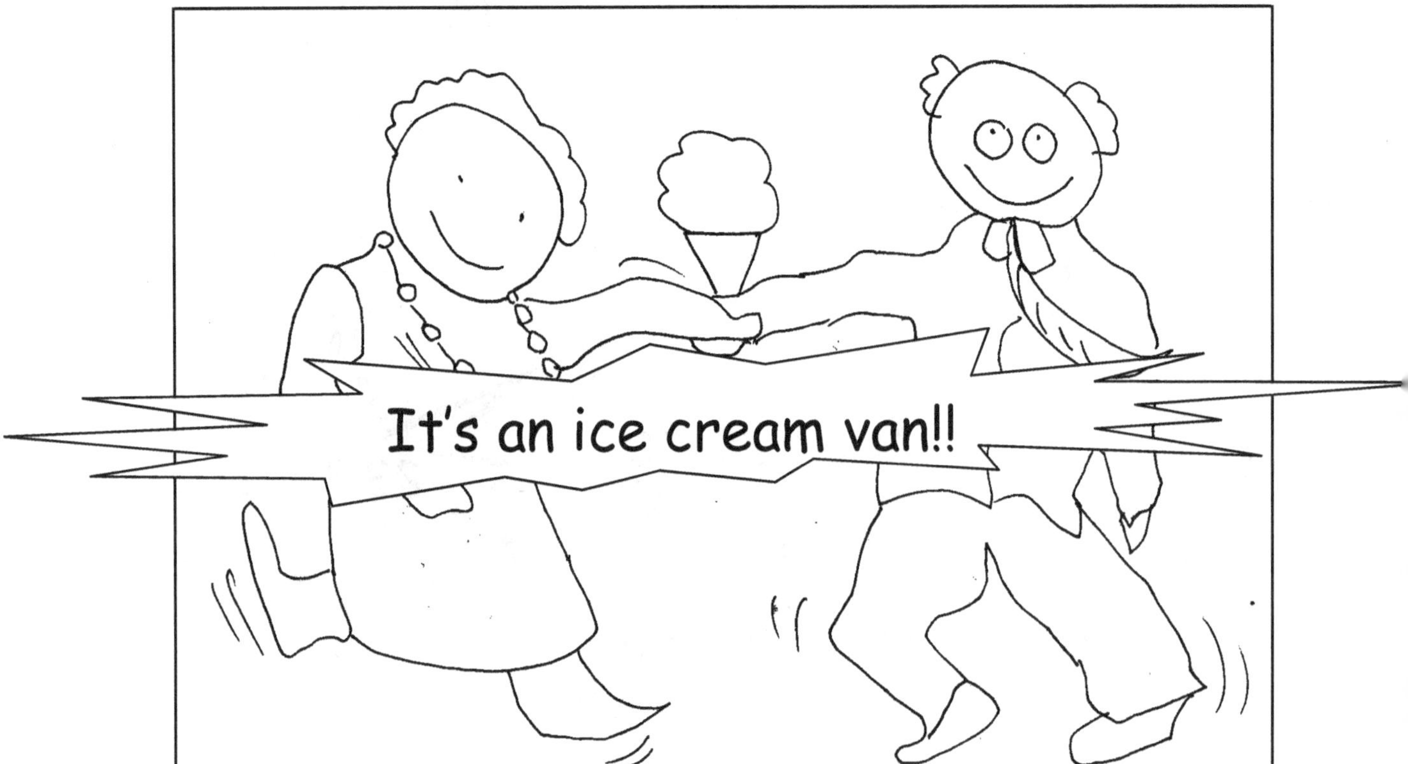

It's an ice cream van!!

COMIC
MATHS
12
John's Ice Creams
ICE CREAMS

John and Sue love ice creams.
ICE CREAMS
Sometimes they share.
Sometimes they **don't**!

Anne, Sue and John like to fight about ice creams!

I have less than Anne!

I have more than Sue!

I have less than **greedy** John!

I have more than **greedy** Sue!!!!

GRAB!!!

*!*!*!*

AND THEN. . .

That is fair!

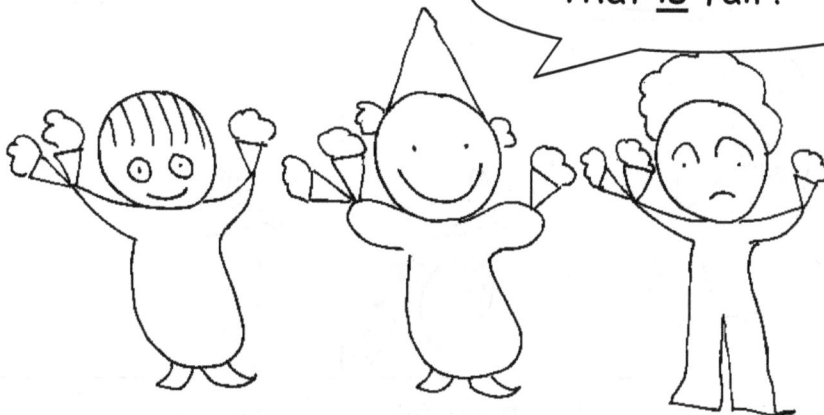

Anne, Sue and John have the same.

Write **SAME**, **LESS** or **MORE**.

Anne has _____ than John.

John has _____ than Anne.

Sue has the _____ as Anne.

Anne has the _____ as Sue.

Sue has _____ than Betty.

Betty has _____ than Sue.

Betty has _____ than Anne.

Anne has _____ than Betty.

## A happy happy ice cream story

| | | |
|---|---|---|
| John has 3 ice creams. | Sue gives him 3 ice creams. | John has 6 ice creams. |

## Draw the pictures for this story

| | | |
|---|---|---|
| | | |
| John has 8 ice creams. | Sue gives him 2 ice creams. | John has 10 ice creams. |

## A happy sad ice cream story

| | | |
|---|---|---|
| John has 3 ice creams. | He drops 2 ice creams. | John has 1 ice cream. |

## Write the story for these pictures

________________________________________

________________________________________

________________________________________

________________________________________

## A happy sad happy ice cream story

| John has 3 ice creams. | He drops 2 ice creams. | Sue gives him 3 ice creams. | John has 4 ice creams. |
|---|---|---|---|

Write the sum for this
happy sad happy ice cream story

Write a story for 8 - 8 + 3 - 3 + 10 - 4 - 3 + 2 -1 - 4 = 0
It is going to be a long one!!

How many ice creams can you hold?
. . . WITHOUT dropping any!!!

# CRAZY BABY! listens to BETTY'S STORY

Once upon a
time there
were lots and
lots of
numbers ....

21

0

8 1

11 52 4 23

54 17 3 9

2 7 99 14

31

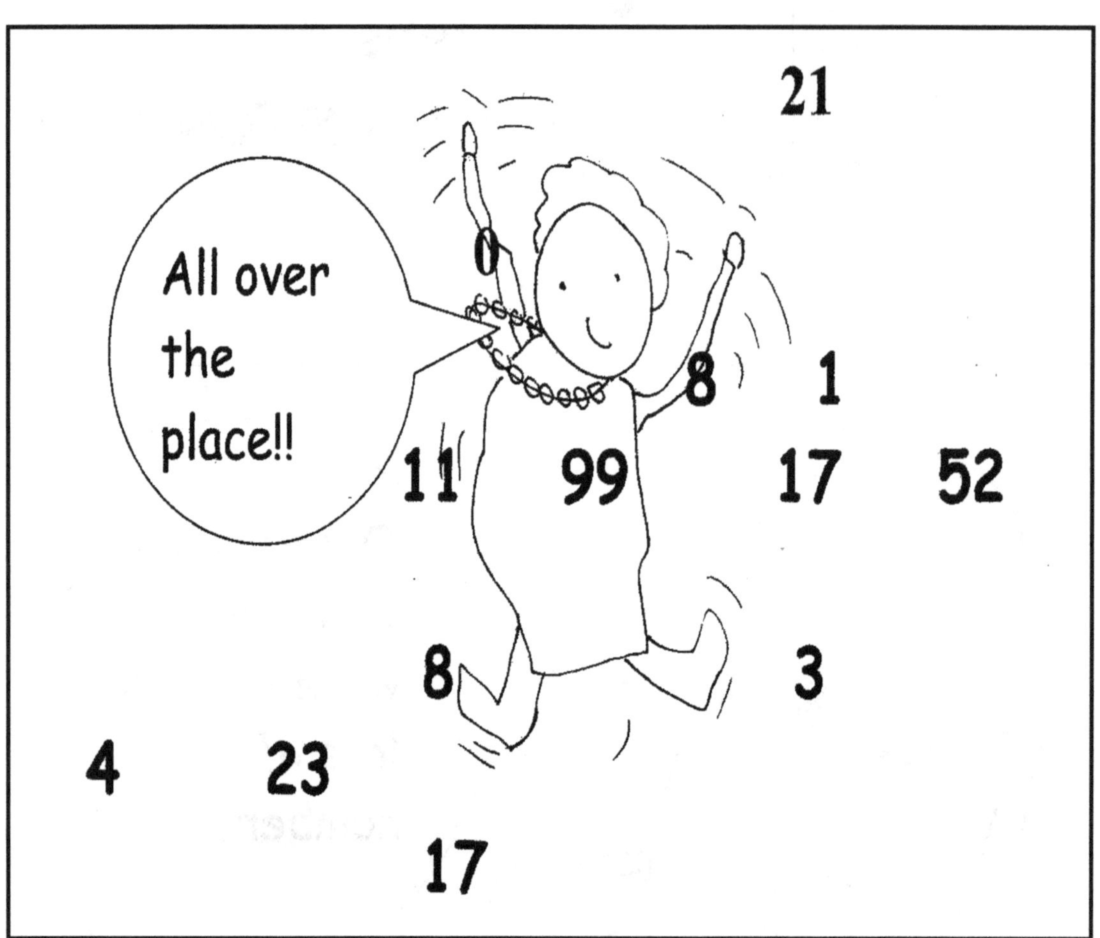

They add and take away with each other . . . but the answers are **always** numbers!!

| | |
|---|---|
| 3 is a | number |
| 2 is a | ________ |
| 3 + 2 = 5 is a | ________ |

Twelve apples in John's pocket!

12
apples in my pocket.
-10
glad to loose ten.
Why John?
because 12 apples was too many.

Twelve pennies in John's pocket!

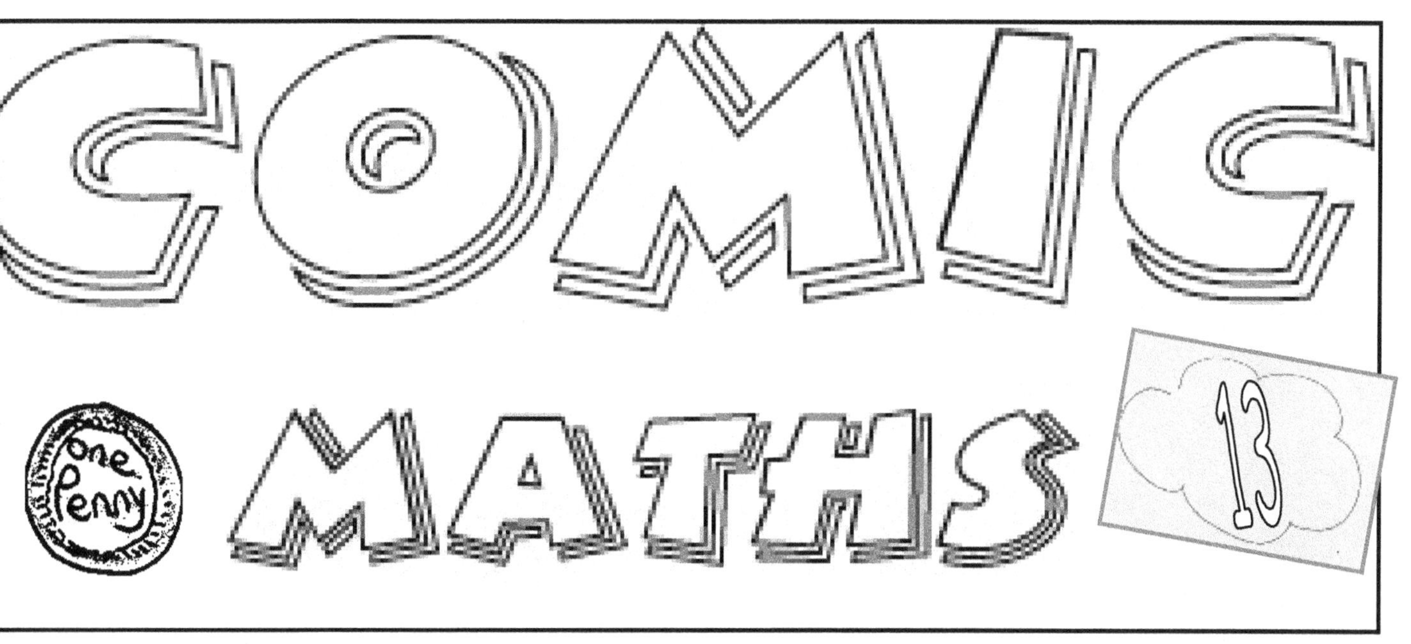


# Paying in PENNIES!

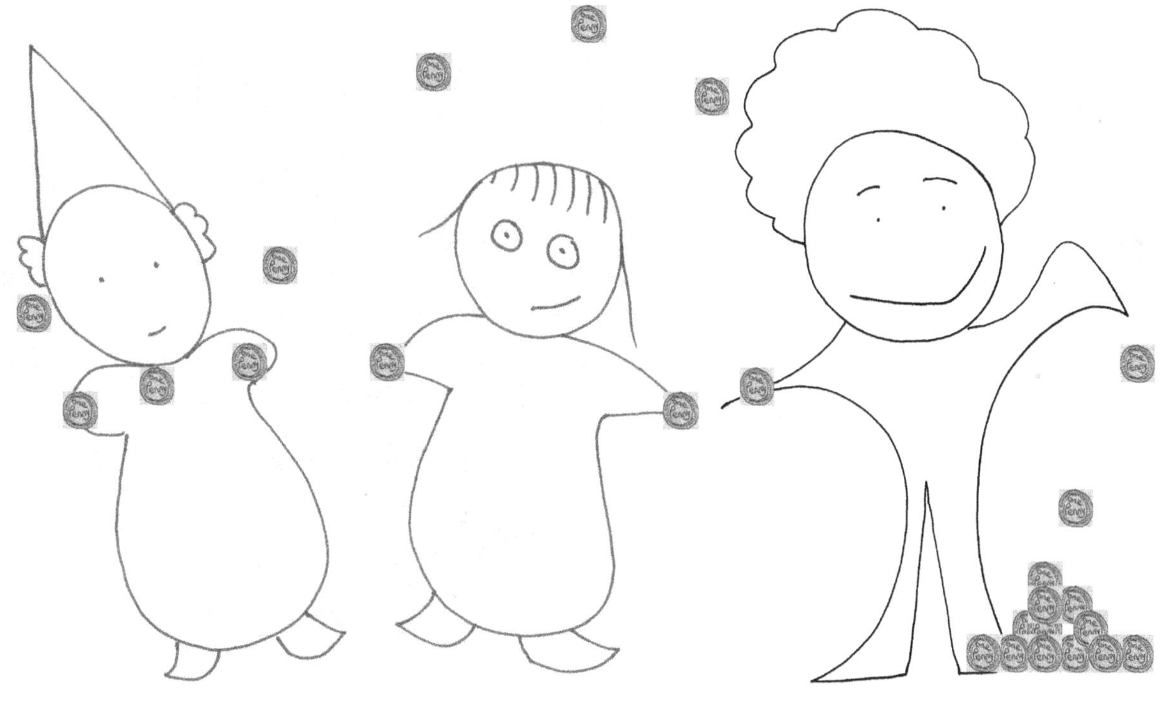

John, Sue and Anne save pennies in a big sack.

Every time they get 100 they give them all to Bill.

Thanks!!

. . . and Bill gives them one big coin!

Thanks Bill!!
A BIG COIN

A toy elephant costs 8 big coins.

How many pennies is this? It is _____ pennies.

A giant carrot costs 2 big coins.

How many pennies is this? It is _____ pennies.

Put in the missing numbers in this table.

| Big Coins | Pennies |
|---|---|
| 1 | 100 |
| 7 | |
| 5 | |
| 11 | |
| 10 | |
| | 600 |
| | 900 |
| | 1200 |
| | 1700 |
| | 2200 |

How many pennies in half a big coin? ___

# CRAZY BABY!
## Counts past
## THE HUNDREDS

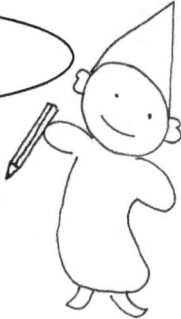

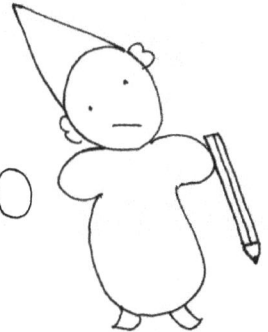

| 98 | 99 | 100 | 101 | |
|---|---|---|---|---|
| 198 | 199 | 200 | | |
| 298 | 299 | | | |
| 398 | | | | |

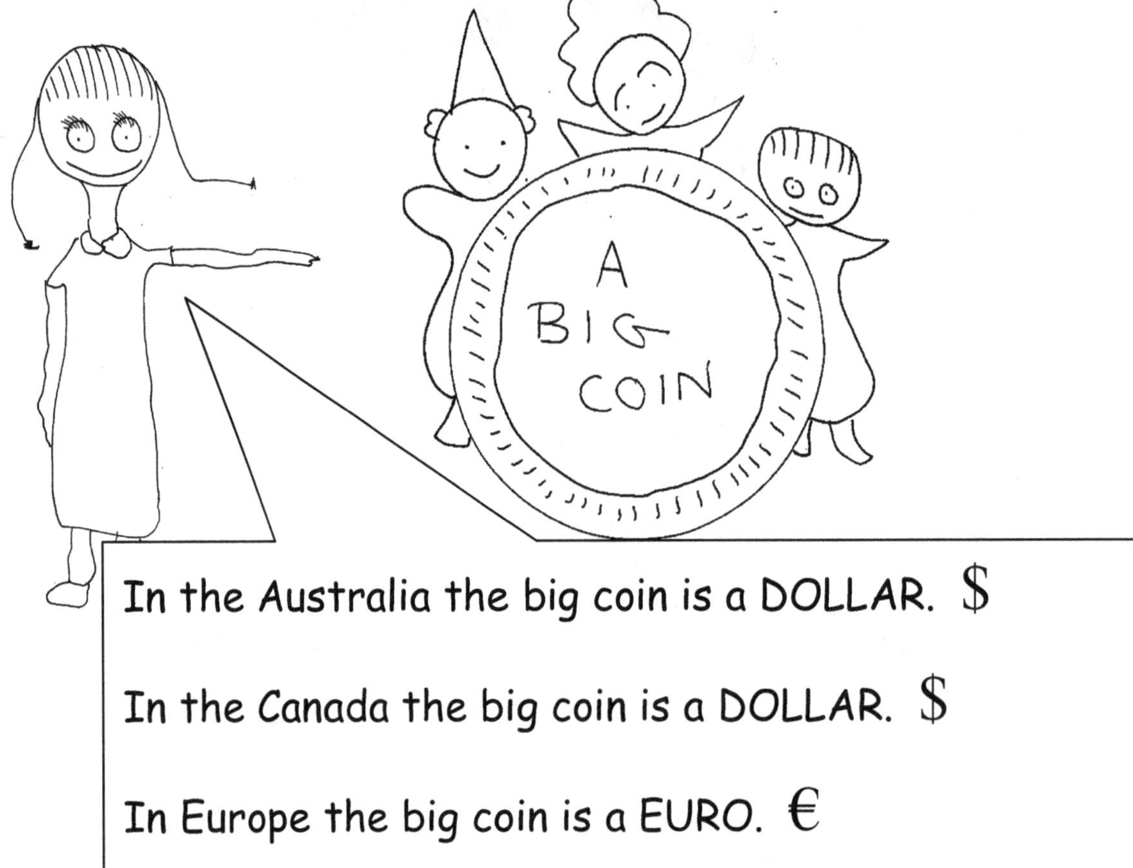


In the Australia the big coin is a DOLLAR. $

In the Canada the big coin is a DOLLAR. $

In Europe the big coin is a EURO. €

In the United Kingdom the big coin is a POUND. £

In the United States the big coin is a DOLLAR. $

Where do you live? Tick a box! ✓

Australia? ☐
Canada? ☐
Europe? ☐
United Kingdom? ☐
United States? ☐
Somewhere else? ☐

My big coin is called a

____________________.

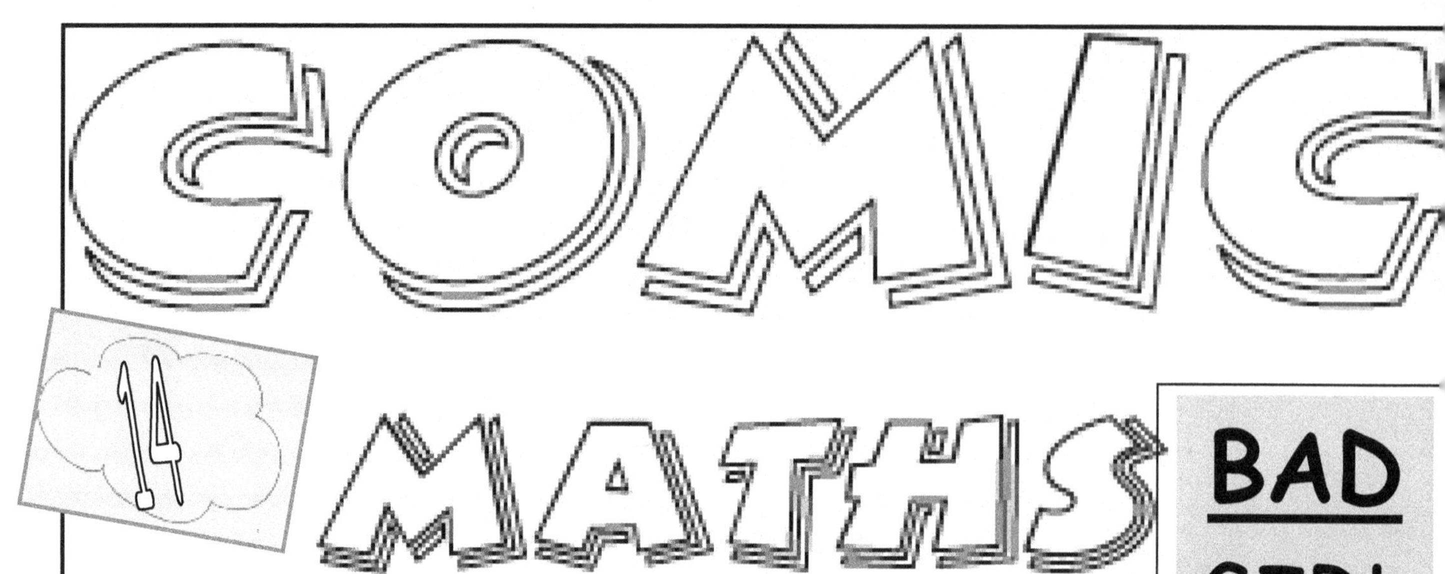
COMIC
14
MATHS
BAD
GIRL
BETTY

Sometimes I get my sums wrong just to make people angry. Sometimes I dance . . . and that can make them angry too!!!
Don't dance.

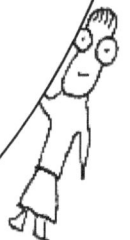

John, Sue and Granddad were playing sums in the garden.

AND ALONG CAME BETTY!!

... dancing, thinking and singing!!

4 + 1 = 41
3 + 3 = 33
1 + 2 = 12
four add one is forty one
three add three is thirty three
one add two is twelve
GIRL
BAD
BETTY

Do these sums really quickly <u>without</u> dancing.

1 + 1 =

2 + 8 =

4 + 7 =

9 + 1 =

3 + 3 =

7 + 7 =

6 + 2 =

4 + 2 =

8 + 3 =

4 + 1 =

4 + 4 =

6 + 3 =

5 + 3 =

2 + 4 =

3 + 2 =

6 + 4 =

7 + 2 =

4 + 5 =

7 + 3 =

2 + 7 =

I hope you didn't do what BAD GIRL BETTY did!!!

Do this sum really quickly <u>while</u> dancing! 6 + 5 =

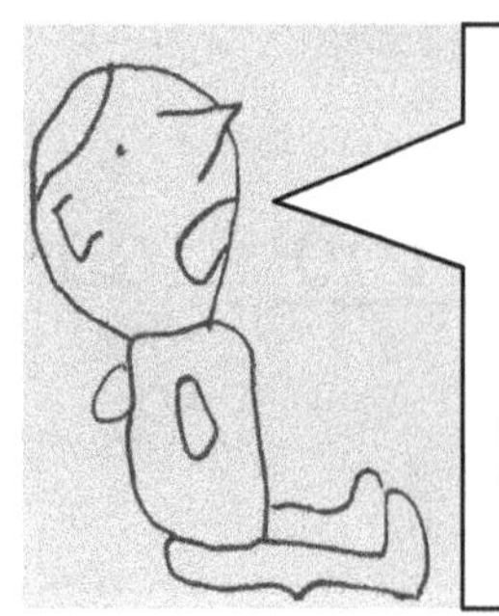

# CRAZY BABY!

goes wider and longer

Make your tens and units sums very **long** like this ... or very **wide** like this!

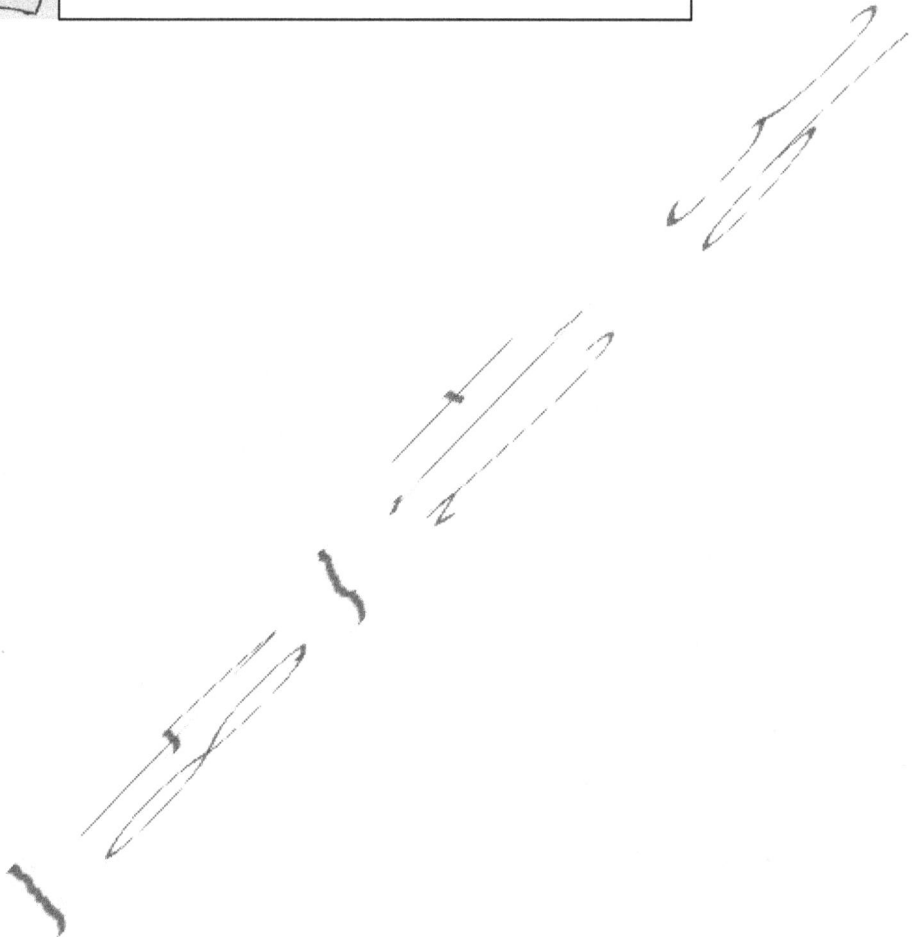

Why is the answer always 48?

Sue, what would you do if you saw a monster in the middle of the night?
Cry!
I would measure it!!

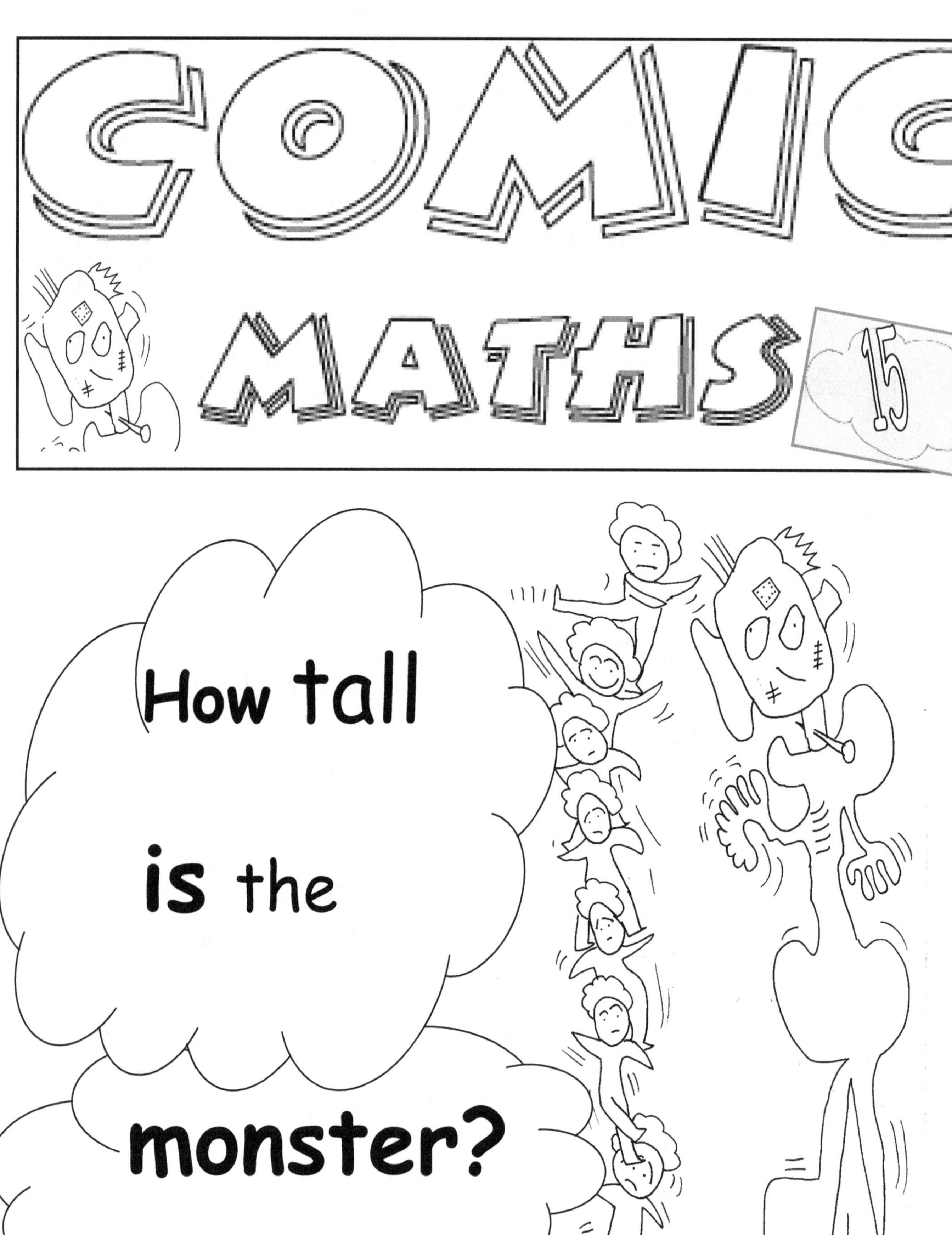
COMIC
MATHS
15
How tall
is the
monster?

**BE SAFE** Ask a grown-up

Measuring can be fun.
The Monster is <u>7</u> Johns tall and very ugly!

. . . but it takes

just 2 John's

to make a Granddad

. . . and
don't say
I'm **ugly**!

We all think that Kilo is a heavy person,
but how heavy **is** Kilo?

Lots and
lots and lots
of Mili's!!!!!

... and how heavy is little Anne?

Did you know that John can fill his drink up 100 times from Granddad's big drink?

100 drinks!!!
Thanks Granddad!!

. . . and best of all,
John, Sue and Anne can COVER
Bill's shop window with 16 sticky smiley face squares!!

## TALL QUESTIONS

How tall is the Monster?

The Monster is ___John's tall

How tall is Granddad?

Granddad is __ Johns tall

## HEAVY QUESTIONS

How heavy is Kilo?

Kilo is ________________________________ Milli's heavy

How heavy is little Anne?

Anne is ___ Milli's heavy.

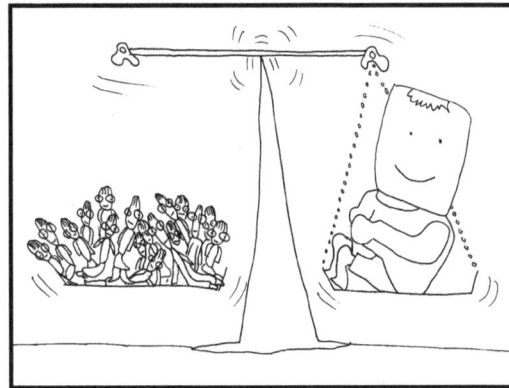

## DRINK QUESTIONS

How big is Granddad's drink?

Granddad's drink is ____ John drinks.

What size of drink

would stop you being thirsty?

I would need ____ John drinks!!

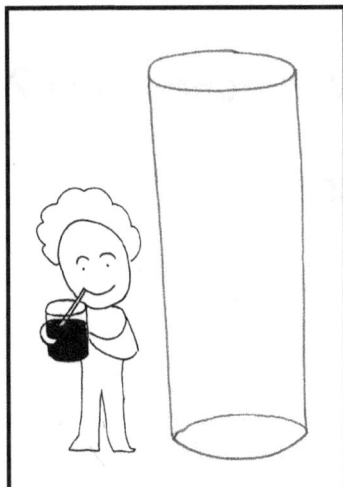

## FLAT QUESTIONS

What is the area of Bill's shop window?

Bill's shop window is _____ smiley face squares.

Make your own smiley face square.

**BE SAFE** Ask a grown-up

What is the area of the biggest window in your house?

_____ of my smiley face squares.

What is the area of the smallest window in your house?

_____ of my smiley face squares.

**COPY ME!**

CRAZY BABY!
measures everyone ...
We measured everyone and I was the biggest!
Why?

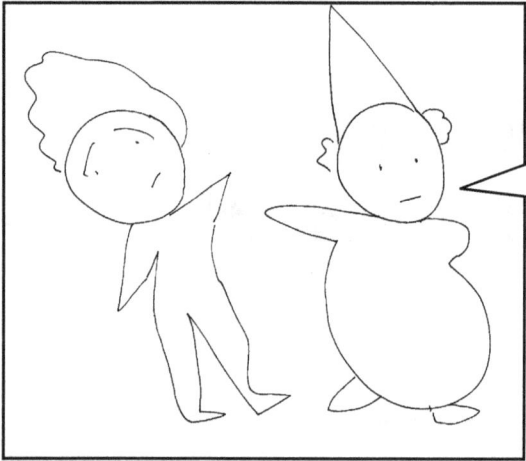

Sue ... you have got a ROUND hat!
John ... you have got a FLAT face!
!
Granddad ... you have got a FLAT face and a ROUND bottom!

# COMIC MATHS

16

FLAT face

ROUND bottom!

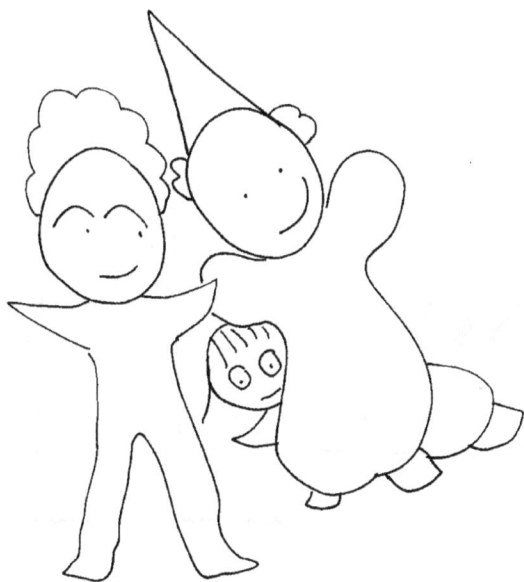

John drew a FLAT castle. The best FLAT castle ever!!

Some of the shapes John used have 3 sides.
Find them and colour them in.

Some of the shapes John used have 4 sides.
Find them and colour them in.

There are 12 shapes with 4 sides here. .
Do you believe him? ___

Sue and Anne attack John's FLAT castle!
Now some shapes have 5 sides. Colour them in.

Cardboard boxes have FLAT faces.

OK, I have a FLAT face but I can smile!

Granddad's glass has a ROUND bottom!

Hello!

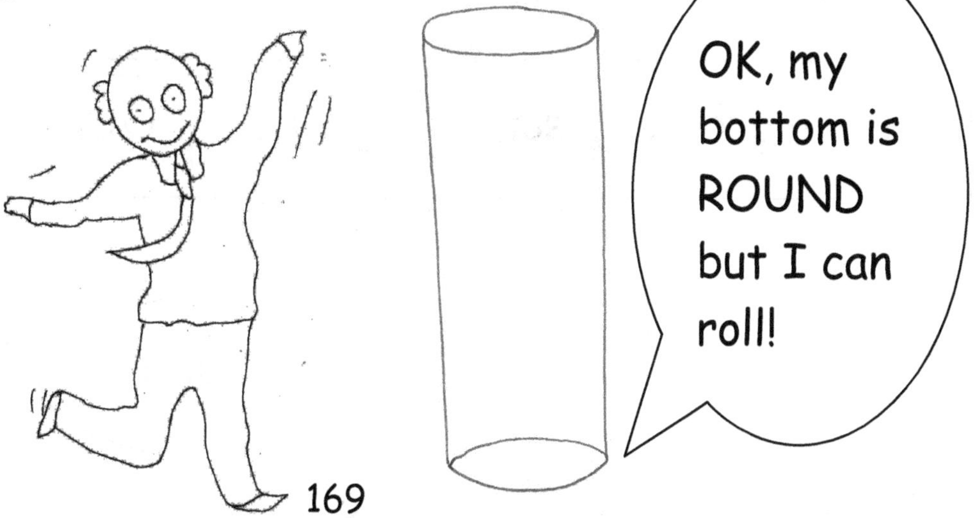

OK, my bottom is ROUND but I can roll!

FLAT
face.

Show a grown-up something with a FLAT face.

ROUND
bottom.

Show a grown-up something with a ROUND bottom.

Well done!

# CRAZY BABY!

## goes upside down

Upside down is the best in town!!

Do you like things upside down? _____

**BE SAFE** Ask a grown-up

I bought you a present!
Thanks.
Did you open the present?
Not yet!

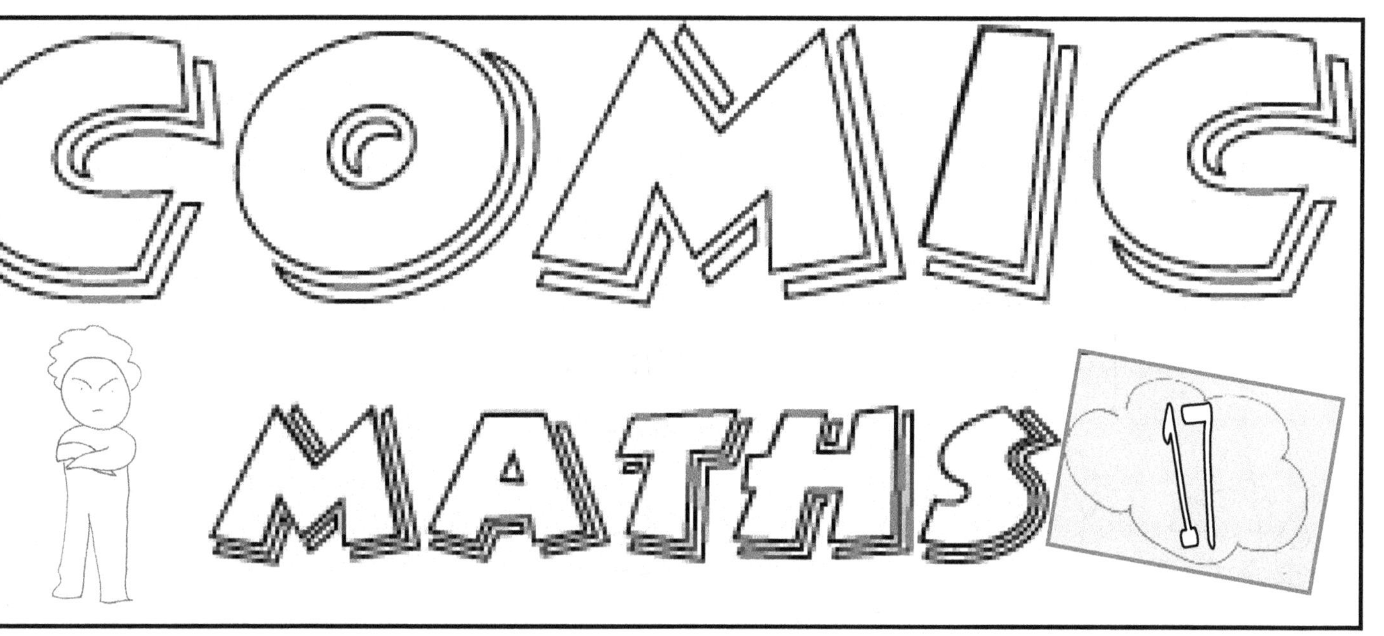

# A Box of People

Anne, Sue and John find a box.

Look! A box!
I wonder what's inside it. .
People!!!
Careful, we are only little people!

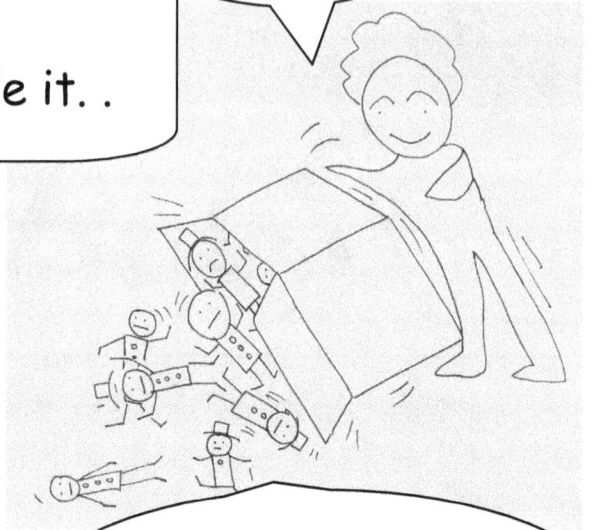

Anne counted them.
John made friends with them.
Sue was a bit scared by them!

I want to go home!
18 of them!?

Anne put the little people into 3 rows of 6.

Line up people!!

Easier to count them now.

John said ...

They all have hats.

Anne and Sue said ...

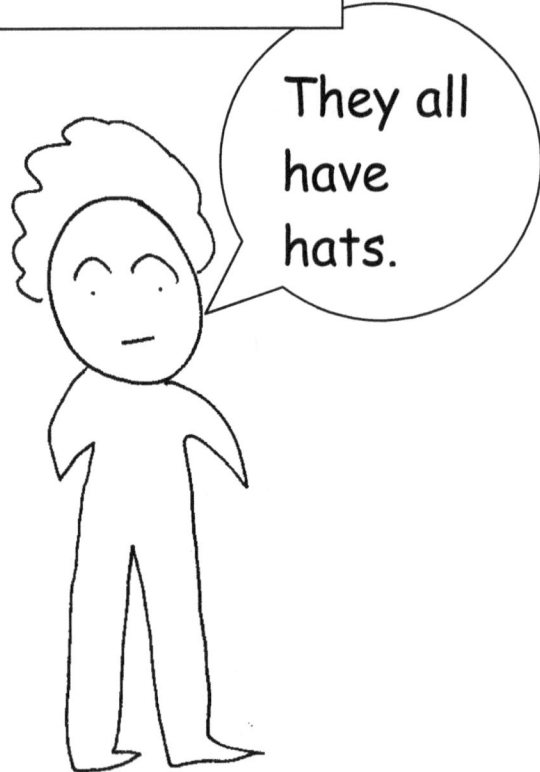

No they don't!!

**You count.** How many ...

| Have a hat? | |
|---|---|
| Don't have a hat? | |

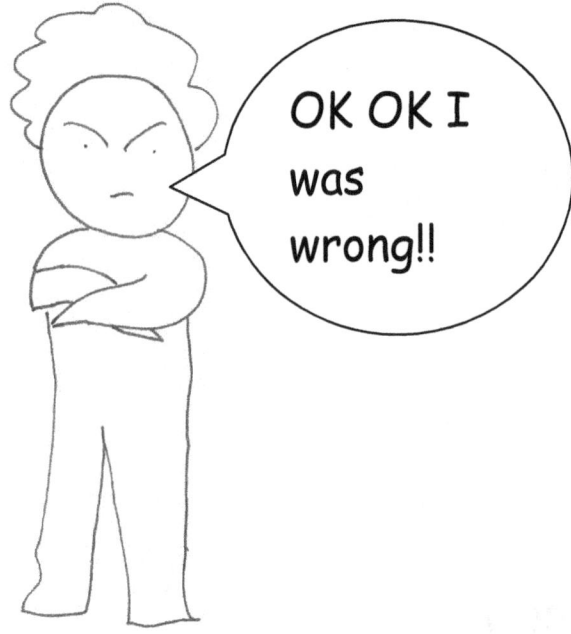

OK OK I was wrong!!

John said ...

Anne and Sue said ...

...but they all have 3 buttons, don't they?

**You count.** How many of the people have . . .

| 3 buttons? | |
|---|---|
| 2 buttons? | |
| 1 button? | |

OK I was wrong **again**
SORRY SORRY SORRY
SORRY SORRY SORRY
**SORRY!!!**

Anne and Sue said ...
There are 9 people with a hat and 3 buttons.

| | 1 Button | 2 Buttons | 3 Buttons |
|---|---|---|---|
| Hat | | | 9 |
| No Hat | | | |

Write the other numbers in.

CRAZY BABY!
asks about 100
Have you ever wondered what a hundred is?
NO
Have you?

# BIG ROBERT SAYS . . .

Do this!

Find 2 friends

Dress up as Anne, John and Sue

Have an ice cream fight!!!!!

BE SAFE Ask a grown-up

Write all the numbers from 1 to 100
Slowly
Really fast!!!


Have a writing race with a friend.

See **00** Say **hundred**

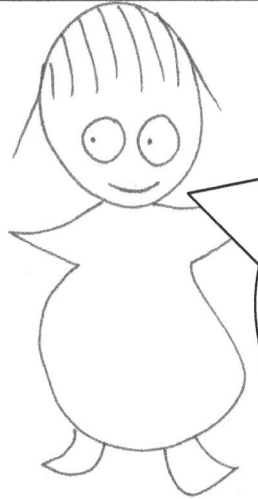

300

3 hundred

Say these numbers.

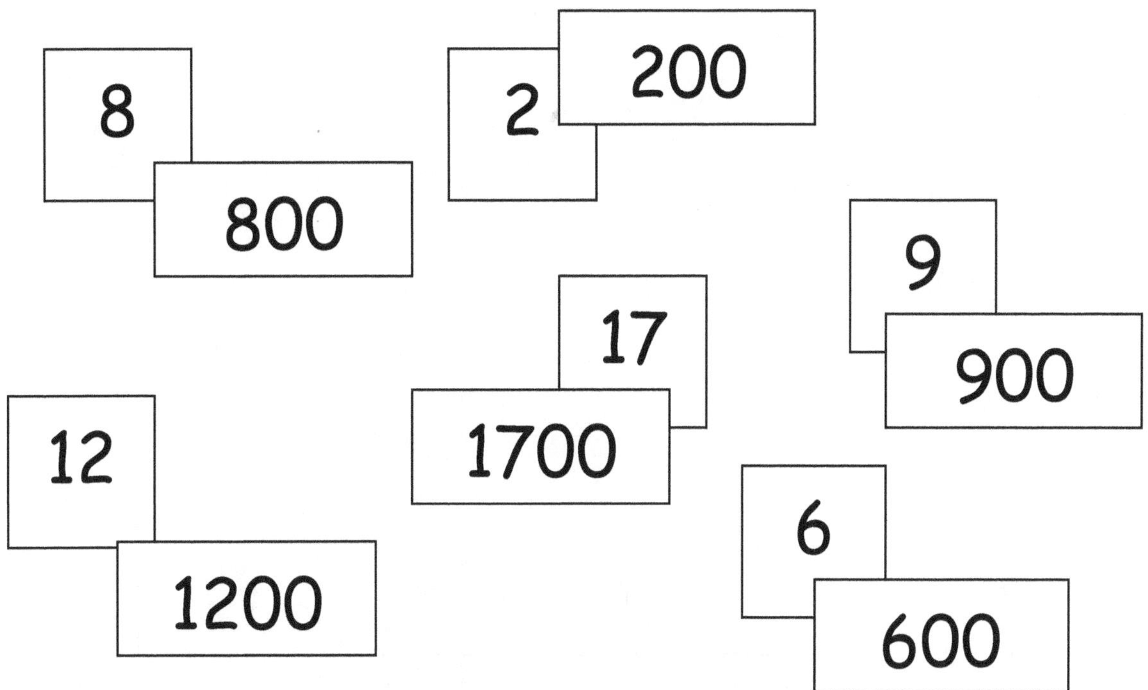

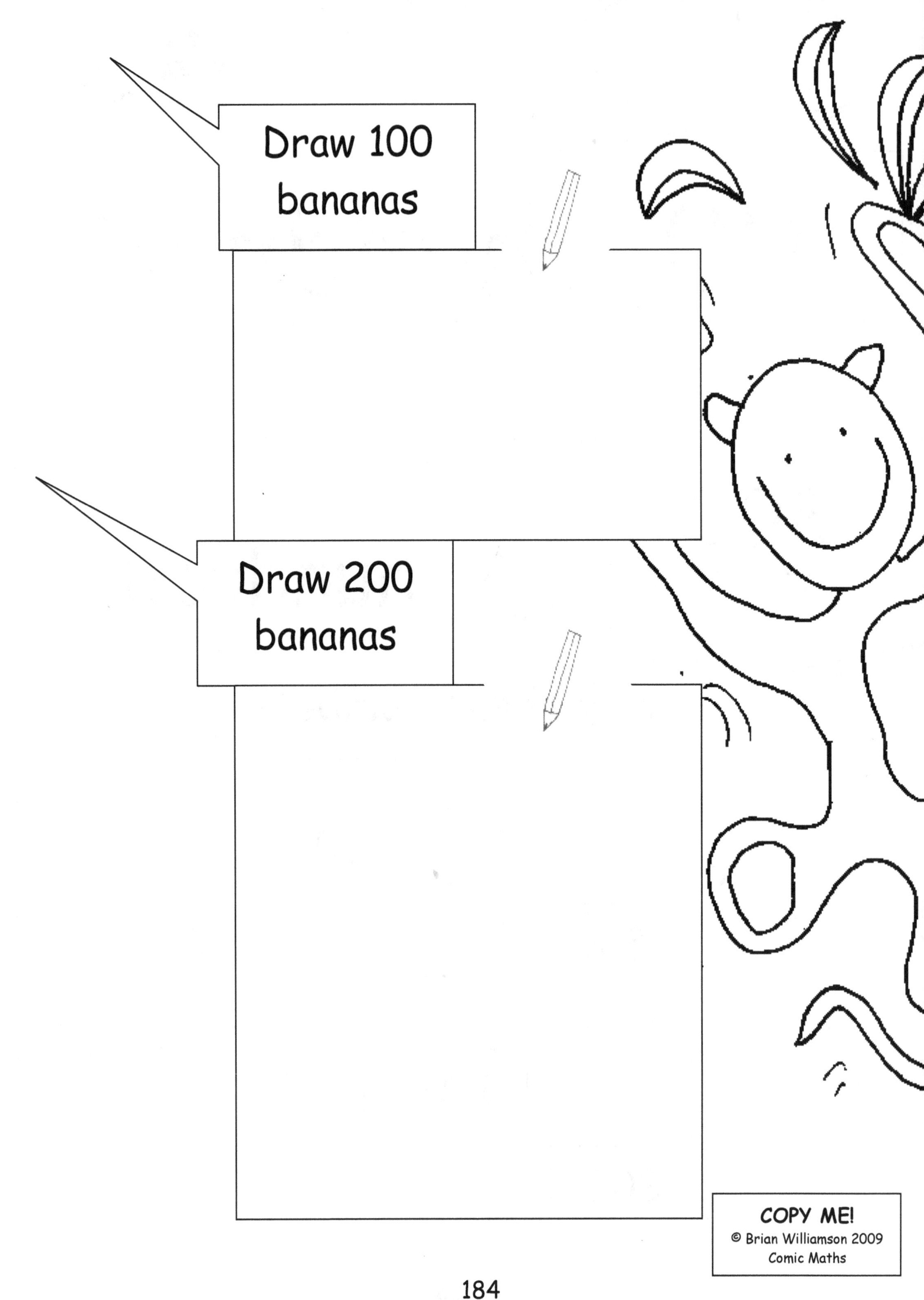
Draw 100
bananas
Draw 200
bananas

# WORK OUT!

Now you...

| | | | |
|---|---|---|---|
| 6= | 6 | | see it! |
| 6 − 6 = | | | don't! |
| 6 − 6 + 6 = | | | see it! |
| 6 − 6 + 6 − 6 = | | | don't! |
| 6 − 6 + 6 − 6 + 6 = | | | see it! |

COPY ME!

5 + 5 =

10

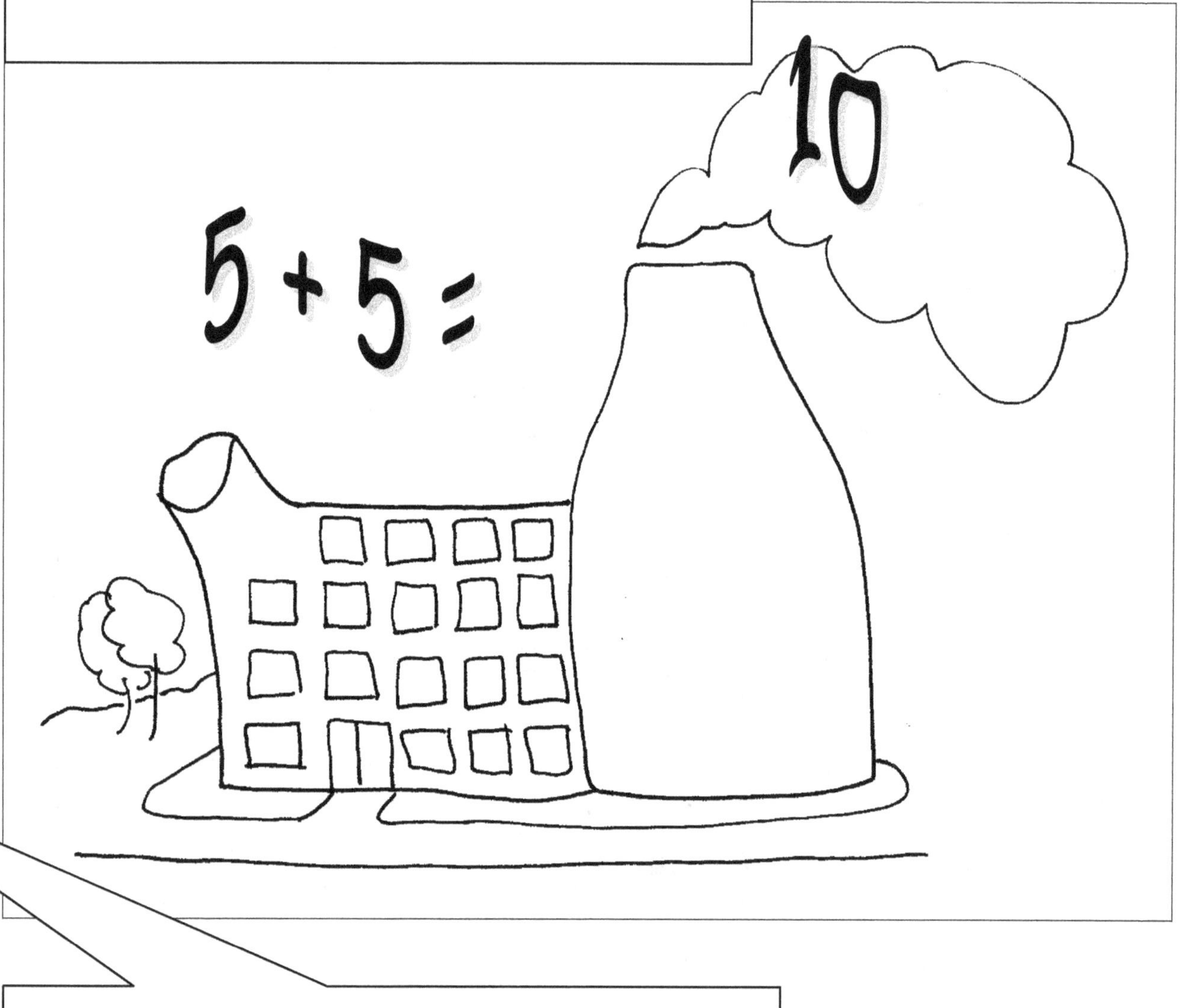

I make them. You do them!

I made these...
... just for you!

Sue's turn.

Anne's turn.

COPY ME!

BIG ROBERT SAYS ...

Your turn.

Draw you!

Your turn.

**COPY ME!**



Your turn.

Make your own!

Your turn.

Your turn.

Your turn.

**COPY ME!**

I think the sum factory has done too many sums!!

Ask a grown-up to play my sum factory game with you.

Teach a grown-up add and take sums.
See the next two pages for help.

Tick this box when the grown-up understands. ☐

BIG
ROBERT
SAYS ...

Add
2
+ 1
3

Add
Add
3 2
+ 2 1
5 3
Add
Add
Add
4 3 2
+ 3 2 1
7 5 3

Take
5
- 1
4
Take
Take
8 5
- 2 1
6 4
Take
Take
Take
Take
4 8 5
- 3 2 1
1 6 4

Charlie has 12 bananas.

He eats 4.

The vet gives him 9.

He throws 3 away.

He finds 1 under his seat.

He looses 5.

A little girl gives him 2.

He gives 4 away to a friend.

He wins 3 in a lucky dip.

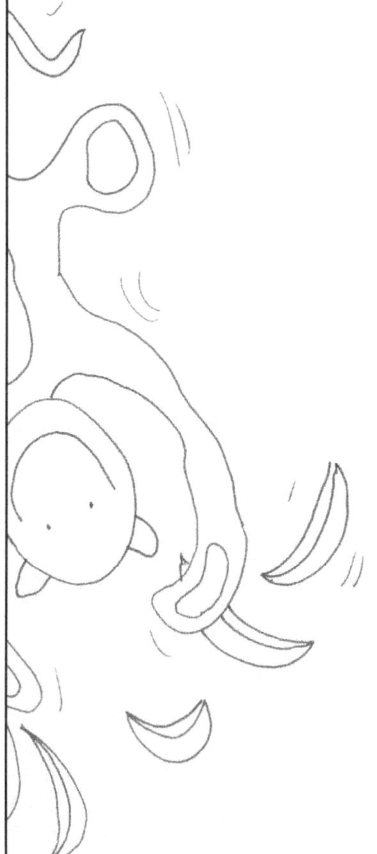

How many bananas

does Charlie have now? ___

COPY ME!

Make a picture using ...
Squares
Rectangles and ......
Triangles
COPY ME!
© Brian Williamson 2009
Comic Maths

# Draw a shape and write the sides inside!!

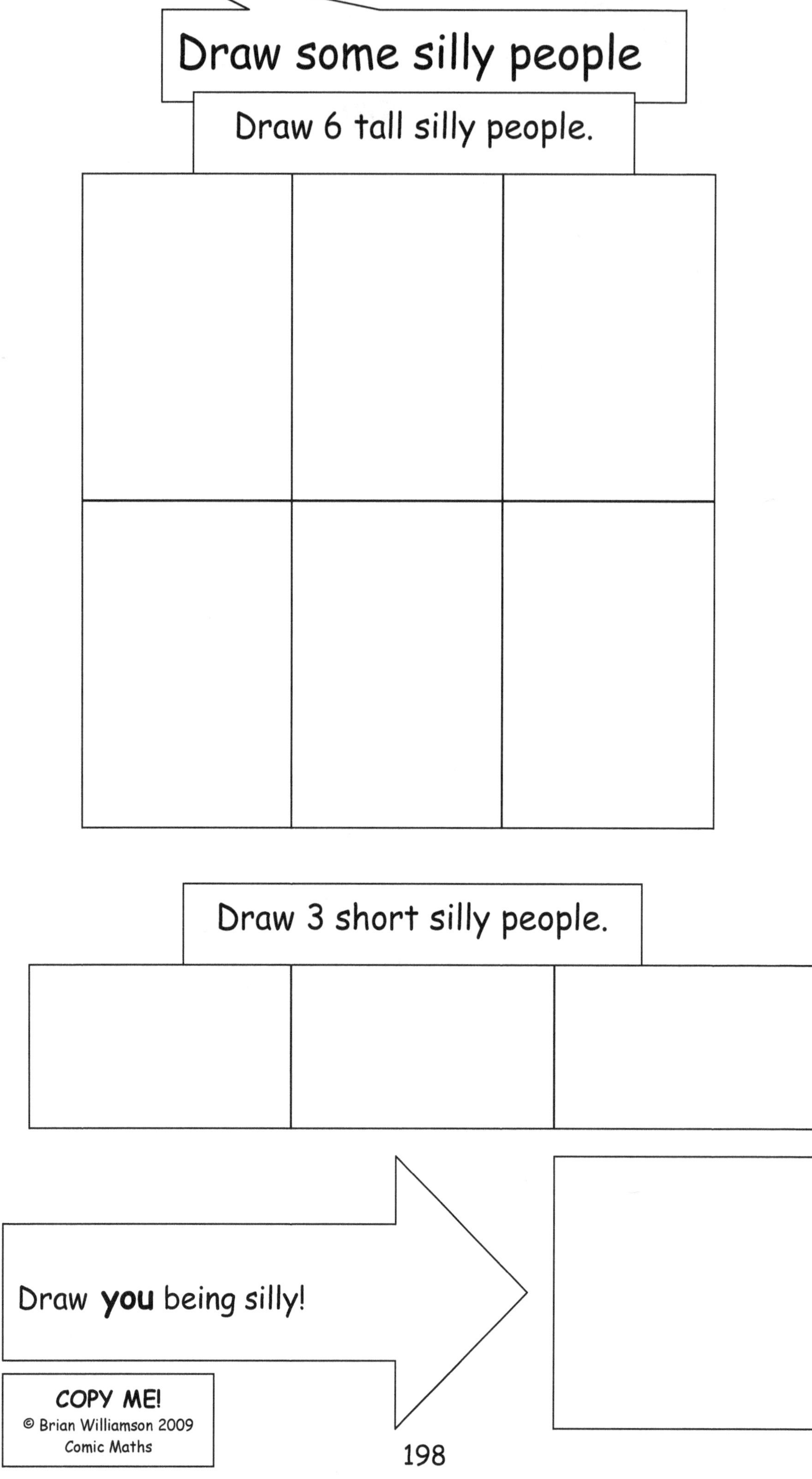
Draw some silly people
Draw 6 tall silly people.
Draw 3 short silly people.
Draw **you** being silly!

COPY ME!

Betty, does dancing make you fall over?

Sometimes!!

COMIC
18
MATHS
Bang!
Thud!
Smack!
JOHN FALLS OVER!!!
Thud!
Bang!
Smack!

18
John walks.
John counts.
1
0
10
John walks and counts.
2
0
10
John
3
0
10
keeps
4
0
10
on ...

5
0
10
counting.
6
0
10
When
7
0
10
John
8
0
10

18

ten he just goes on!

10 11 20

10 12 20

10 13 20

. . . until one bad day

he tripped over Horace the Hedgehog!!

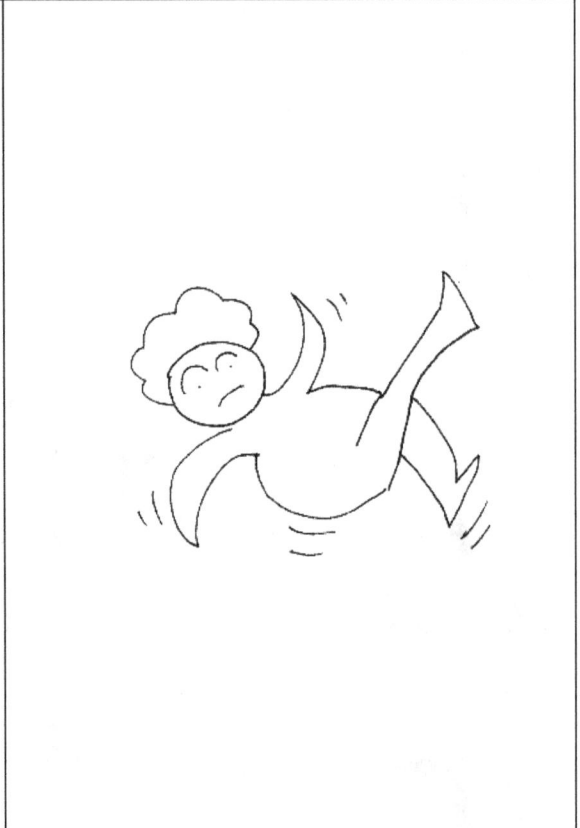

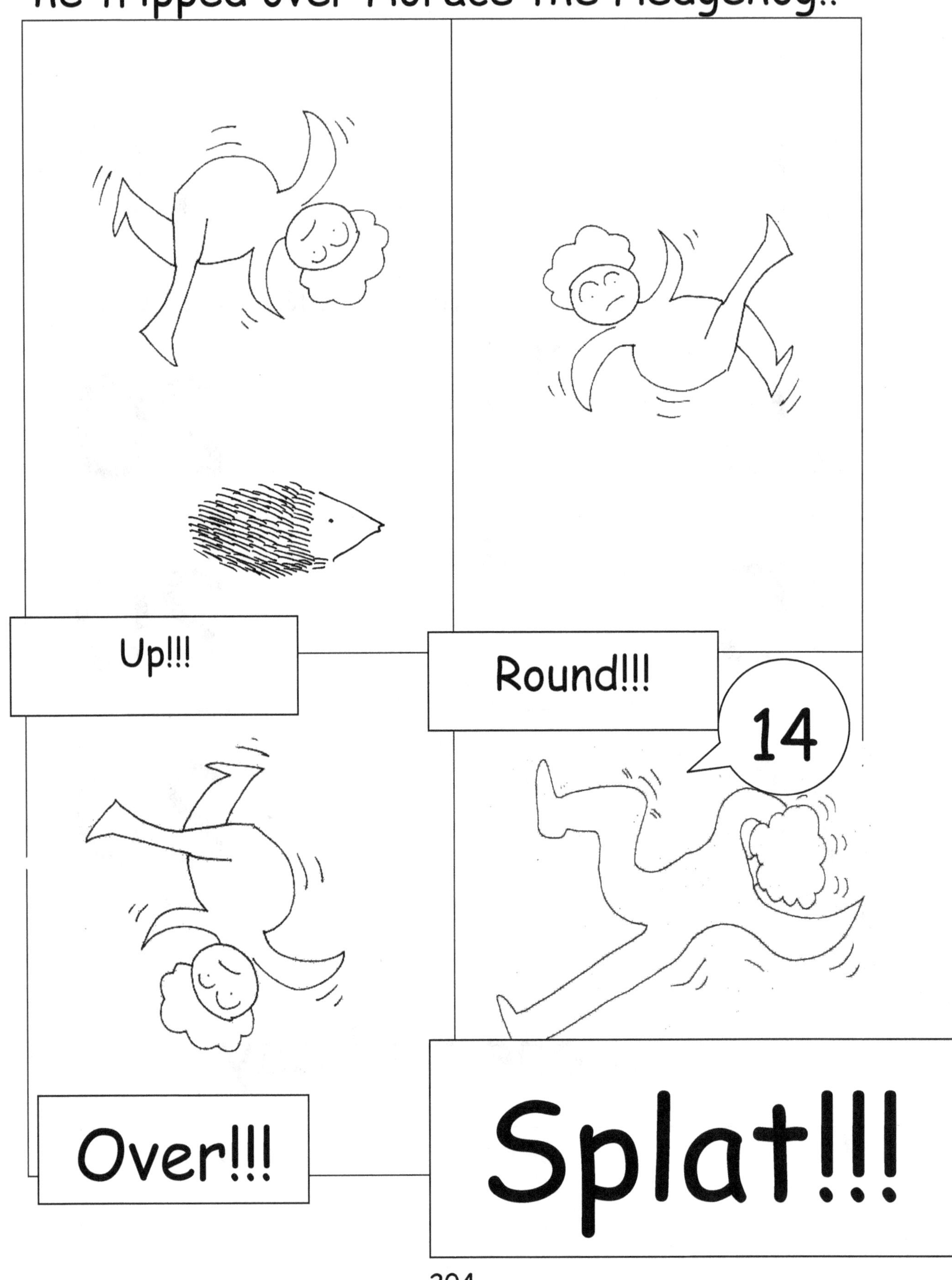

Up!!!
Round!!!
14
Over!!!
Splat!!!

Number 10 came running to help ...

because number 10 was the closest.

Look who comes running to help now.

18

# Who will come running to help?

39

Number ___

21

Number ___

19

Number ___

67

Number ___

!!!!!!

That John needs to be more careful!!

COPY ME!

CRAZY BABY!

makes John think!!

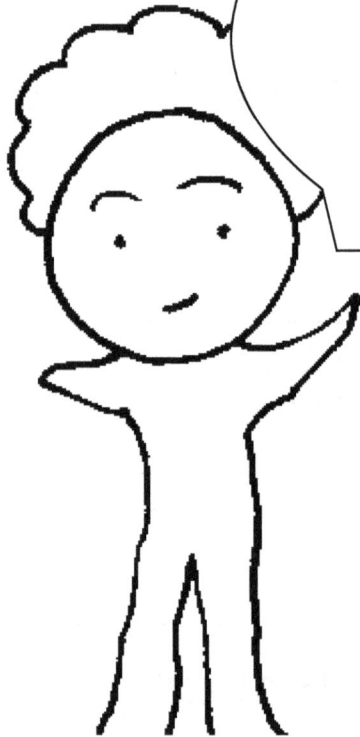

HELP!! You are stretching my brain . . .

. . . as far as

mars!

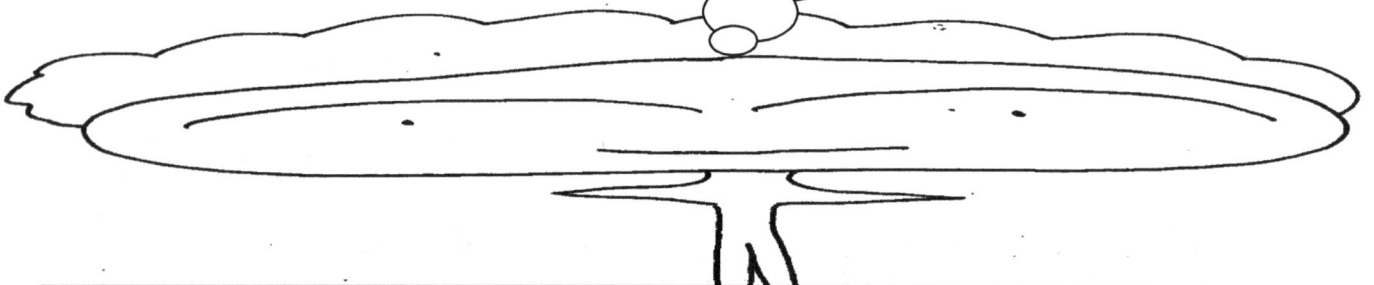

What stretches your brain?

I am worried about my

... chin, Sue.

Oh no! A spot!!

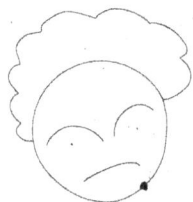

COMIC
MATHS
19
Spotty
Chins!
They are catching!!!

John gets one spot on his chin. Oh no!
One John times one spot equals one.

Kilo and Granddad get one spot each.

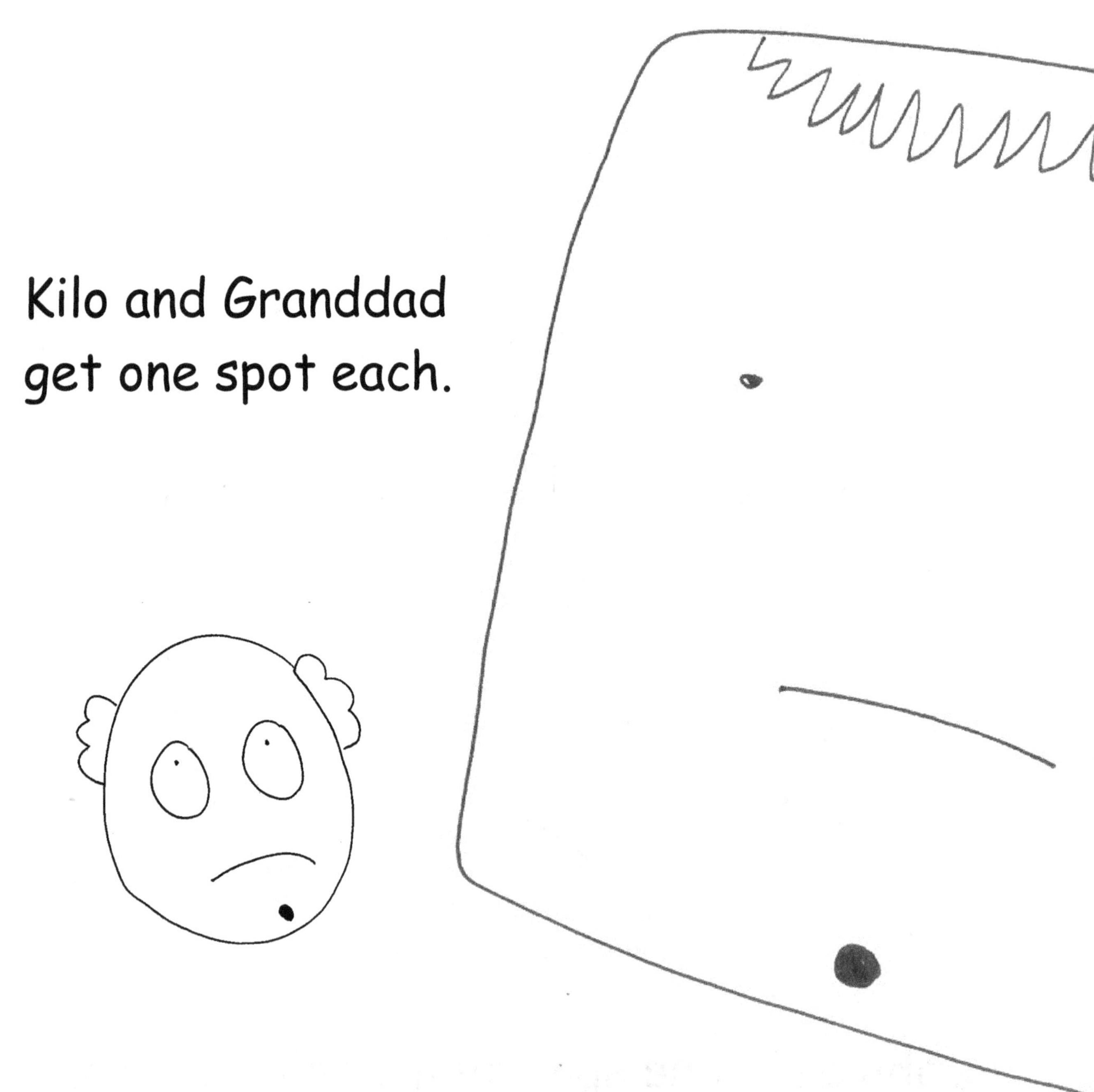

Two times one equals two.

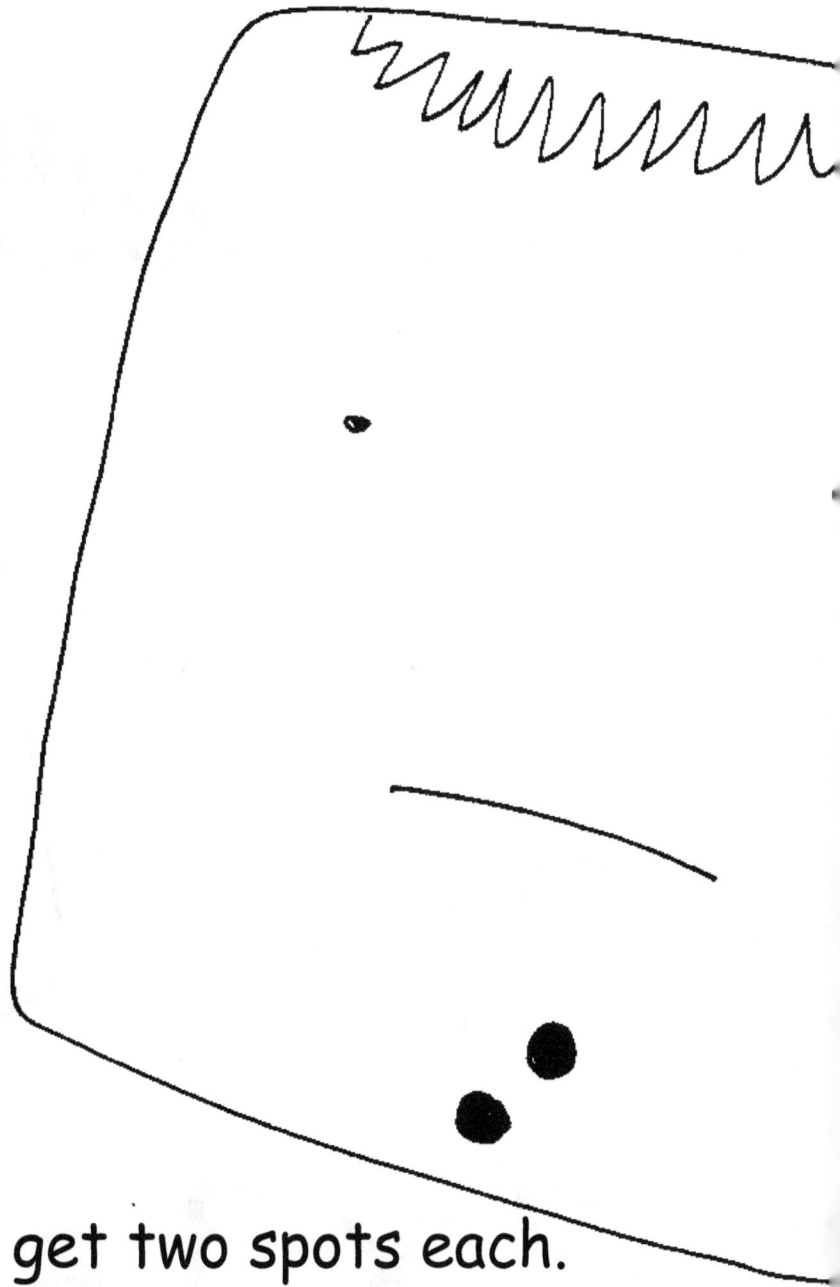

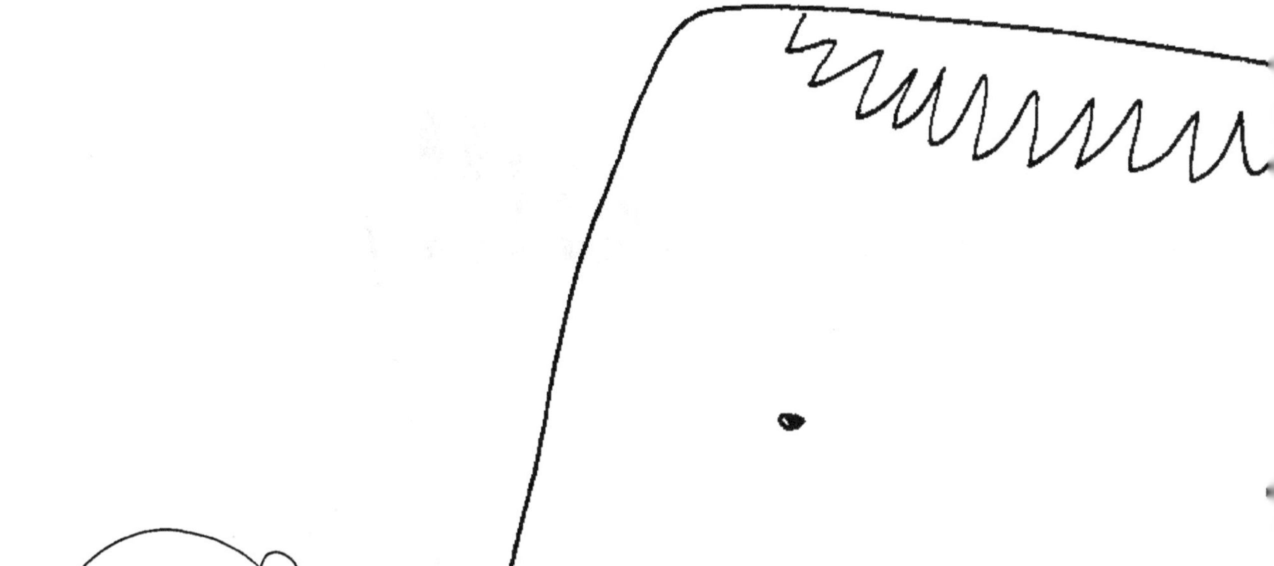

Kilo and Granddad get two spots each.

Two times two equals four.

... and worse!!!

2 x 3 = 6

Anne, Anne's mum and Sue get three spots each.

3 x 3 = 9

John gets 3 spots and so do all the boys ...

# ... in the Comic Maths Football Team!

$$11 \times 3 = 33$$

Think of spotty chins and work these out!!

1 x 3 =

2 x 3 =

3 x 3 =

4 x 3 =

5 x 3 =

6 x 3 =

7 x 3 =

8 x 3 =

9 x 3 =

10 x 3 =

11 x 3 =

12 x 3 =

# CRAZY BABY!

one times one

ONE TIMES ONE
That is a funny thing to say to someone!!

What is ONE TIMES ONE? __

My baby doll.

My toy train.

COMIC
MATHS
20
Granddad's Sharing Hands

It can be hard ... to share 1 ice cream

... between 3 children!

# and

It can be hard ...
to share 3 ice creams
between 2 children.

... Sometimes
not even a Granddad can sort it out!

BUT ...

Sharing 3 ice creams between 3 children is easy for any Granddad to do.

1 for you    1 for you and ...    1 for you!!

Share 3 ice creams between 3 children.

# $3 \div 3 =$

They have __ each.

Share 6 ice creams between 3 children.

$$6 \div 3 =$$

They have __ each.

Share 9 ice creams between 3 children.

$$9 \div 3 =$$

They have __ each.

Share 12 ice creams between 3 children.

$$12 \div 3 =$$

They have __ each.

Sometimes sharing is easy.

Sometimes sharing is hard!!

CRAZY BABY!
shares nothing!
I have nothing to share with you ten ...

... so we all get nothing!!!!

$0 \div 10 =$

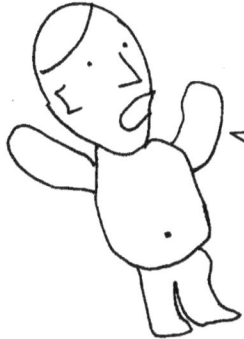

I want
more baby dolls.

I want
more toy trains.

I want
more ideas.

We want more of **everything**!

Bill sells everything in his everything Shop!

Bird cages

Giant carrots

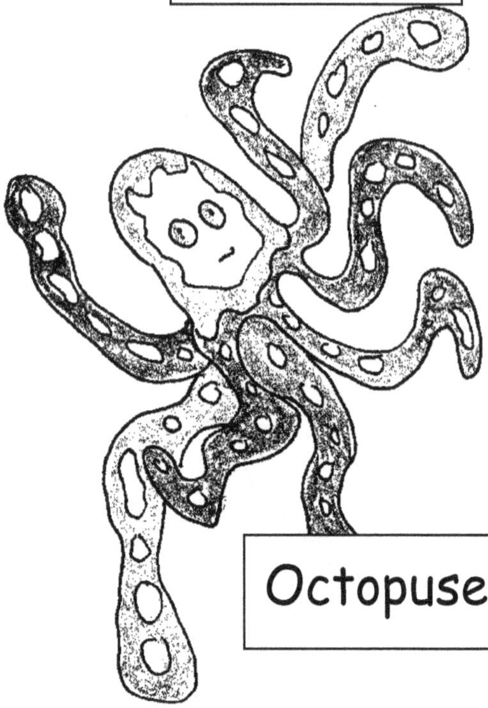

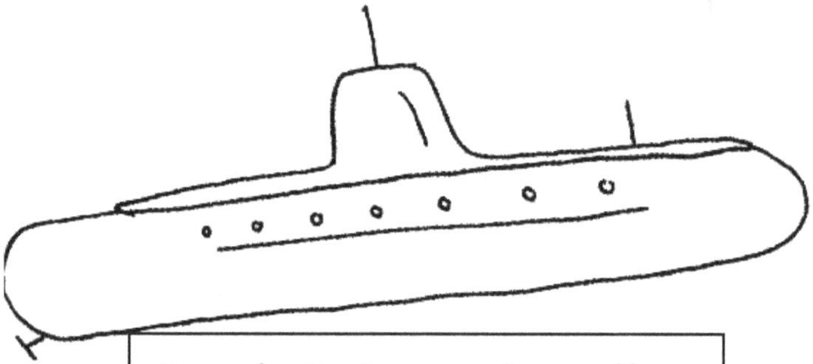

Octopuses

Real Submarines!!

Write something Bill does not sell.

Sorry, I sell those!!
I sell **everything**!!

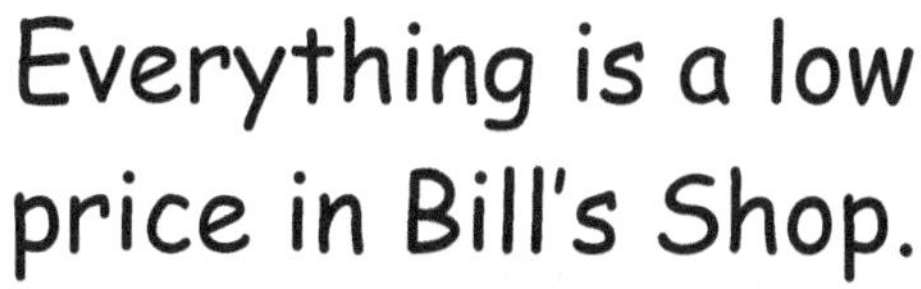

Everything is a low price in Bill's Shop.

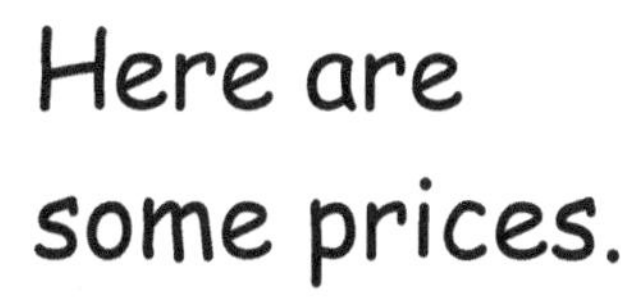

Here are some prices.

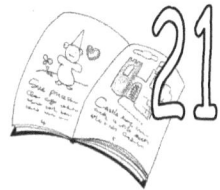

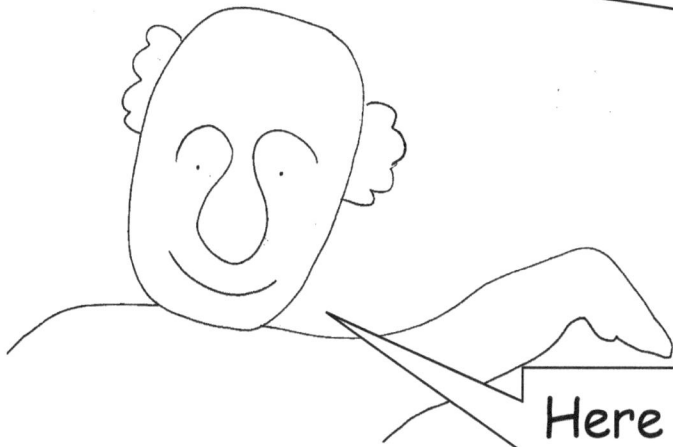

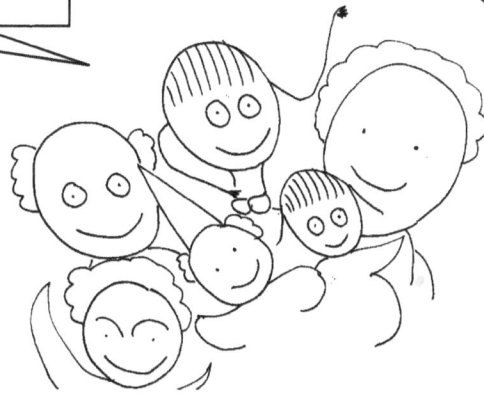

| Giant Carrot | 40 pennies |
|---|---|
| Octopus | 60 pennies |
| Real Submarine | 45 pennies |
| Necklace | 25 pennies |
| Apple | 5 pennies |
| Banana | 10 pennies |
| Picture | 90 pennies |
| Set of Pencils | 15 pennies |
| Girl's Top | 65 pennies |
| Bird Cage | 55 pennies |
| Computer | 95 pennies |
| Robot | 45 pennies |
| Paint Brush | 35 pennies |
| Tin of Paint | 40 pennies |

Betty buys a giant carrot and an octopus.

How many pennies should she give to Bill?
She should give Bill _____ pennies.

John buys 2 robots and a banana.

How many pennies should he give Bill?
He should give Bill _____ pennies.

Charlie the Monkey buys ...

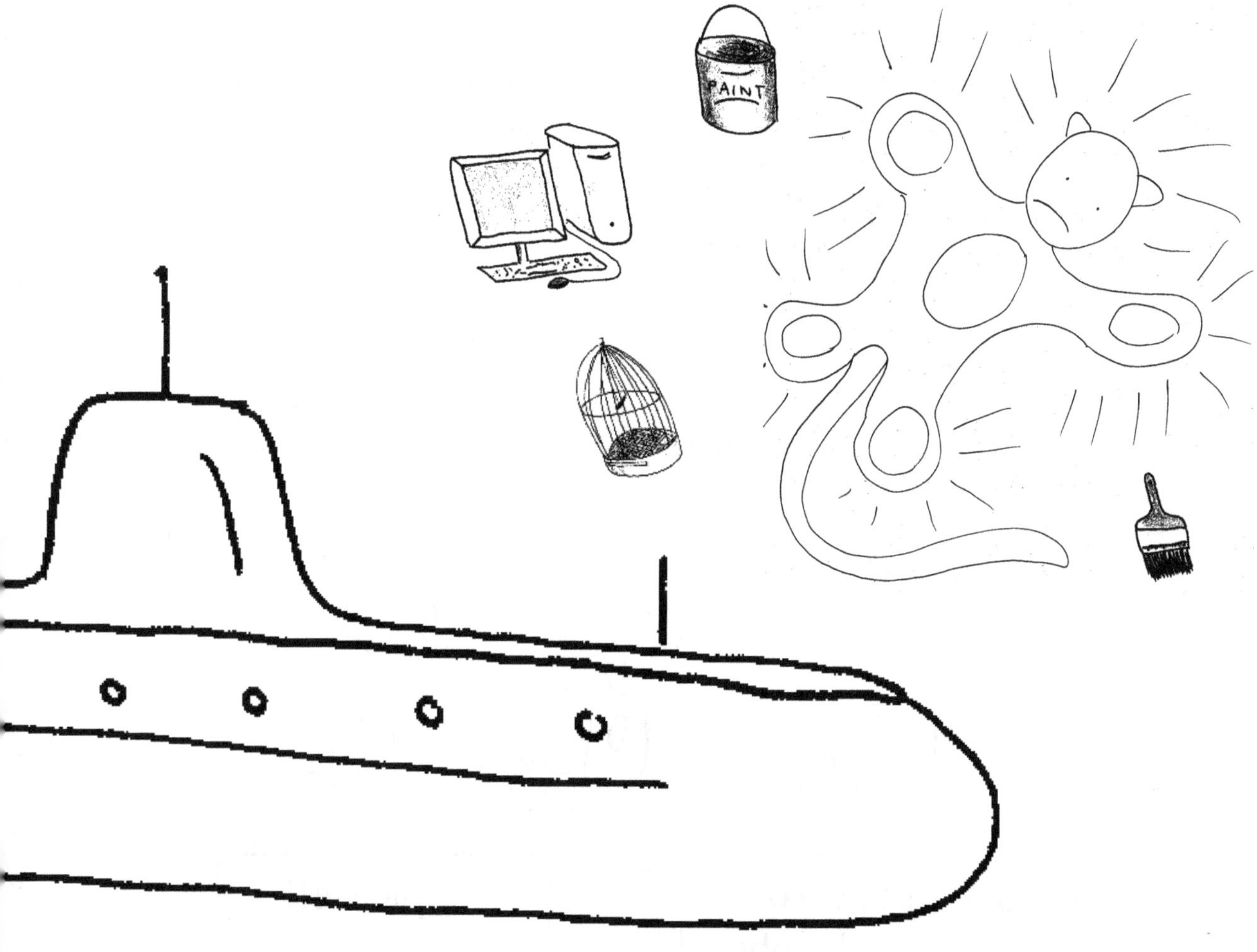

How much money should Charlie give to Bill?
Charlie should give Bill _____ pennies.

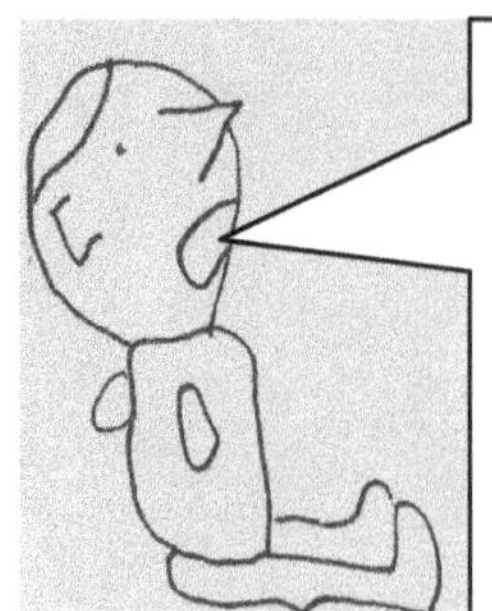

# CRAZY BABY! goes shopping.

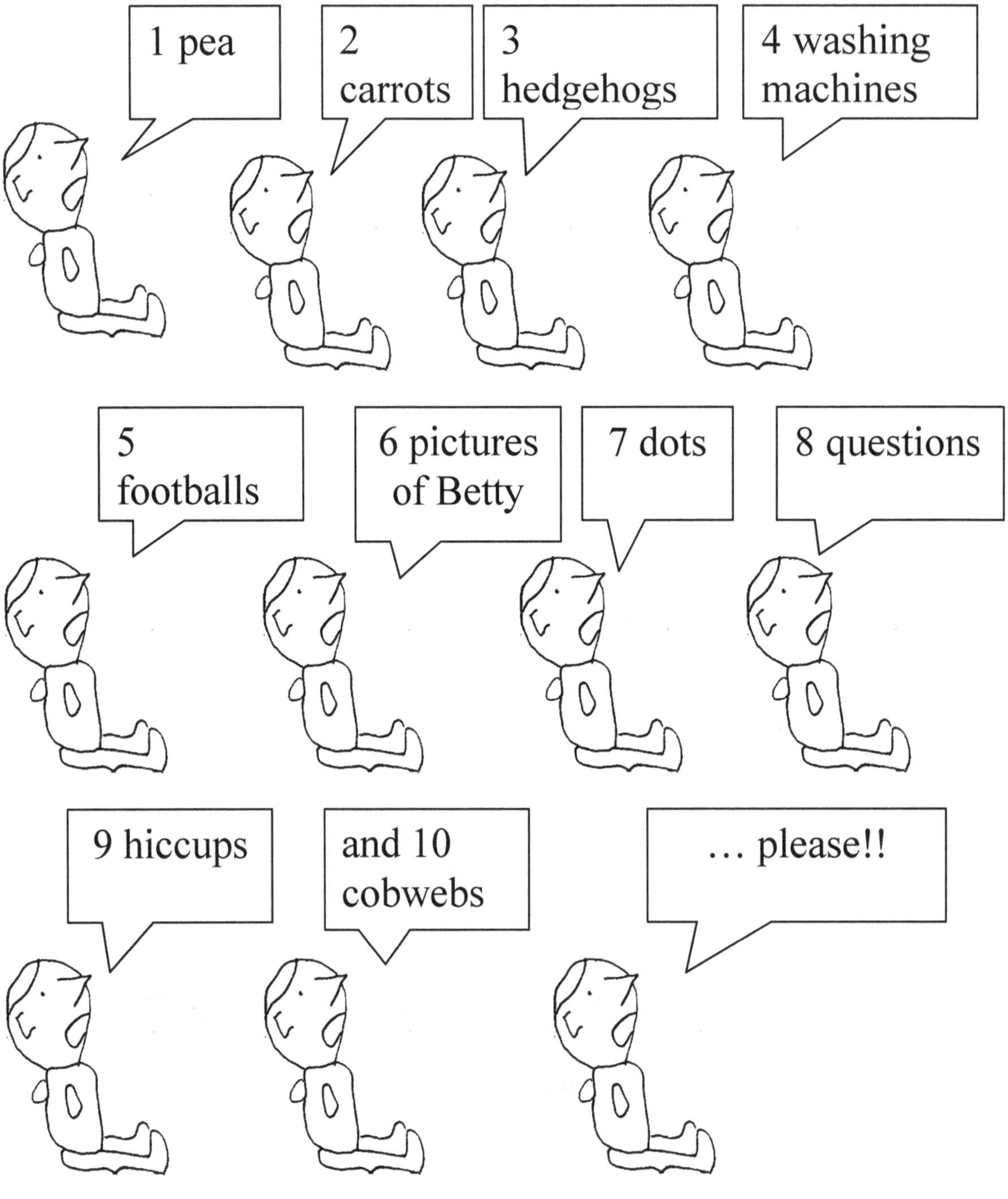

1 pea

2 carrots

3 hedgehogs

4 washing machines

5 footballs

6 pictures of Betty

7 dots

8 questions

9 hiccups

and 10 cobwebs

… please!!

How many things does **CRAZY BABY!** buy? ____.

I am 6
and I am running to 7.
I am 7.

19 year olds
are so big ....
they disappear!

# Sue is five

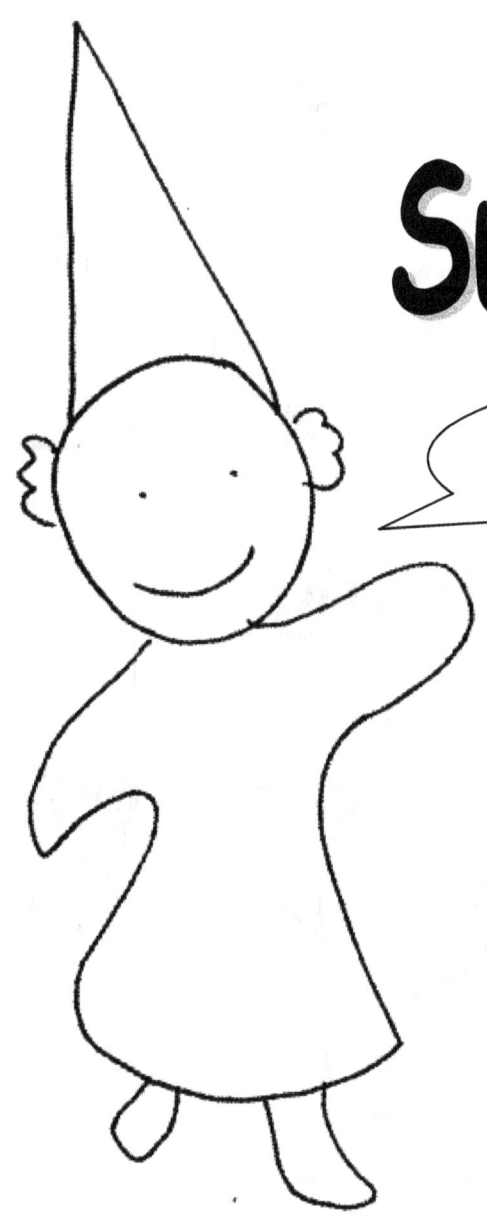

I was

five.

5

but now I am

five and a half.

$5\frac{1}{2}$

I am just waiting to be 6.

On her $5\frac{1}{2}$ birthday Sue shared 11 buns between 2 elephants!!

How many buns did each elephant get?

Nelly has ... ___ buns

Gladys has ... ___ buns

and that makes ... ___ buns altogether.

COPY ME!

# CRAZY BABY!

halves a cherry cake

or

If someone hasn't got the cherry they start to moan!!

Should the cherry be cut in half? ________

How many sleeps to your birthday John?
4 sleeps Bill and Betty!
1
2
3
4
5
6
John's Birthdayometer

How many bananas have you eaten, Charlie?
1
2
3
4
5
6
4 bananas John and Anne!
Charlie's Bananaometer

COMIC
MATHS
kilo
23
7 meters
6 meters
5 meters
4 meters
3 meters
2 meters
1 meter
Monster Mesures


The monster is 7 meters tall.
Tall for a monster!

Kilo runs 1000 meters and that is quite a long way!
A Kilo meter!!
kilo
Kilo lifts 1000 grams!!
A Kilo gram
kilo
Kilo drinks 1000 litres of juice!!
A Kilo litre
... but then Kilo has to go to the toilet for 1000 hours!!!
A Kilo hour
The area of Kilo's t-shirt is 1000 smiley face squares.
Kilo squares!!
All the Kilo measures are named after me!!
Kilo

| Put **1000** of **Milli**'s pencil cases in a line. They will be 1 meter long!! | If **1000 Millis** get weighed they only weigh 1 gram. | **1000** of **Milli**'s drinks make a litre!! |
|---|---|---|
| 1 **Milli**metre!!! | 1 **Milli**gram!!! | Not much. |
| **Milli** can drink **1000** drinks in 1 second!! | ... and her pillow is just 1 **milli**metre long and 1 **milli**metre wide. | All the **Milli** measures are named after me!! |
| 1 **milli**second. That's fast!!! | | |

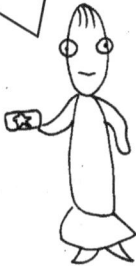

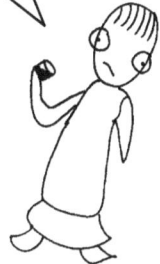

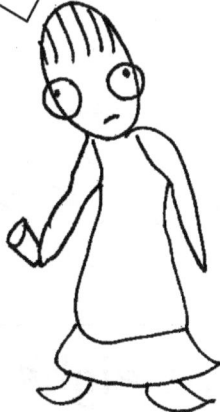

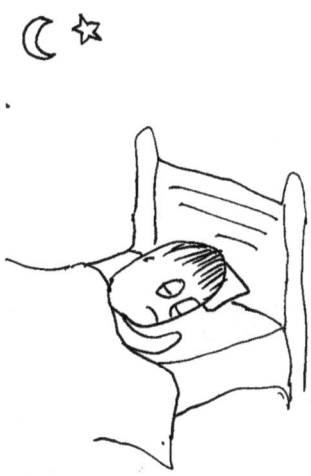

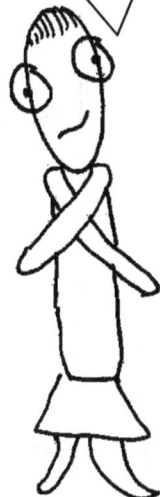

# Colour in the picture if you believe it.

John's leg is 6 hours long.

The ice cream van is 6 meters long.

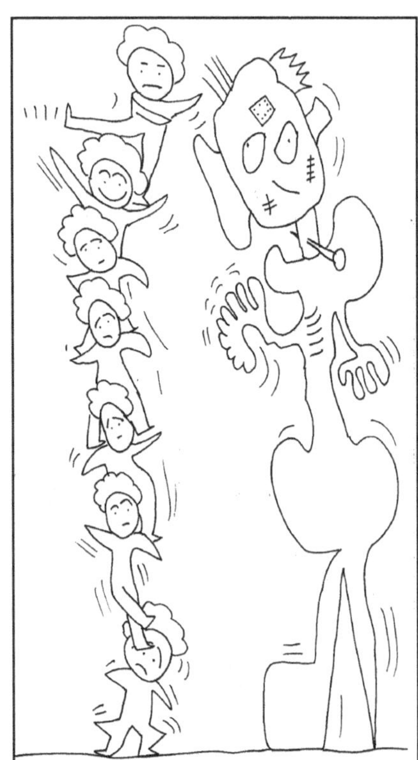

The monster is 7 stones high.

Betty weighs 10 stones.

The ice cream van weighs 1 ton.

John's drink is 6 miles long.

John's drink is 1 litre.

Betty weighs 10 hours.

John's leg is 60 centimetres long.

The monster is 7 Johns high.

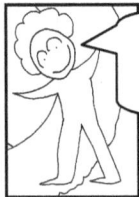

Birthdays!!

| August | | | | | | |
|---|---|---|---|---|---|---|
| M | T | W | T | F | S | S |
| 1 | 2 | 3 | 4 | 5 | 6 | 7 |
| 8 | 9 | 10 | 11 | 12 | 13 | 14 |
| 15 | 16 | 17 | 18 | 19 | 20 | 21 |
| 22 | 23 | 24 | 25 | 26 | 27 | 28 |
| 29 | 30 | 31 | | | | |

On August 11 it will be 10 days before my birthday.

August $31^{st}$ is Anne's birthday!

Milli drinks 100 drinks in 1 second!!

If 1000 Millis get weighed they only weigh 1 gram.

Kilo runs 1000 meters and that is quite a long way.

Kilo lifts 100 grams!!

**COPY ME!**

# CRAZY BABY!

Says" ALIEN is 2"

Am I
2 houses
tall?
I weigh
2 tons?
0
3
1
2

If ALIEN was shorter ...
how many houses tall would he be? _____ houses tall.

If ALIEN was heavier ...
how many tons would he weigh? _____ tons.

Anne is very clever
She can do lots of tricks!
But sometimes she forgets things!
Who are you??
I am Charlie the Monkey!!

COMIC
MATHS
24
NAME THOSE SHAPES!
NAME THOSE SHAPES!
NAME THOSE SHAPES!
Play our game and
be a winner!

Anne and her mum make up a game called ....

NAME THOSE SHAPES!
I know what this is...
and I can write its name HERE!!
_ _ _ _ _ _

I can name 2 shapes.
24
I can name 3!!

I can name 4!!!!!!
THEN NAME THOSE SHAPES!!

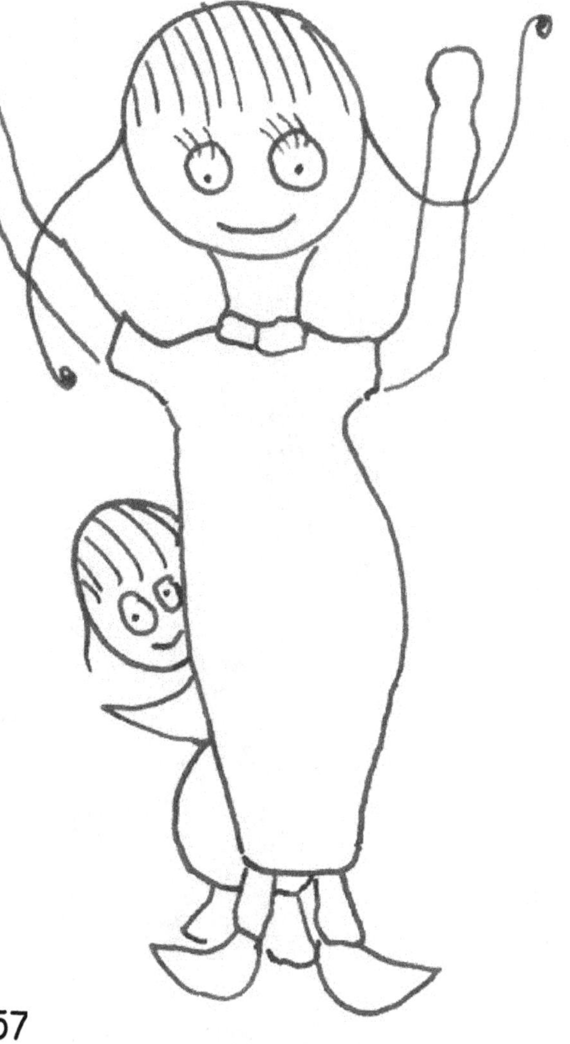

Mum wins!

Play **NAME THOSE SHAPES!** with these shapes.

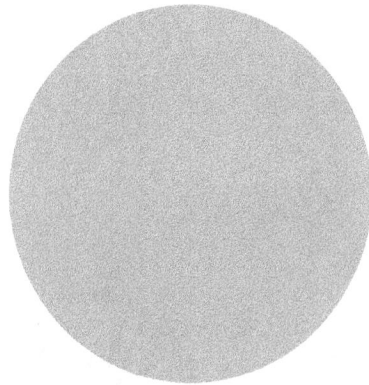

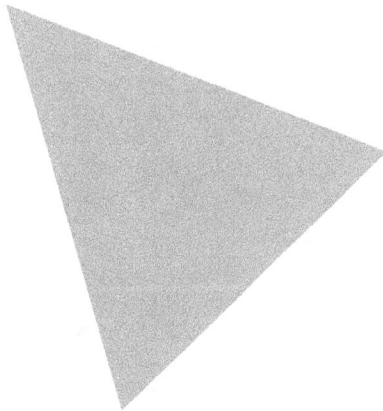

# CRAZY BABY! gets ... stung!!!!!

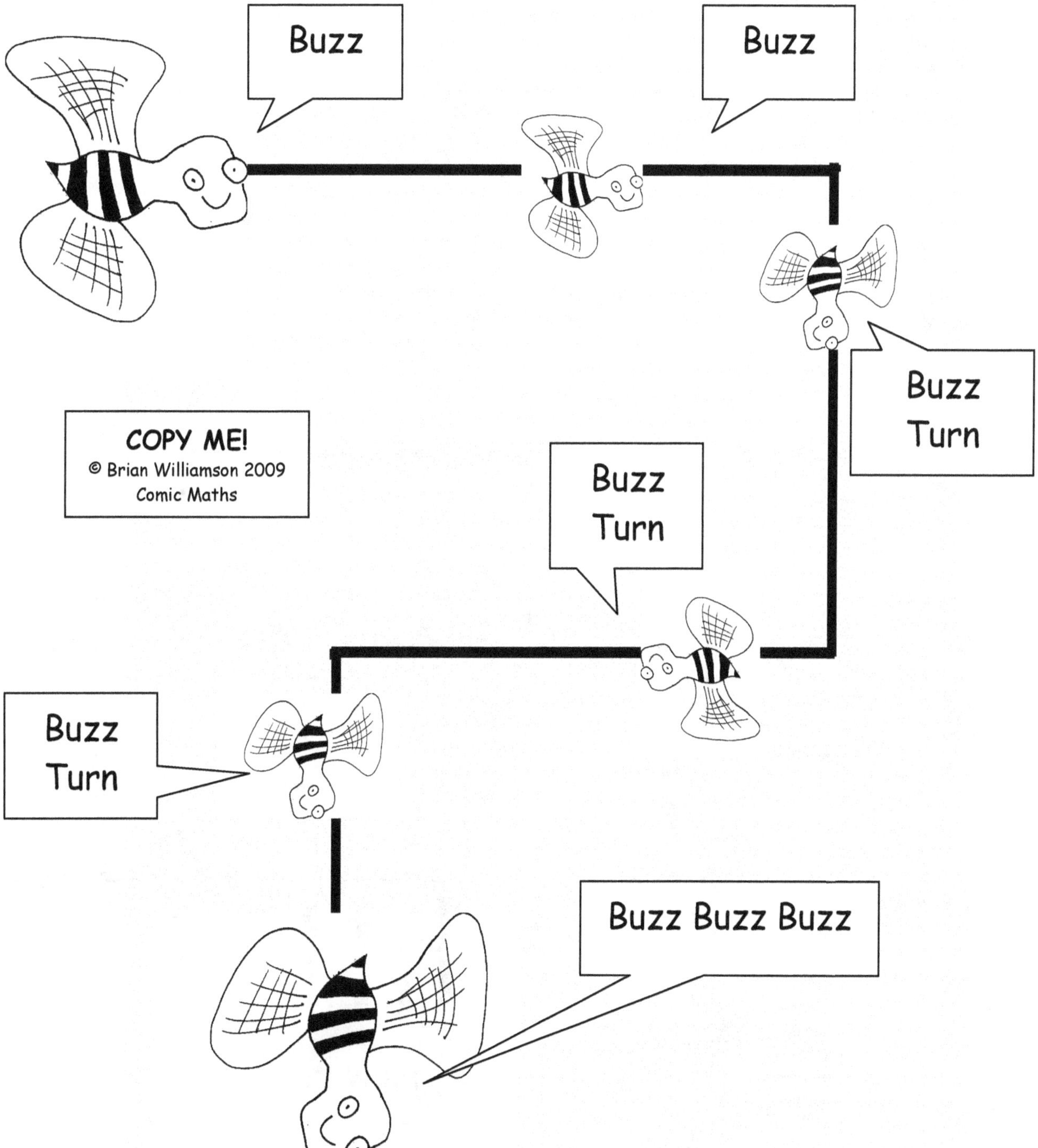

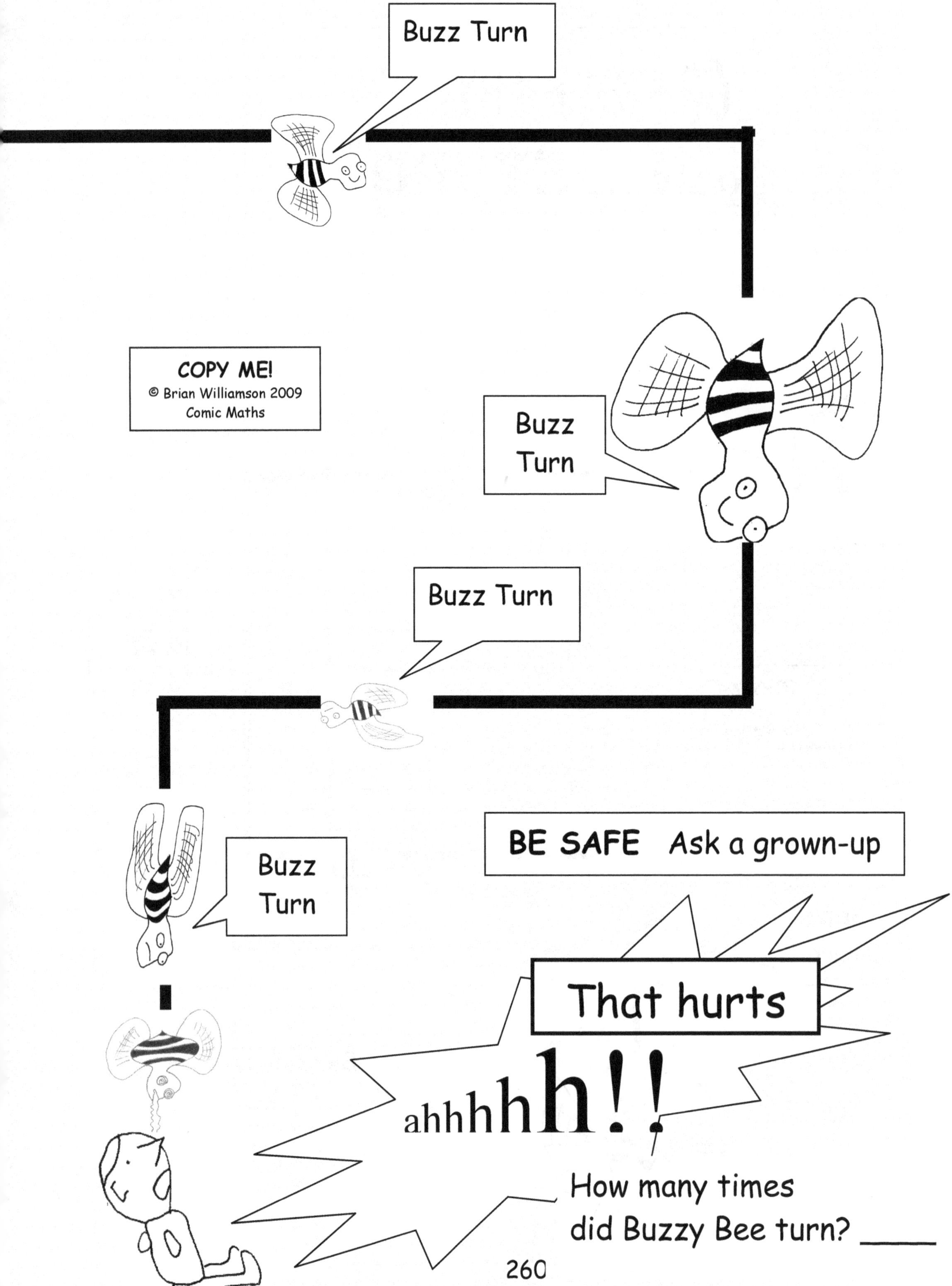

Buzz Turn

COPY ME!


Buzz
Turn

Buzz Turn

Buzz
Turn

BE SAFE Ask a grown-up

That hurts

ahhhhh!!

How many times
did Buzzy Bee turn? ____

Charlie, why are you good at guessing and laughing at mistakes?

Granddad, why are you good at thinking of clever funny ideas?

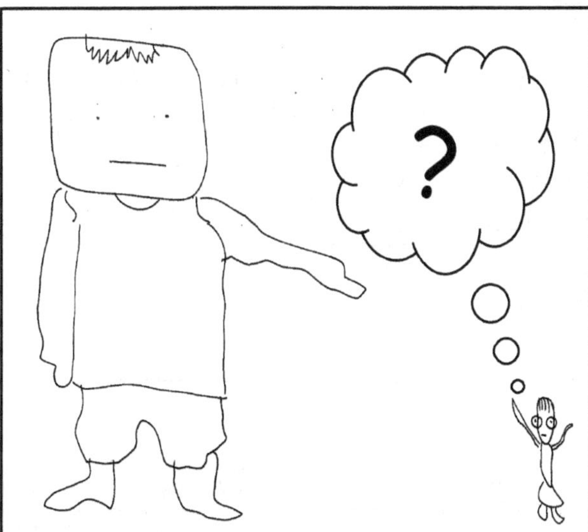


Milli, why are you good at finding small small mistakes?

Anne's mum, why are you good at listening to children?

# The Comic Maths Family

# Did you know ... people are different?

Granddad is different to Sue!

I am a girl.
I am a boy!

Milli is different to Charlie the Monkey!

I wear glasses.
I wear bananas!

# Did you know ...
# people are the same?

Granddad is the same as Sue!

I have fluffy hair.
I have fluffy hair.

Milli is the same as Charlie the Monkey!

I like to dance.
I like to dance.

Find 4 friends.
How are they the same?
How are they different?

25

Ask your friends questions!

Do you like ice cream?

Tick ✓ or cross ✗ in each box.

| Name of your friend | Likes ice cream | Likes to dance | Wears glasses | Has fluffy hair | Is a boy | Reads Comic Maths |
|---|---|---|---|---|---|---|
| | | | | | | |
| | | | | | | |
| | | | | | | |
| | | | | | | |

COPY ME!

Anne, John, Sue, Granddad and Kilo say ice cream is **brilliant**!!

Anne's mum, Betty and Charlie the Monkey say ice cream is **OK**.

Bill and Milli
say that ice cream is **horrible**!!

How many people think ice cream is?

| | | |
|---|---|---|
| **brilliant**! | | ____ people |
| **OK** | | ____ people |
| **horrible**!! | | ____ people |
| and that's | | ____ people altogether!! |

COPY ME!

Finish the Comic Maths Ice Cream Bar Chart.

The Comic Maths Ice Cream Bar Chart

People

| | | | |
|---|---|---|---|
| 5 | | | |
| 4 | | | |
| 3 | | | |
| 2 | | | |
| 1 | | | |

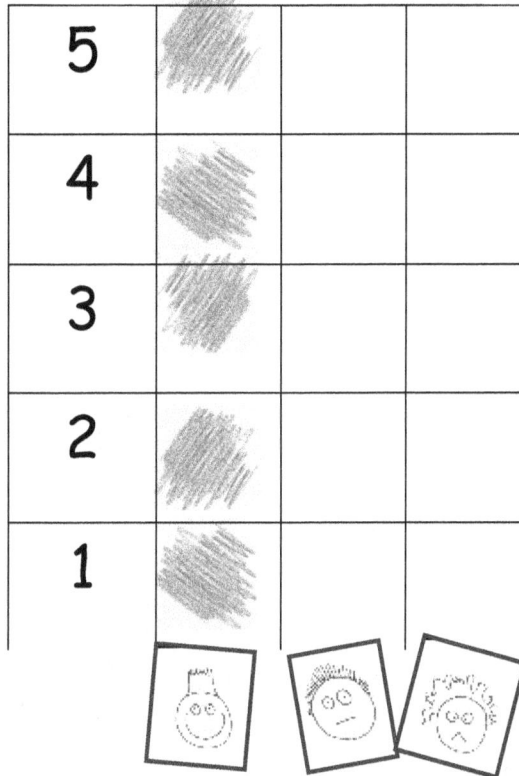

Draw the face

that shows what most people think of ice cream.

COPY ME!

BIG
ROBERT
SAYS …
BIG
ROBERT!!!
BIG
ROBERT!!!
BIG
ROBERT!!!

# Anne's Special Job!

Count in your head 1 2 3 .... up to 1000

Without moving your mouth.

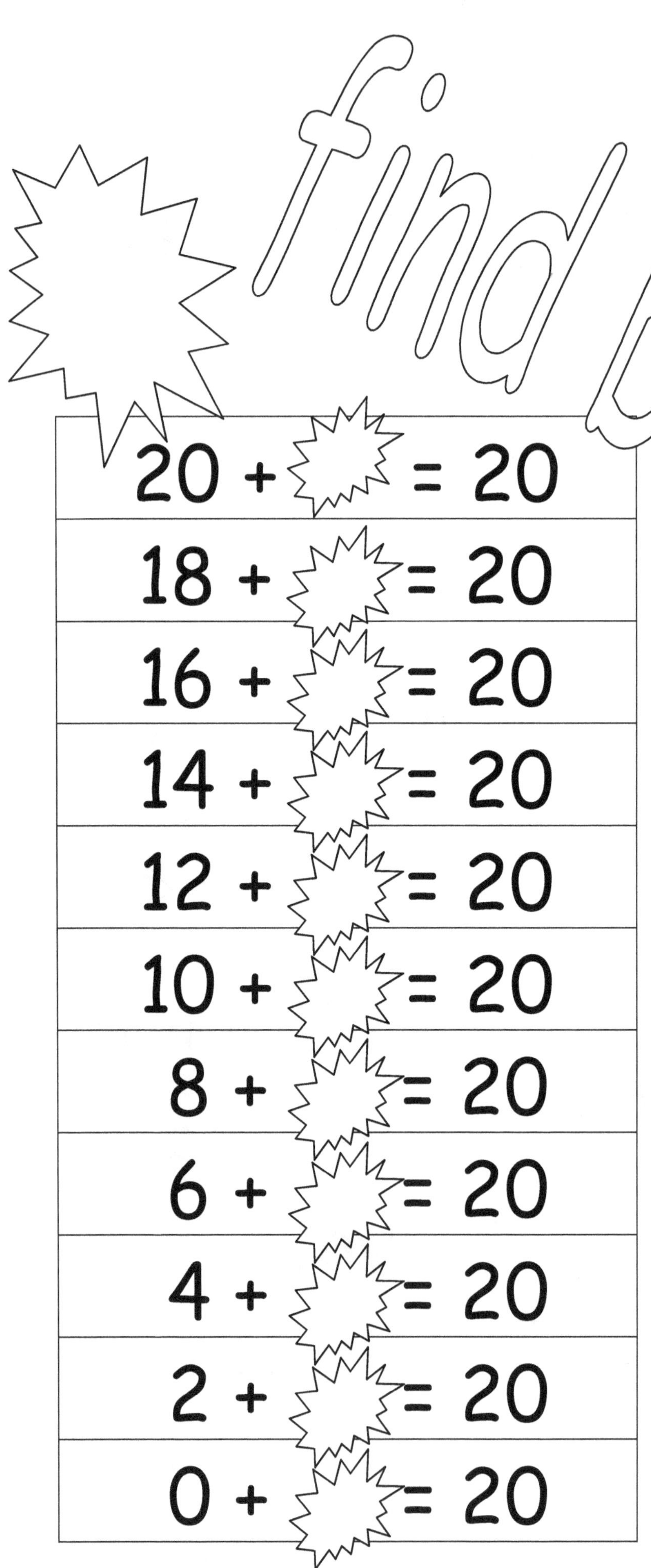


**COPY ME!**

find blob!
BIG ROBERT SAYS ...
19 + = 20
17 + = 20
15 + = 20
13 + = 20
11 + = 20
9 + = 20
7 + = 20
5 + = 20
3 + = 20
1 + = 20

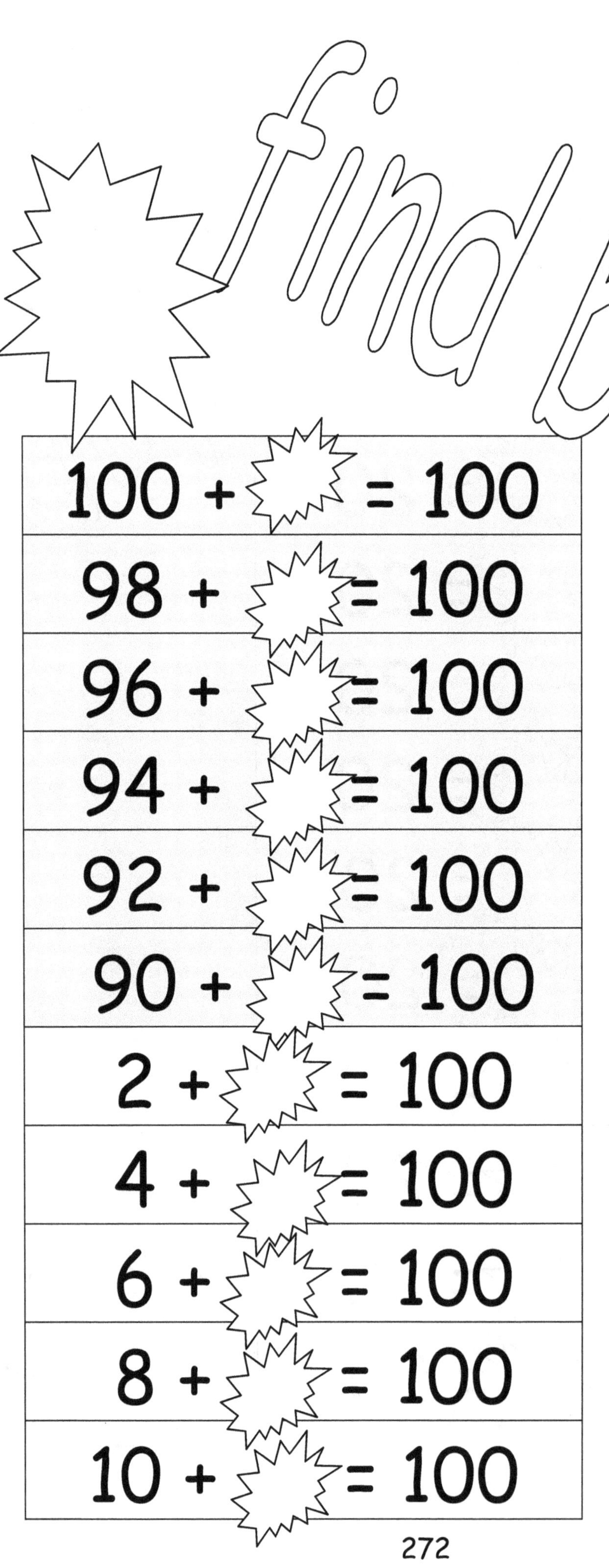


**COPY ME!**



Comic Maths

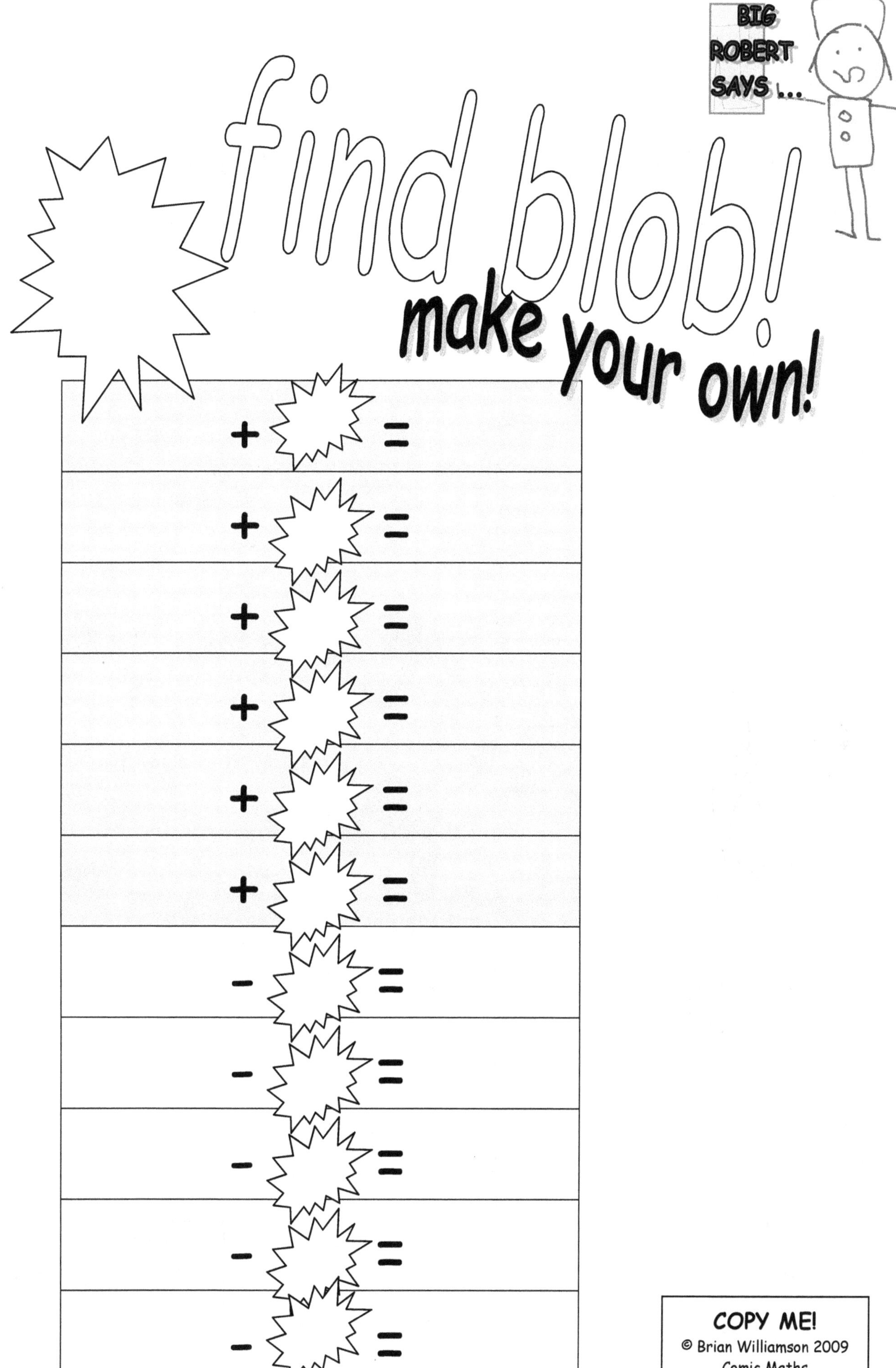
BIG ROBERT SAYS ...
find blob!
make your own!
+ =
+ =
+ =
+ =
+ =
+ =
- =
- =
- =
- =
- =

Draw 1000 very small bananas!
That makes me very happy!
COPY ME!
© Brian Williamson 2009
Comic Maths

Say **99**

```
    5   3
+   4   6
  _______

  _______
```

```
    3   7        1   5        7   1
+   6   2   +    8   4   +    2   8
  _______      _______      _______

  _______      _______      _______
```

# Beat the **CLOCK**!

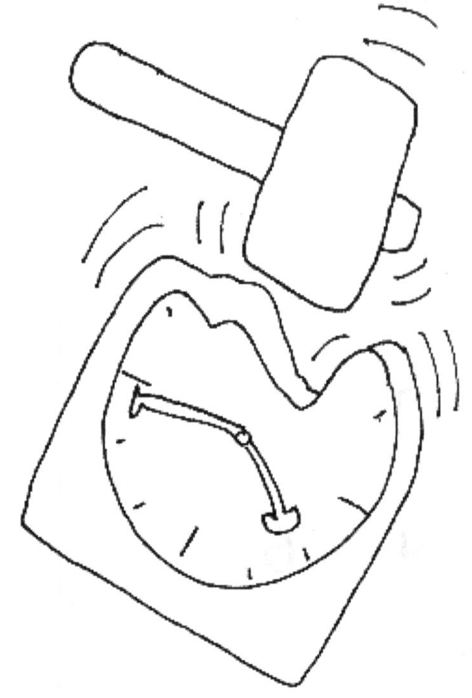

Do these sums in 5 minutes

| | |
|---|---|
| 1 + 2 = | 5 - 1 = |
| 3 + 3 = | 8 + 2 = |
| 11 + 9 = | 20 - 6 = |
| 30 + 4 = | 48 - 10 = |
| 60 + 40 = | 80 - 6 = |

Ask a grown-up to time you.

COPY ME!

## Do these sums in 3 minutes

| | |
|---|---|
| 2 + 2 = | 5 - 3 = |
| 4 + 2 = | 7 + 3 = |
| 12 + 7 = | 19 - 5 = |
| 31 + 7 = | 47 - 10 = |
| 59 + 40 = | 75 - 6 = |

## Do these sums in 1 minute!

| | |
|---|---|
| 3 + 2 = | 8 - 3 = |
| 7 + 2 = | 2 + 8 = |
| 14 + 2 = | 19 - 7 = |
| 29 + 11 = | 37 - 10 = |
| 50 + 35 = | 70 - 6 = |



Ask a grown-up to time you.

# Count the BUMPS!

3 people with 3 bumps on their head make ___ bumps.

5 people with 4 bumps on their head make ___ bumps.

10 people with 3 bumps on their head make ___ bumps.

8 people with 7 bumps on their head make ___ bumps.

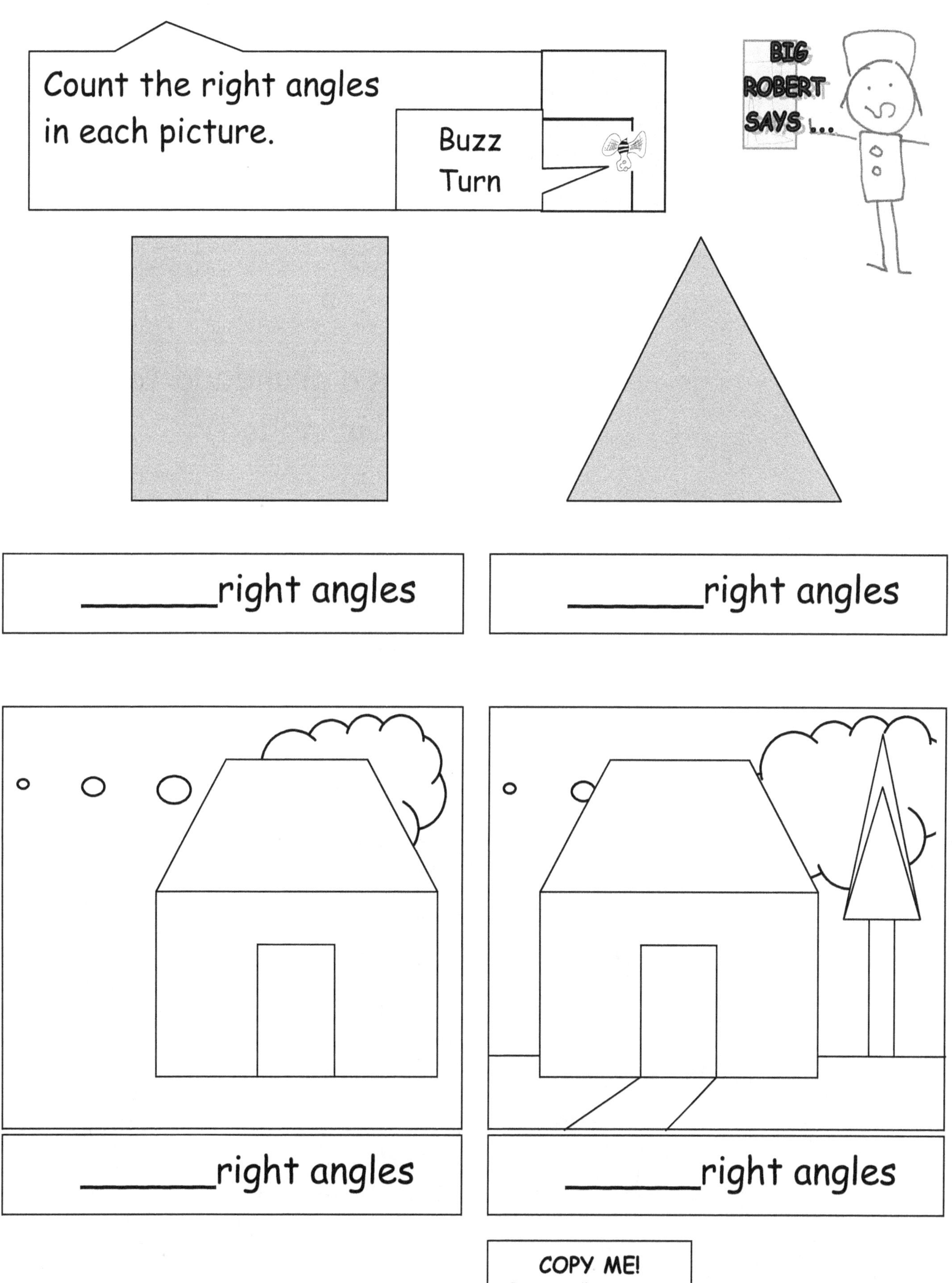
Count the right angles in each picture.
Buzz Turn
BIG ROBERT SAYS ...
_______right angles
_______right angles
_______right angles
_______right angles

Ask an aunty to be Betty

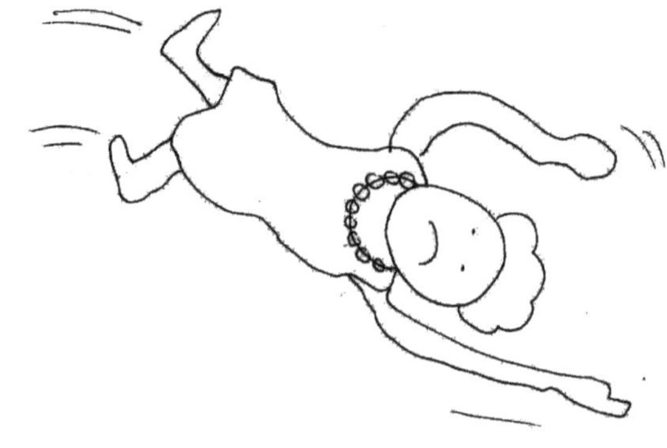

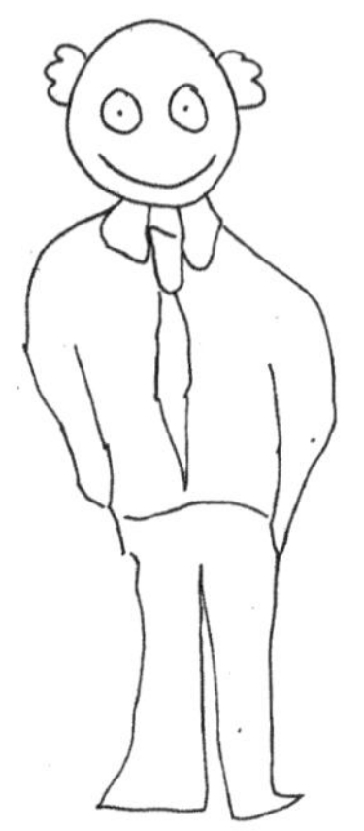

Ask a granddad to be Granddad

Find someone to be Bill and play shop!

EVERYTHING

BILL'S SHOP

OPEN

Play

**YOU and I Symmetry!!**

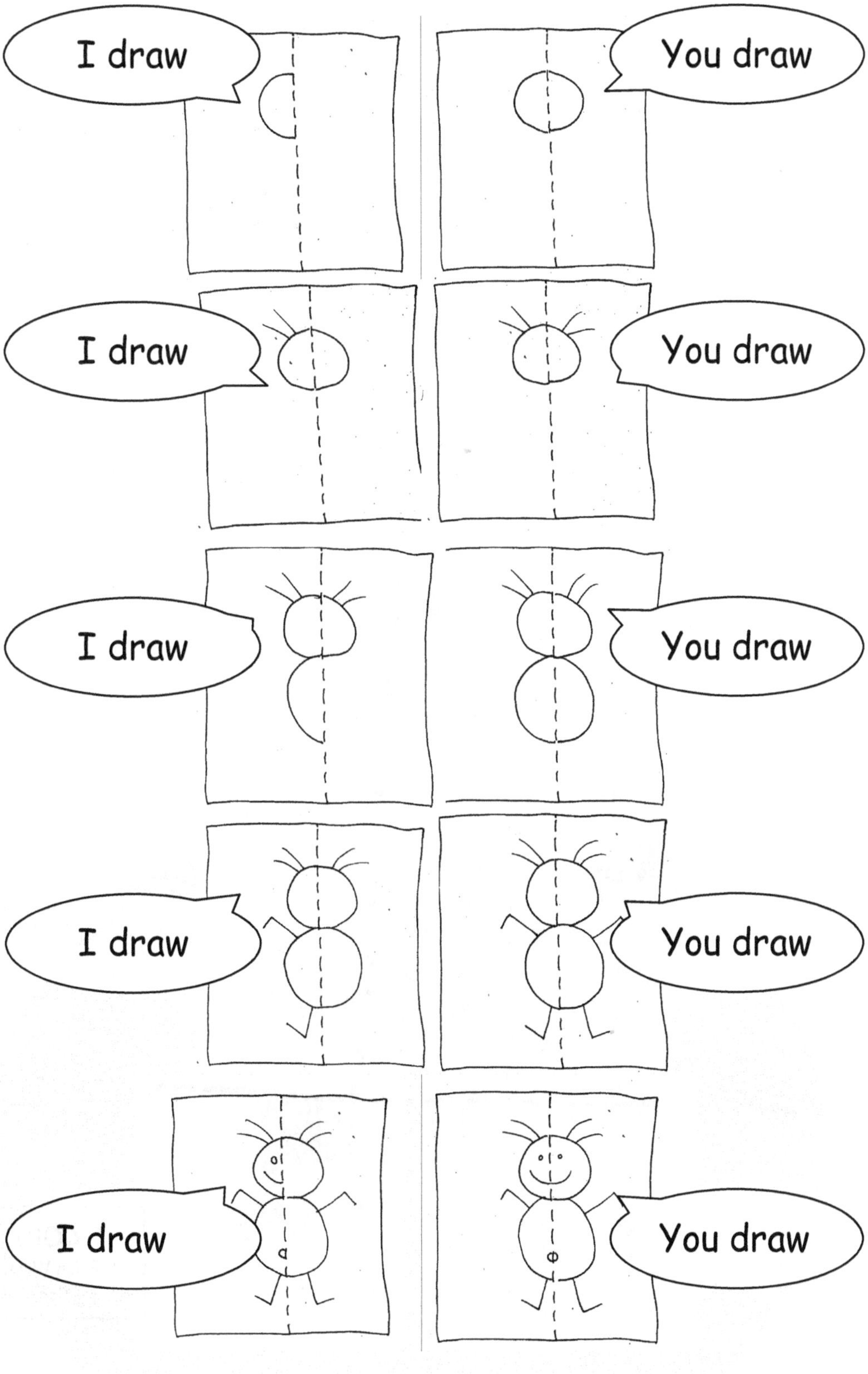

I draw

You draw

I draw

You draw

I draw

You draw

I draw

You draw

I draw

You draw

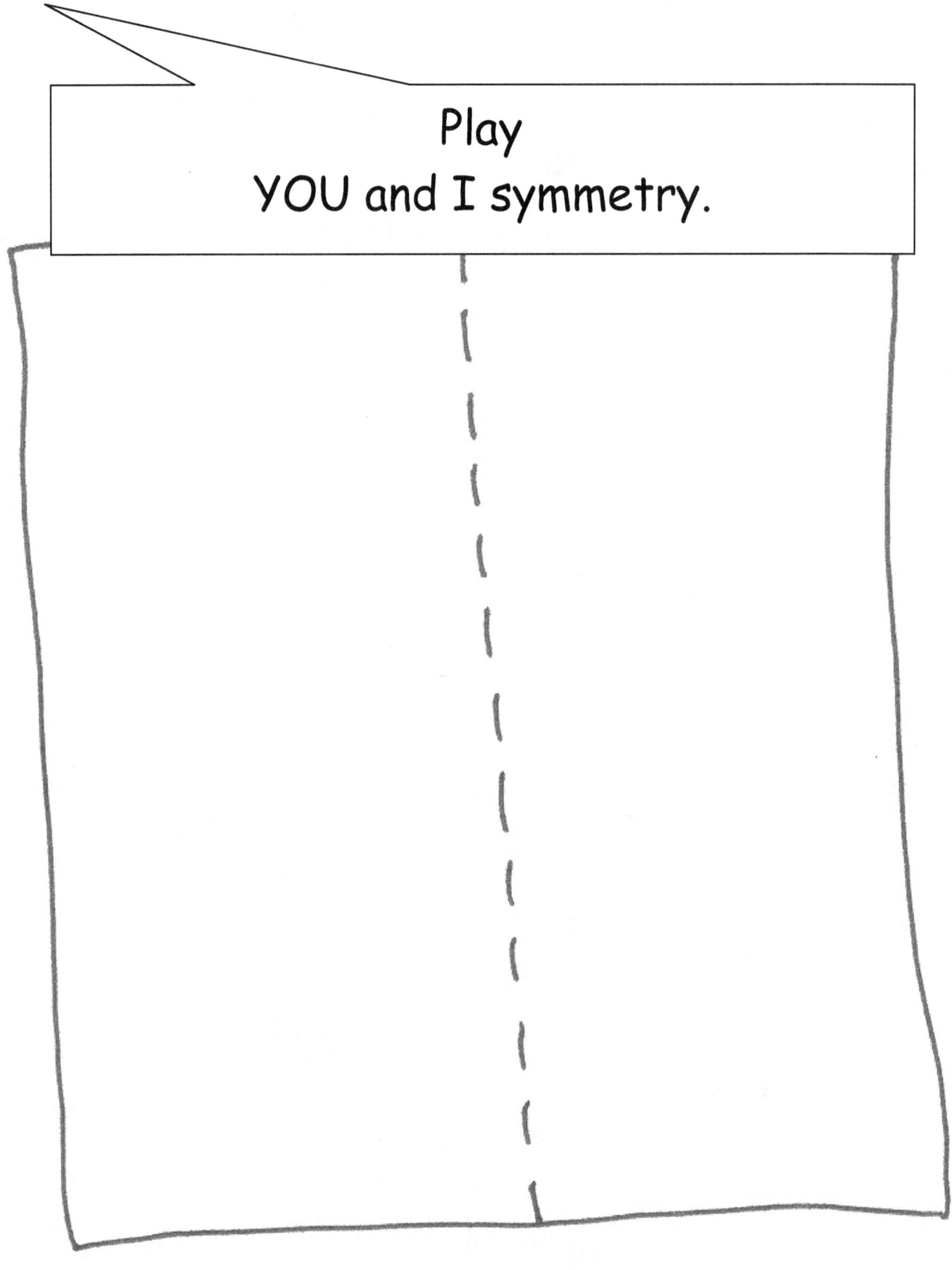
Play
YOU and I symmetry.

**COPY ME!**

# Draw the other half.

Write down the names and ages of 5 people in your family.

| Name | Age | |
|---|---|---|
| | | |
| | | |
| | | |
| | | |
| | | |
| Add them up → | | |

Now that's **really** old!!

# CRAZY BABY!

Next year . . .

Next year we will be doing sums like . . .

456732 +
3436864345543 ÷
3435768 -
6764565 $\frac{1}{2}$ x 99 + $\frac{1}{2}$

Will the sums be hard next year? ____

COPY ME!

Comic Maths

Good luck!

The Comic Maths
Colouring Book

COMIC
MATHS

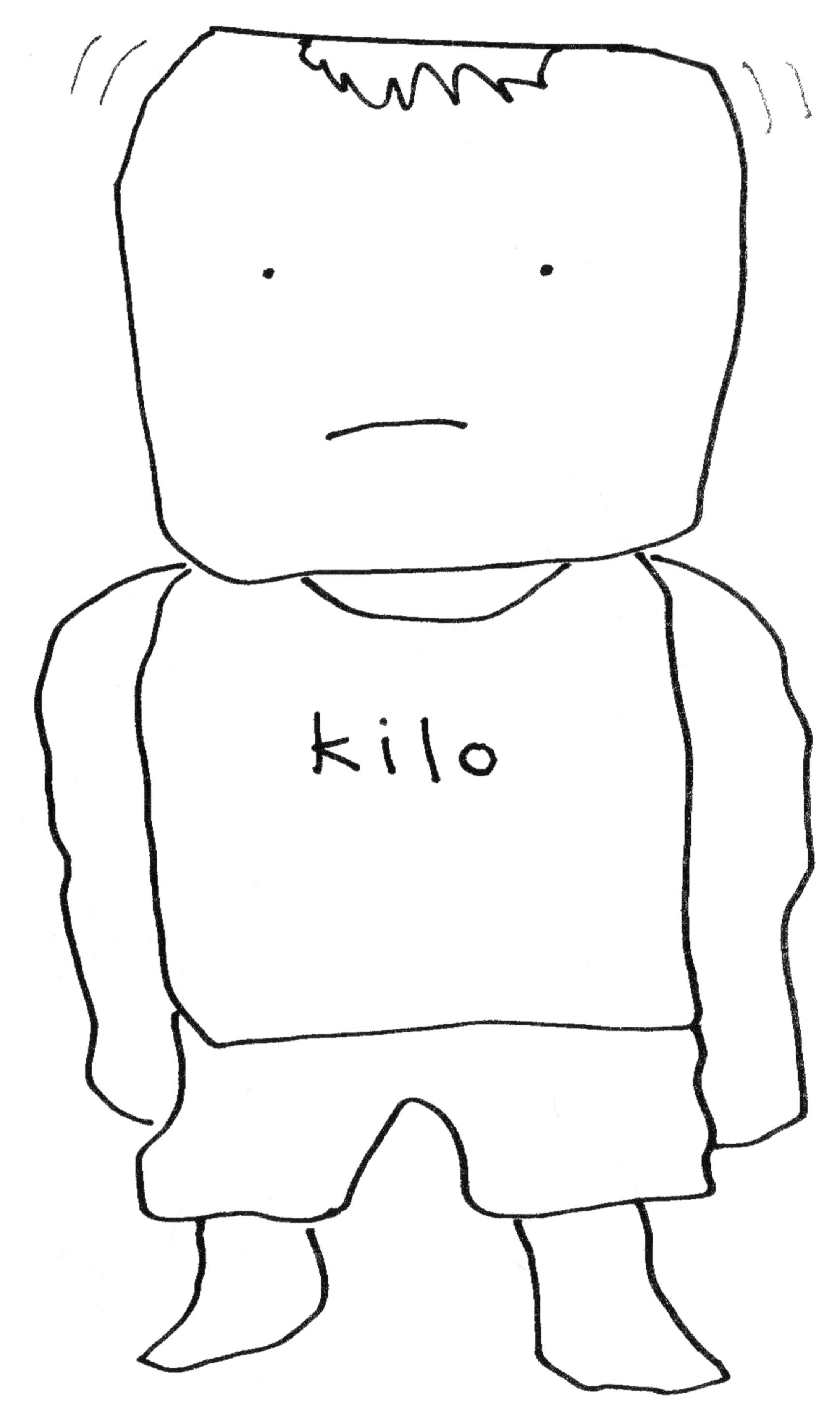
kilo

ICE

CREAMS

Pete Sam

Jack Chris Joe Mike

Alan Brian John George Mark

COMIC MATHS

EVERYTHING
BILL'S SHOP
OPEN
PAINT

Extra Sums
for Greedy People!

1
2
3
1

1. Find a piece of paper
2. Find a pencil
3. Draw a crazy baby
4. Draw 4 hedgehogs
5. Draw 4 flowers that have 4 petals and 4 leaves
6. Draw 4 buzzy bees
7. Draw 4 fluffy clouds
8. Colour it all in!

Colour and count the number of pieces these jigsaws.

There are ________ pieces.

There are ________ pieces.

There are ________ pieces.

There are ________ pieces.

Draw football pictures for the numbers 15, 20 and 25.

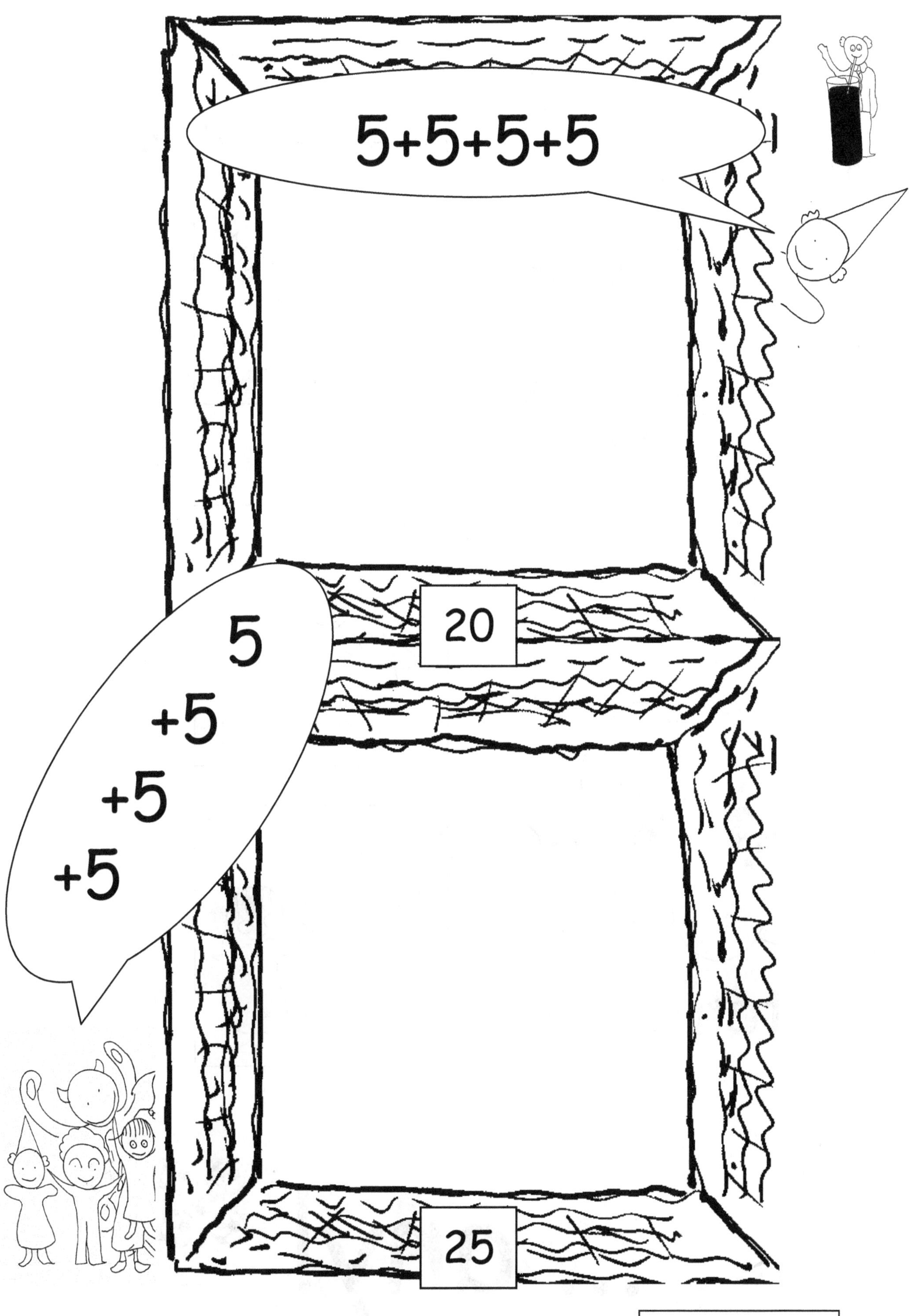
5+5+5+5
20
5
+5
+5
+5
25

Close your eyes
really tight!
Think of footballs... one

... five ...

... ten ...

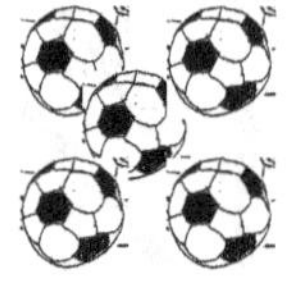

# ... any!

# Play Writing

Draw a face made out of the numbers
0, 0, 1, 3, 5 and 7.

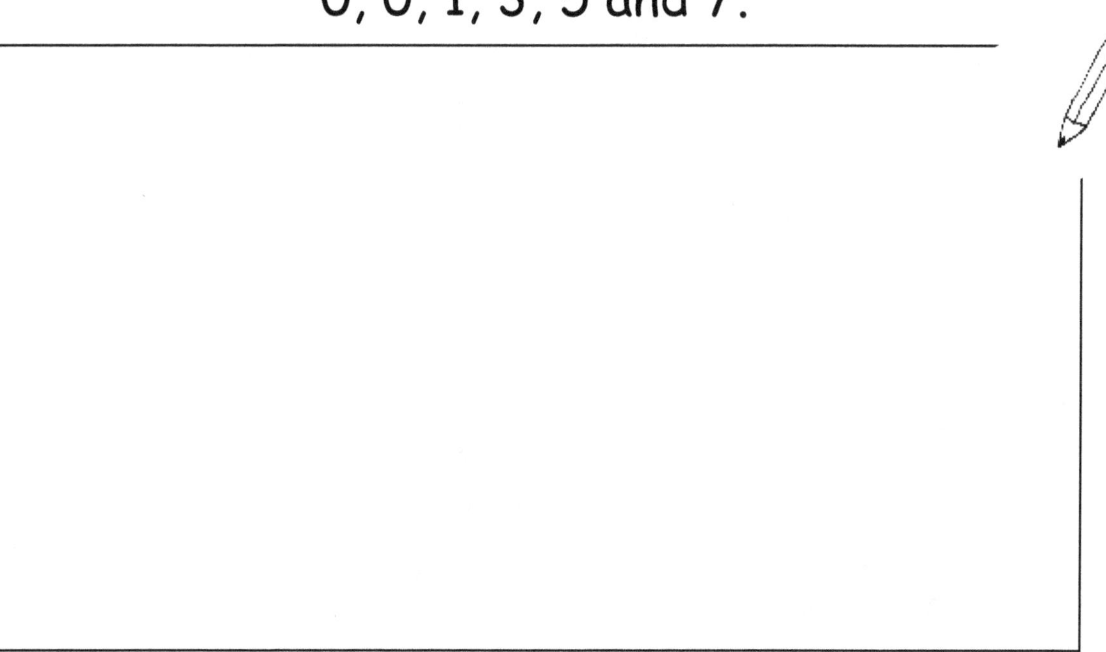

Copy this swan and make a two!

COPY ME!

# Charlie the Monkey

# the Mad Guesser!!!

Be Charlie and surprise a friend!!

Look
There are
66 fingers and
14 thumbs
on my hand!

CRAZY
NUMBERS
*-!*!+*!>*<!

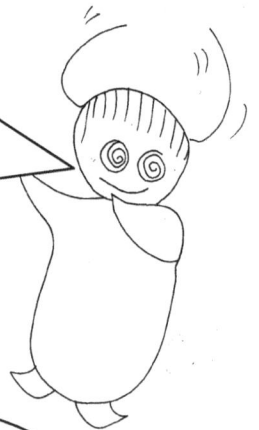

Look
You have __ noses on your face and you are wearing ___ pairs of trousers.

Look
There are ___ windows in that house and ___ chimney pots.

# wHAT cOMES nEXT?????

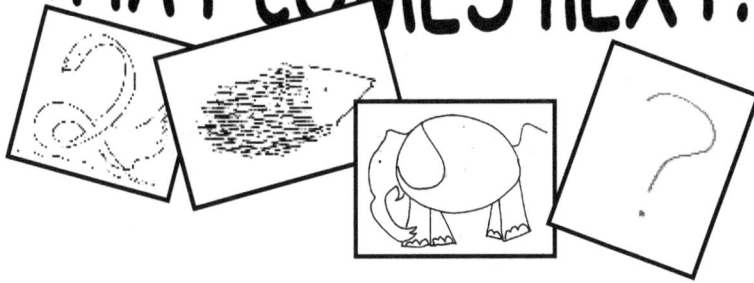

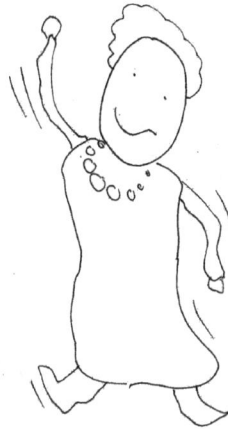

A B C D E ___

A C E G I ___

2 4 6 8 10 ___

5 10 15 20 25 ___

6 11 16 21 26 ___

10 20 30 40 50 ___

100 90 80 70 60 ___

M T W T F ___

J F M A M ___

1 2 3 1 2 3 1 2 ___

My square is bigger than your square!
7

Line up with your friends in order of nose size.

Line up with your friends in order of foot size.

# Bedtime

Wear a watch!

Ask a grown-up the time at
1 o'clock,
2 o'clock,
3 o'clock,
4 o'clock,
5 o'clock,
6 o'clock,
7 o'clock,
8 o'clock,
9 o'clock,
and 10 o'clock.

# CARDBOARD CASTLES

Have a fight with a cardboard box.
Who won? ________________

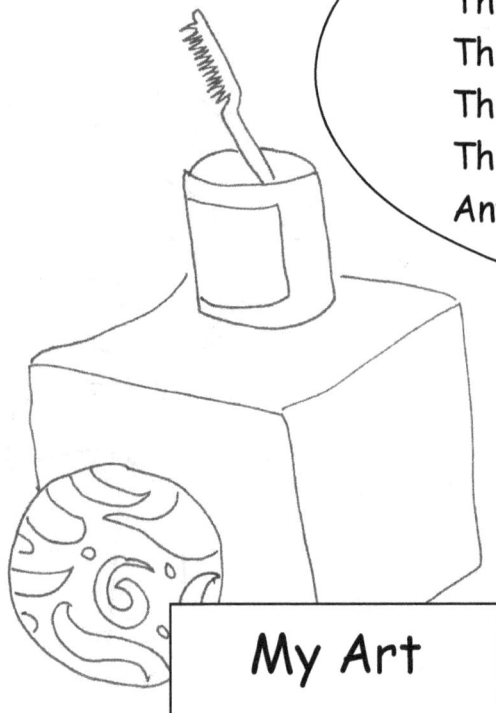

**BE SAFE** Ask a grown-up

Make art out of things and talk about it.

My Art

As you see ...
The tooth brush is inside the tin.
The tin is on top of the box.
The ball is at the side of the box.
This is my art. I made it.
Any questions?

10
Silly People!!!
have a party!!

BE SAFE Ask a grown-up

Tell anyone you think is silly to stand in the corner.

How many?

Tell the silly boys to say "boy silly".

How many?

Tell the girls to jump up and down.

How many?

Tell anyone who has one head to put their hand up.

How many?

Who's on the tops of the age of4?

Put these numbers in order.
Smallest first.

7   66   5   80   2   49   33   6

__ __ __ __ __ __ __ __

Put these numbers in order.
Largest first.

7   66   5   80   2   49   33   6

__ __ __ __ __ __ __ __

Write the names of four people you know.

__________ __________ __________ __________

Write the names of four things.

__________ __________ __________ __________

Use these words to make up stories for these sums

$3 + 5 = 8$

| |
|---|
| ________________________________________ |
| ________________________________________ |
| ________________________________________ |

$$6 + 12 - 7 = 11$$

$$1 - 1 + 3 + 20 - 6 = 17$$

COPY ME!

# Paying in PENNIES!

Put in the missing numbers in this table.

| Big Coins | Pennies |
|---|---|
| $\frac{1}{2}$ | 50 |
| $1\frac{1}{2}$ | |
| $2\frac{1}{2}$ | |
| $3\frac{1}{2}$ | |
| $9\frac{1}{2}$ | |
| $6\frac{1}{2}$ | 650 |
| | 850 |
| | 1250 |
| | 1750 |
| $22\frac{1}{2}$ | 2250 |

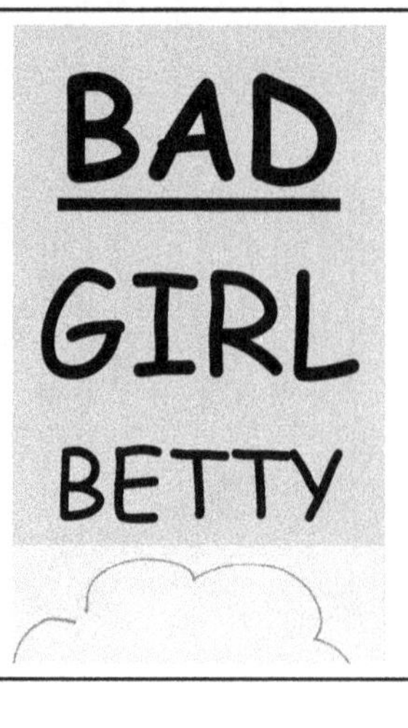


Why was Betty a bad girl?

Do these sums while dancing.

10 + 10 + 10 =

8 + 2 + 8 + 2 + 8 + 2 =

6 + 4 + 6 + 4 + 6 + 4 =

4 + 6 + 4 + 6 + 4 + 6 =

2 + 8 + 2 + 8 + 2 + 8 =

10 + 10 + 10 =

# How tall is the monster?

Find 10 small things that weight the same.
My made up name for a small thing is a ______________.
Find 1 big thing that weighs the same as them.
My made up name for a big thing is a _____________.

| 10 small things = 1 big thing.<br>10 _____________ = 1 _____________ |
|---|

Find 10 small cups that hold the same.
My made up name for a small cup is a _____________.
Find 1 big cup that holds the same as them.
My made up name for a big cup is a _____________.

| 10 small cups = 1 big cup.<br>10 _____________ = 1 _____________ |
|---|

Shade in the solids that can stand up on their own? A pencil can.

| pencil | string | eraser |
|---|---|---|
| bottle | tub of cream | scissors |
| toilet roll | umbrella | penny |
| football | hat | coat |
| shoe | sock | spoon |
| mug | towel | box |
| piece of paper | house | car |
| cloud | drop of water | elephant |
| key | hamster wheel | book |
| clock | teddy bear | walking stick |

Shade in the solids that can roll along the ground?

**A pencil can.**

| pencil | string | eraser |
|---|---|---|
| bottle | tub of cream | scissors |
| toilet roll | umbrella | penny |
| football | hat | coat |
| shoe | sock | spoon |
| mug | towel | box |
| piece of paper | house | car |
| cloud | drop of water | elephant |
| key | hamster wheel | book |
| clock | teddy bear | walking stick |

Anne, Sue and John find another box.

Use the numbers on the next page to draw the 12 people that came out of this box?

| | 1 Button | 2 Buttons | 3 Buttons |
|---|---|---|---|
| Hat | 3 | 4 | 1 |
| No Hat | 2 | 2 | 0 |

Draw the 12 people here.

COPY ME!

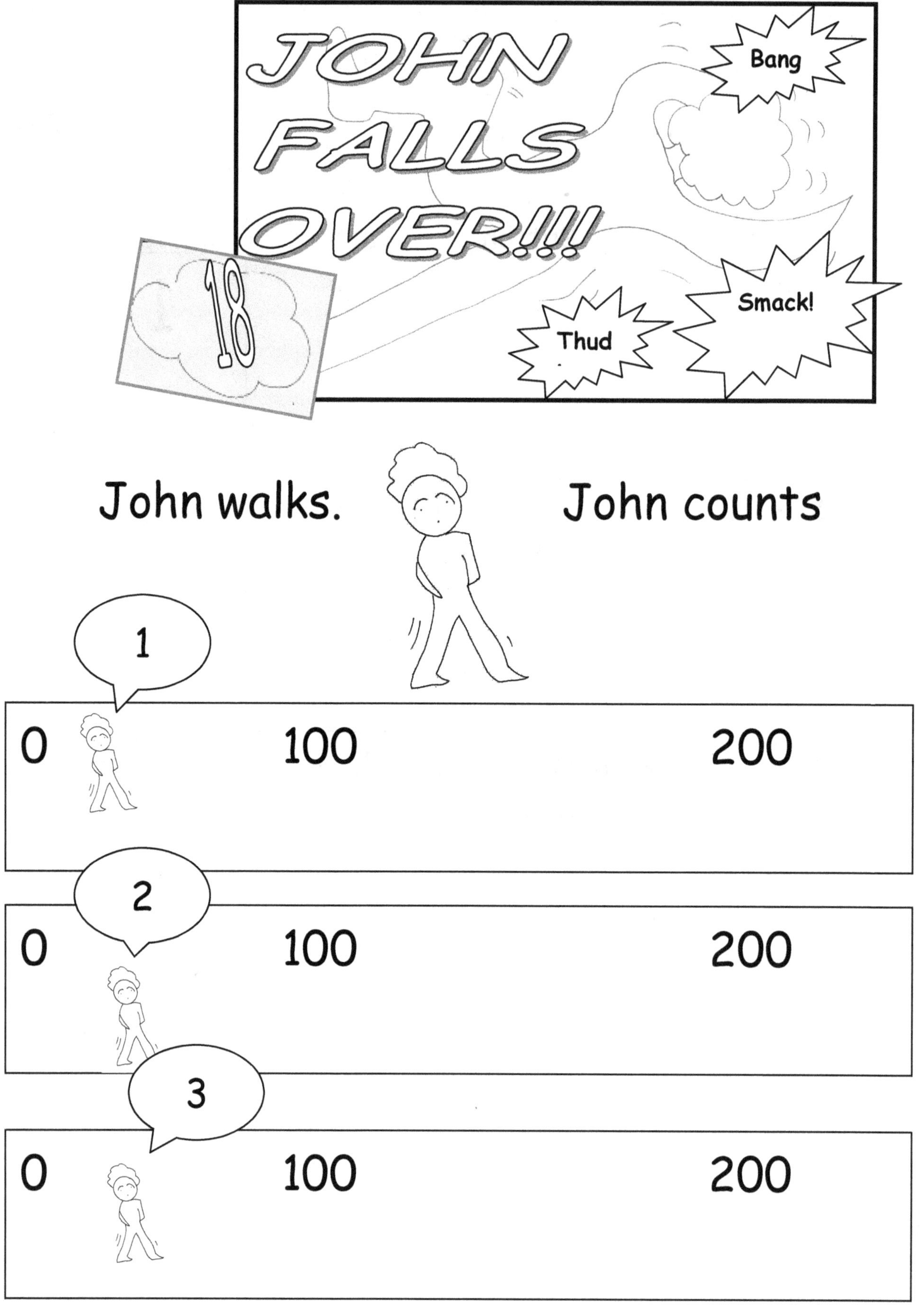
JOHN FALLS OVER!!!
18
Bang
Thud
Smack!
John walks.
John counts
1
0
100
200
2
0
100
200
3
0
100
200

# Who will come running to help?

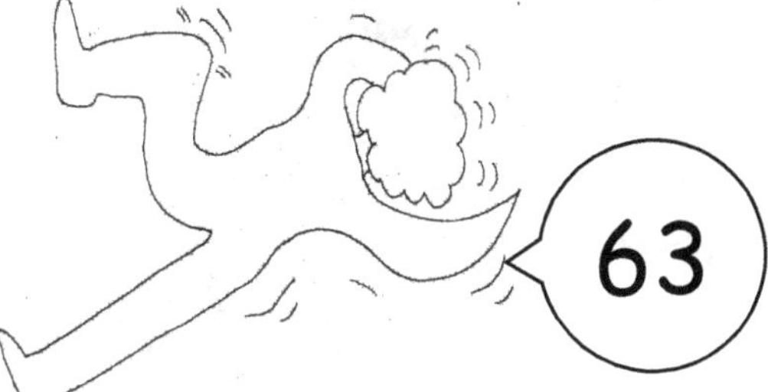

63

Number <u>100</u>

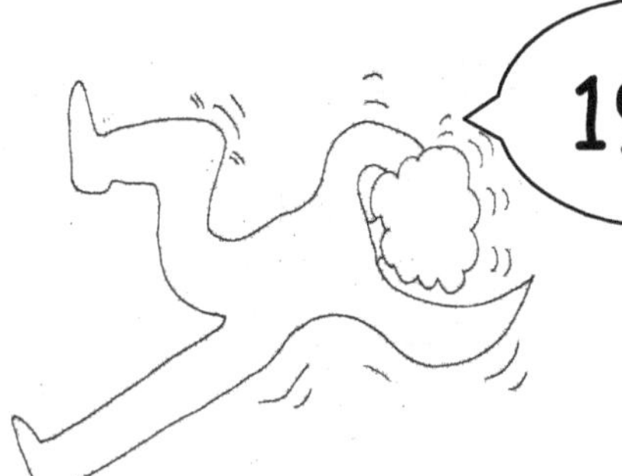

199

Number ___

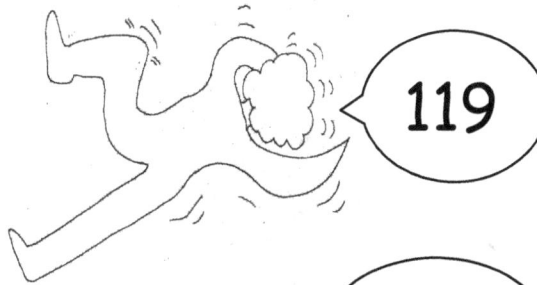

119

Number ___

249

Number ___

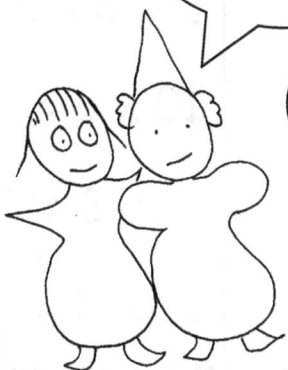

That John needs to be more careful.

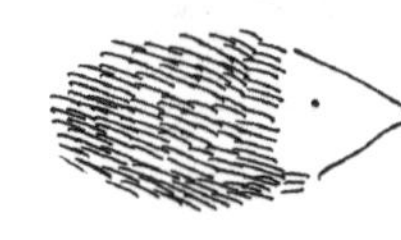

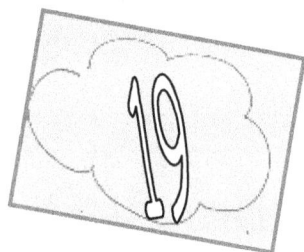

Think of spotty chins.
Find the missing answers!

| | | |
|---|---|---|
| 1 x 1 = 1 | 1 x 2 = | 1 x 3 = 3 |
| 2 x 1 = | 2 x 2 = 4 | 2 x 3 = |
| 3 x 1 = 3 | 3 x 2 = | 3 x 3 = 9 |
| 4 x 1 = | 4 x 2 = 8 | 4 x 3 = |
| 5 x 1 = 5 | 5 x 2 = | 5 x 3 = 15 |
| 6 x 1 = | 6 x 2 = 12 | 6 x 3 = |
| 7 x 1 = 7 | 7 x 2 = | 7 x 3 = 21 |
| 8 x 1 = | 8 x 2 = 16 | 8 x 3 = |
| 9 x 1 = 9 | 9 x 2 = | 9 x 3 = 27 |
| 10 x 1 = | 10 x 2 = 20 | 10 x 3 = |
| 11 x 1 = 11 | 11 x 2 = | 11 x 3 = 33 |
| 12 x 1 = | 12 x 2 = 24 | 12 x 3 = |

  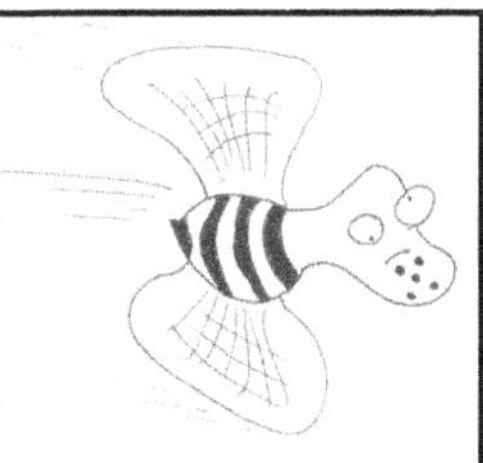 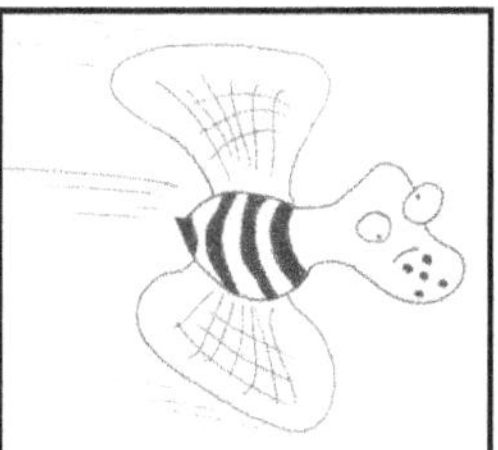

 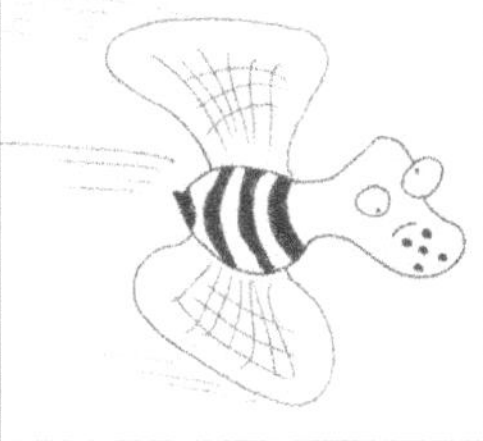  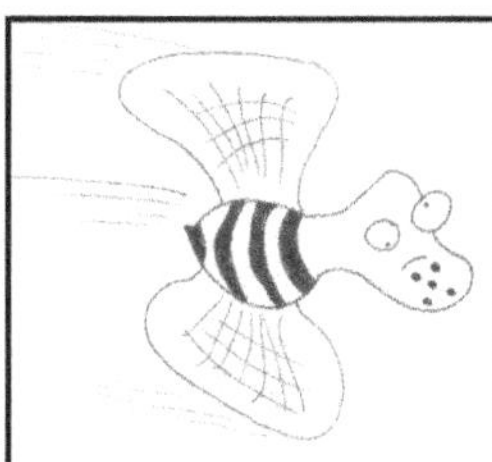

| | | |
|---|---|---|
| 1 x 4 = | 1 x 5 = 5 | 1 x 6 = |
| 2 x 4 = 8 | 2 x 5 = | 2 x 6 = 12 |
| 3 x 4 = | 3 x 5 = 15 | 3 x 6 = |
| 4 x 4 = 16 | 4 x 5 = | 4 x 6 = 24 |
| 5 x 4 = | 5 x 5 = 25 | 5 x 6 = |
| 6 x 4 = 24 | 6 x 5 = | 6 x 6 = 36 |
| 7 x 4 = | 7 x 5 = 35 | 7 x 6 = |
| 8 x 4 = 32 | 8 x 5 = | 8 x 6 = 48 |
| 9 x 4 = | 9 x 5 = 45 | 9 x 6 = |
| 10 x 4 = 40 | 10 x 5 = | 10 x 6 = 60 |
| 11 x 4 = | 11 x 5 = 55 | 11 x 6 = |
| 12 x 4 = 48 | 12 x 5 = | 12 x 6 = 72 |

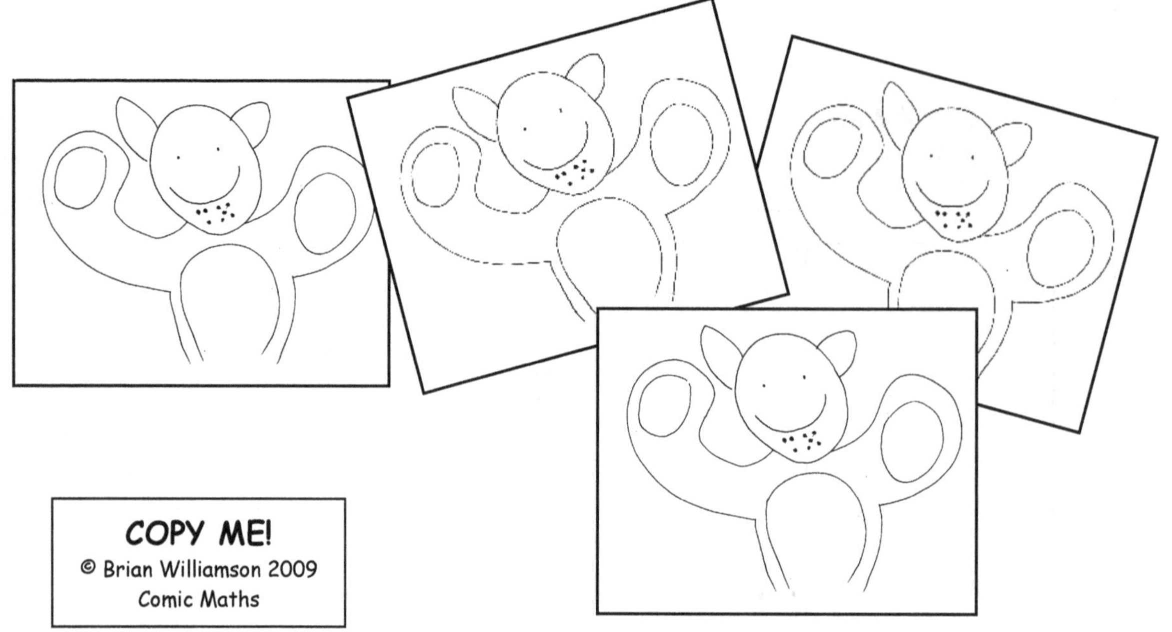


| 1 x 7 = 7 | 1 x 8 = | 1 x 9 = 9 |
|---|---|---|
| 2 x 7 = | 2 x 8 = 16 | 2 x 9 = |
| 3 x 7 = 21 | 3 x 8 = | 3 x 9 = 27 |
| 4 x 7 = | 4 x 8 = 32 | 4 x 9 = |
| 5 x 7 = 35 | 5 x 8 = | 5 x 9 = 45 |
| 6 x 7 = | 6 x 8 = 48 | 6 x 9 = |
| 7 x 7 = 49 | 7 x 8 = | 7 x 9 = 63 |
| 8 x 7 = | 8 x 8 = 64 | 8 x 9 = |
| 9 x 7 = 63 | 9 x 8 = | 9 x 9 = 81 |
| 10 x 7 = | 10 x 8 = 80 | 10 x 9 = |
| 11 x 7 = 77 | 11 x 8 = | 11 x 9 = 99 |
| 12 x 7 = | 12 x 8 = 96 | 12 x 9 = |

| | | |
|---|---|---|
| 1 x 10 = | 1 x 11 = 11 | 1 x 12 = |
| 2 x 10 = 20 | 2 x 11 = | 2 x 12 = 24 |
| 3 x 10 = | 3 x 11 =33 | 3 x 12 = |
| 4 x 10 = 40 | 4 x 11 = | 4 x 12 = 48 |
| 5 x 10 = | 5 x 11 = 55 | 5 x 12 = |
| 6 x 10 = 60 | 6 x 11 = | 6 x 12 = 72 |
| 7 x 10 = | 7 x 11 = 77 | 7 x 12 = |
| 8 x 10 = 80 | 8 x 11 = | 8 x 12 = 96 |
| 9 x 10 = | 9 x 11 = 99 | 9 x 12 = |
| 10 x 10 = 100 | 10 x 11 = | 10 x 12 = 120 |
| 11 x 10 = | 11 x 11 = 121 | 11 x 12 = |
| 12 x 10 = 120 | 12 x 11 = | 12 x 12 = 144 |

# Granddad's Sharing Hands

Colour in easy or hard.

6 ice creams between 2 children.

easy

hard

6 ice creams between 5 children.

easy

hard

8 ice creams between 3 children.

easy

hard

15÷5

easy

hard

21÷2

easy

hard

Share 8 ice creams between 2 children.

$8 \div 2 =$

They have _____ each.

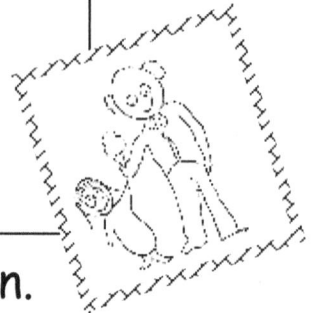

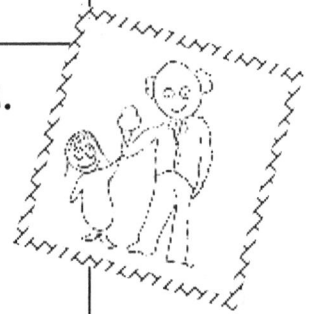

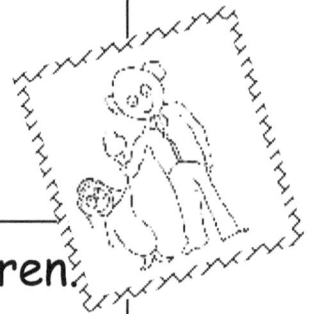

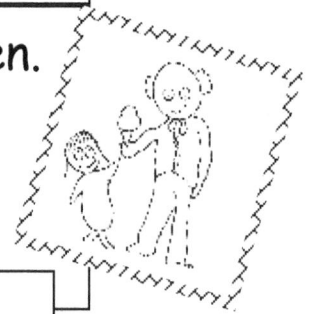

Share 12 ice creams between 3 children.

$12 \div 3 =$

They have _____ each.

Share 6 ice creams between 6 children.

$6 \div 6 =$

They have _____ each.

Share 12 ice creams between 6 children.

$12 \div 6 =$

They have _____ each.

Share 24 ice creams between 6 children.

$24 \div 6 =$

They have _____ each.

Share 48 ice creams between 6 children.

$48 \div 6 =$

They have _____ each.

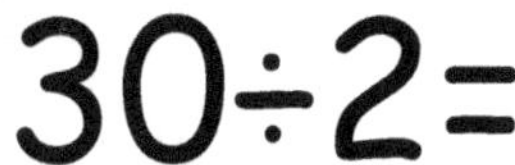

Share 30 ice creams between 2 children.

$30 \div 2 =$

They have _____ each.

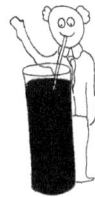

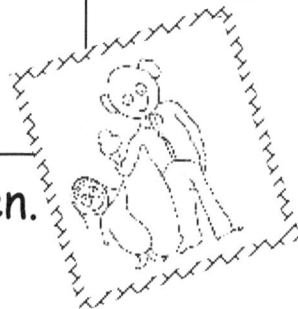

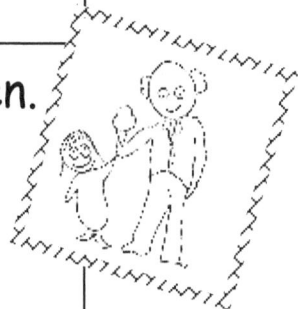

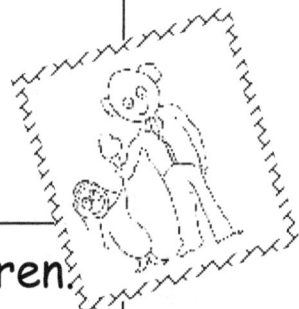

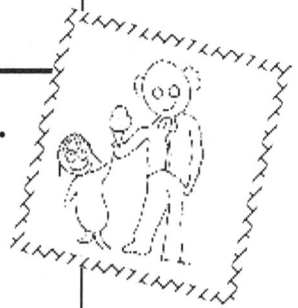

Share 36 ice creams between 4 children.

$36 \div 4 =$

They have _____ each.

Share 40 ice creams between 4 children.

$40 \div 4 =$

They have _____ each.

Share 63 ice creams between 7 children.

$63 \div 7 =$

They have _____ each.

Share 56 ice creams between 8 children.

$56 \div 8 =$

They have _____ each.

Share 0 ice creams between 8 children.

$0 \div 8 =$

They have _____ each.

Share 60 ice creams between 1 child.

$60 \div 1 =$

They have _____ each.

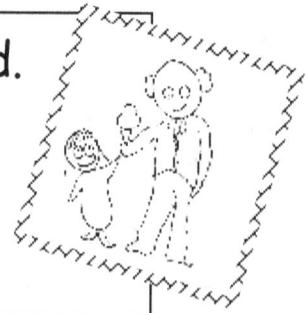

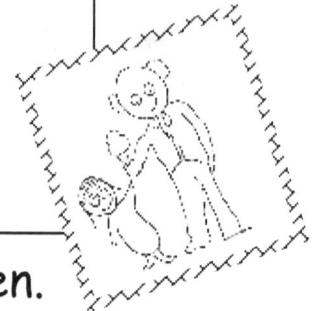

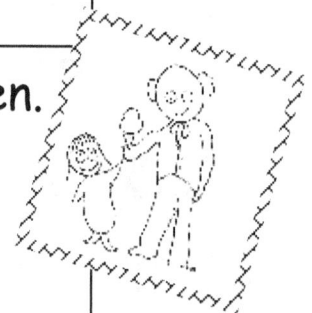

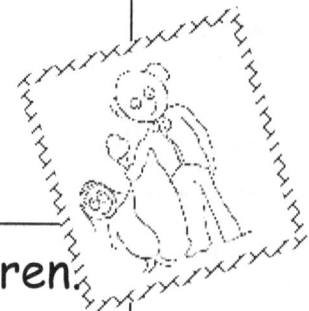

Share 60 ice creams between 2 children.

$60 \div 2 =$

They have _____ each.

Share 60 ice creams between 3 children.

$60 \div 3 =$

They have _____ each.

Share 60 ice creams between 4 children.

$60 \div 4 =$

They have _____ each.

Share 6 ice creams between 5 children.

$60 \div 5 =$

They have _____ each.

Share 60 ice creams between 6 children.

$60 \div 6 =$

They have _____ each.

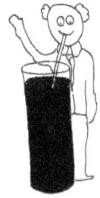

make your own!

Share ice creams between children.

÷ =

They have _____ each.

Share ice creams between children.

÷ =

They have _____ each.

Share ice creams between children.

÷ =

They have _____ each.

Share ice creams between children.

÷ =

They have _____ each.

Share ice creams between children.

÷ =

They have _____ each.

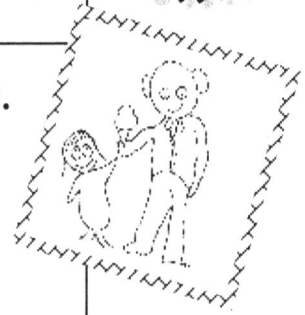

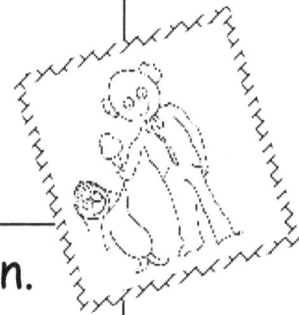

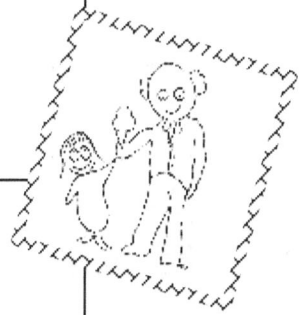

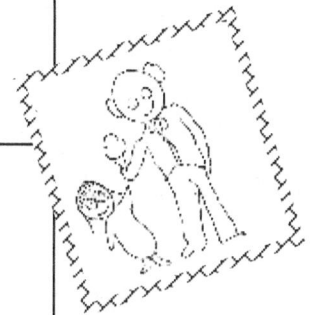

Share ice creams between children.

÷ =

They have _____ each.

COPY ME!

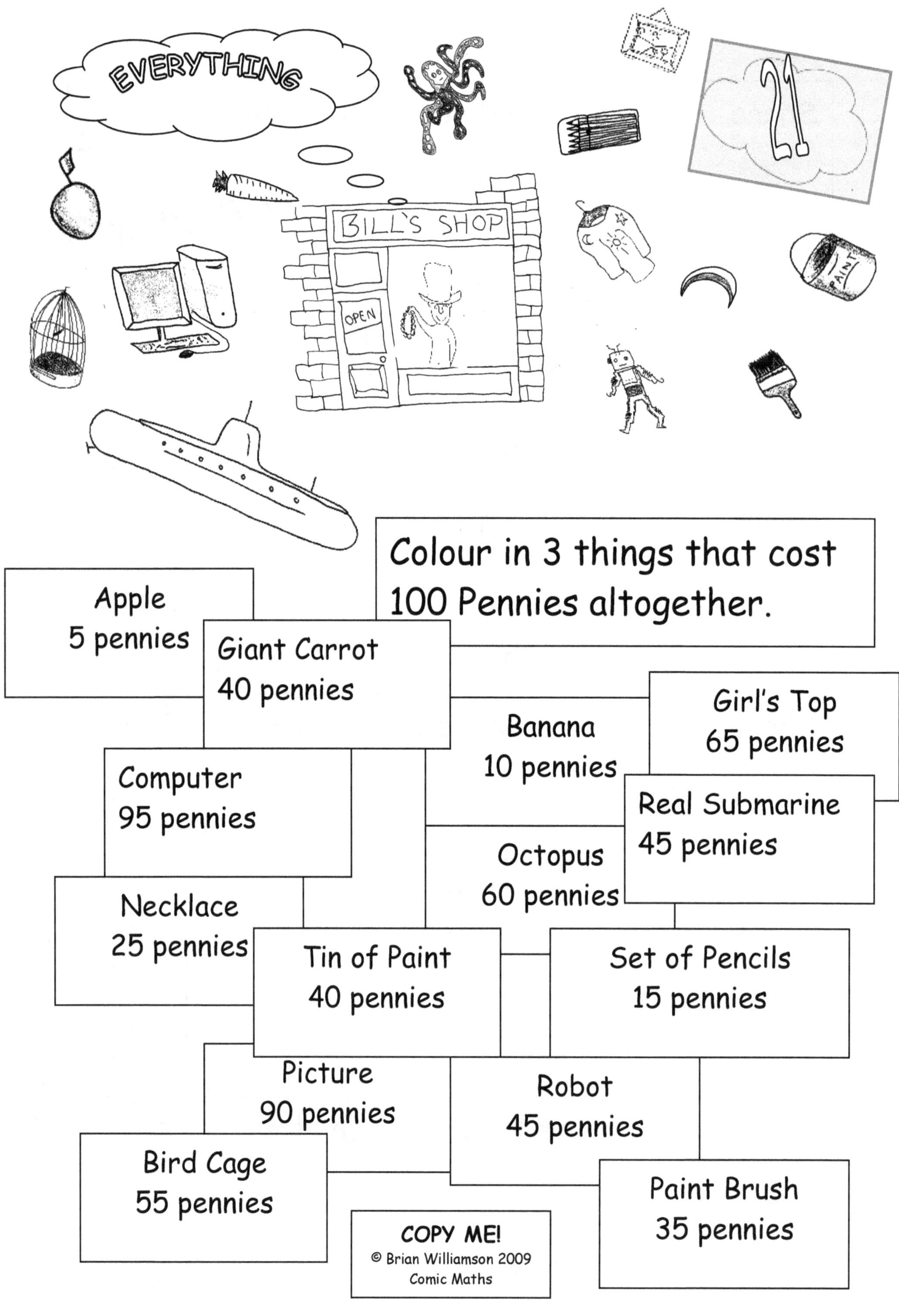
EVERYTHING
21
BILL'S SHOP
OPEN
PAINT
Colour in 3 things that cost 100 Pennies altogether.
Apple
5 pennies
Giant Carrot
40 pennies
Girl's Top
65 pennies
Banana
10 pennies
Computer
95 pennies
Real Submarine
45 pennies
Octopus
60 pennies
Necklace
25 pennies
Tin of Paint
40 pennies
Set of Pencils
15 pennies
Picture
90 pennies
Robot
45 pennies
Bird Cage
55 pennies
Paint Brush
35 pennies
COPY ME!
© Brian Williamson 2009
Comic Maths

Colour in 4 things that cost 100 Pennies altogether.

Picture
90 pennies

Tin of Paint
40 pennies

Octopus
60 pennies

Paint Brush
35 pennies

Girl's Top
65 pennies

Apple
5 pennies

Real Submarine
45 pennies

Banana
10 pennies

Computer
95 pennies

Necklace
25 pennies

Bird Cage
55 pennies

Giant Carrot
40 pennies

Robot
45 pennies

Set of Pencils
15 pennies

Do you think that Bill's shop is a good shop?

What would you buy?

# Fill in the missing numbers

# in CRAZY BABY'S

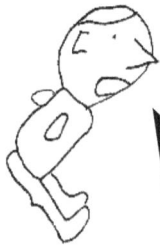

| Shopping List | | | |
|---|---|---|---|
| I want | | Pennies each | Pennies altogether |
| 1 | pea | 10 | 10 |
| 2 | carrots | 9 | |
| 3 | hedgehogs | 8 | 24 |
| 4 | washing machines | 7 | |
| 5 | footballs | 6 | |
| 6 | pictures of Betty | 5 | 30 |
| 7 | dots | 4 | |
| 8 | questions | 3 | |
| 9 | hiccups | 2 | |
| 10 | cobwebs | 1 | |
| Costs this much altogether | | | |

# Sue is five and a half!!!

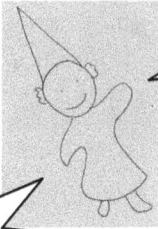

| | |
|---|---|
| $9\frac{1}{2} + \frac{1}{2} =$ | $\frac{1}{2} + \frac{1}{2} =$ |
| $8\frac{1}{2} + 1\frac{1}{2} =$ | $1\frac{1}{2} + 1\frac{1}{2} =$ |
| $7\frac{1}{2} + 2\frac{1}{2} =$ | $2\frac{1}{2} + 2\frac{1}{2} =$ |
| $6\frac{1}{2} + 3\frac{1}{2} =$ | $3\frac{1}{2} + 3\frac{1}{2} =$ |
| $5\frac{1}{2} + 4\frac{1}{2} =$ | $4\frac{1}{2} + 4\frac{1}{2} =$ |
| $\frac{1}{2} + \frac{1}{2} + \frac{1}{2} + \frac{1}{2} =$ | |
| $\frac{1}{2} + \frac{1}{2} + \frac{1}{2} + \frac{1}{2} + \frac{1}{2} + \frac{1}{2} =$ | |
| $\frac{1}{2} + \frac{1}{2} + \frac{1}{2} + \frac{1}{2} + \frac{1}{2} + \frac{1}{2} + \frac{1}{2} + \frac{1}{2} =$ | |
| $1\frac{1}{2} + 1\frac{1}{2} + 1\frac{1}{2} + 1\frac{1}{2} =$ | |
| $2\frac{1}{2} + 2\frac{1}{2} + 2\frac{1}{2} + 2\frac{1}{2} =$ | |
| $3\frac{1}{2} + 3\frac{1}{2} + 3\frac{1}{2} + 3\frac{1}{2} =$ | |
| $\frac{1}{2} + 1\frac{1}{2} + 2\frac{1}{2} + 3\frac{1}{2} + 4\frac{1}{2} + 5\frac{1}{2} =$ | |
| $10\frac{1}{2} - 1\frac{1}{2} + 2\frac{1}{2} - 3\frac{1}{2} + 4\frac{1}{2} - 5\frac{1}{2} =$ | |
| $\frac{1}{2} - \frac{1}{2} + \frac{1}{2} - \frac{1}{2} + \frac{1}{2} - \frac{1}{2} + \frac{1}{2} - \frac{1}{2} + \frac{1}{2} - \frac{1}{2} =$ | |

Find a carrot.
It is _______ long.
It weighs ______.

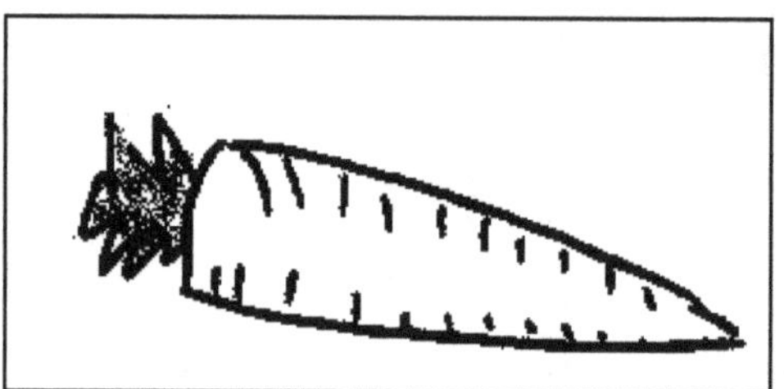

Find three apples.
Find a pint cup.

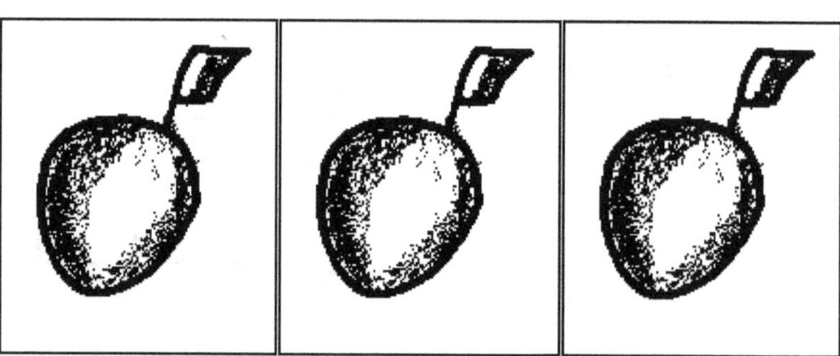

I can fit ___ apples into my pint cup.

Find 30 apples.
Find a gallon bucket.

I can fit ___ apples into my gallon bucket.

Ask a grown-up to take a picture off the wall.

The picture is _____ long and _____ wide.

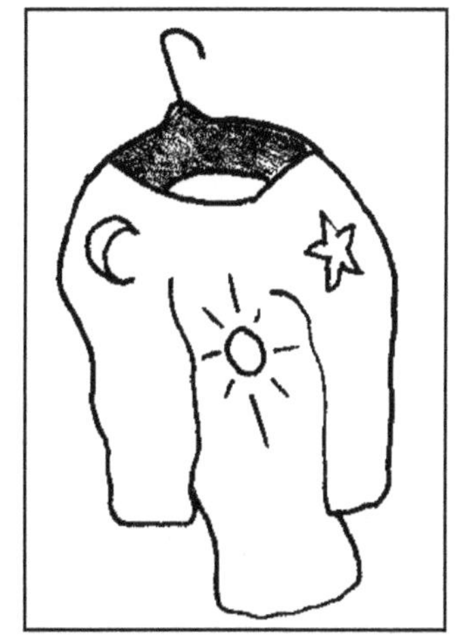

Find a pullover.
Make some paper squares.

Cover the pullover with the paper squares.

The area of the pullover is ___ paper squares.

COPY ME!

# NAME THOSE SHAPES!

Put in the missing letters.

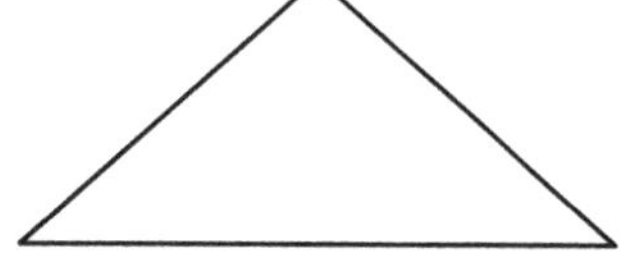

t _ _ a _ _ _ _

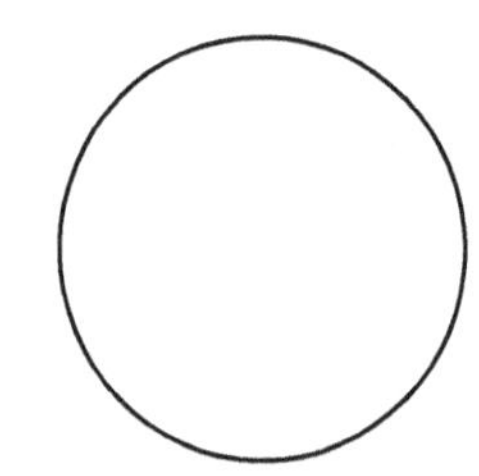

c _ r _ _ _

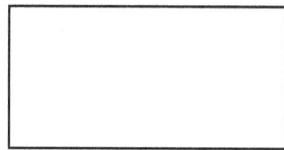

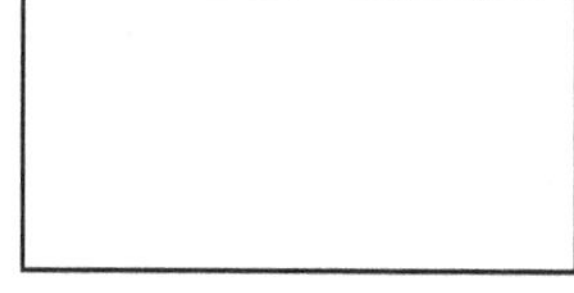

r _ _ _ _ _ _ _ e

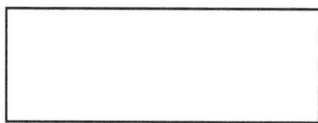

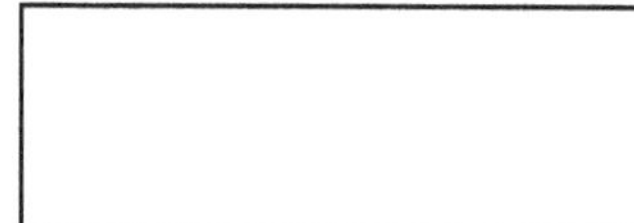

_ e _ _ a _ _ _ _

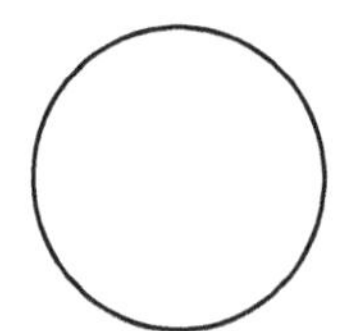

c i _ _ _ _

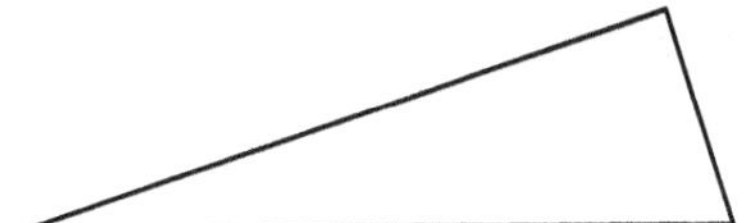

t _ _ _ n _ _ _

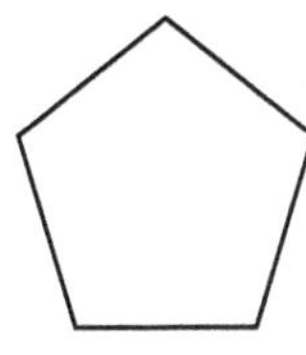

p _ n _ ag _ _

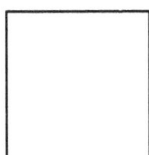

s _ ua _ _

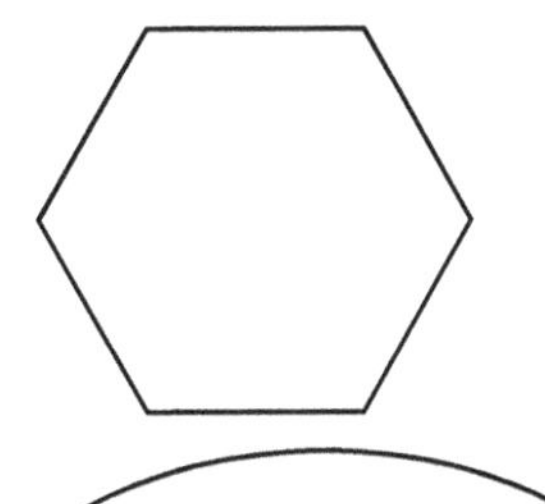

h _ xag _ _

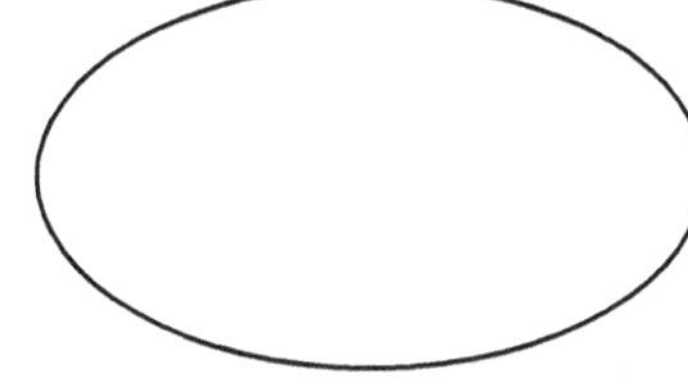

o _ a _

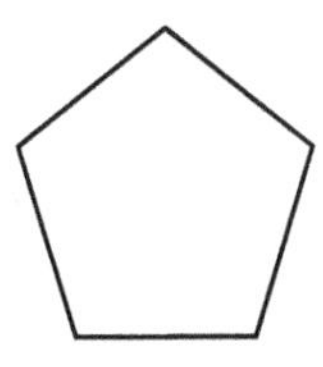

_ e _ t _ _ on

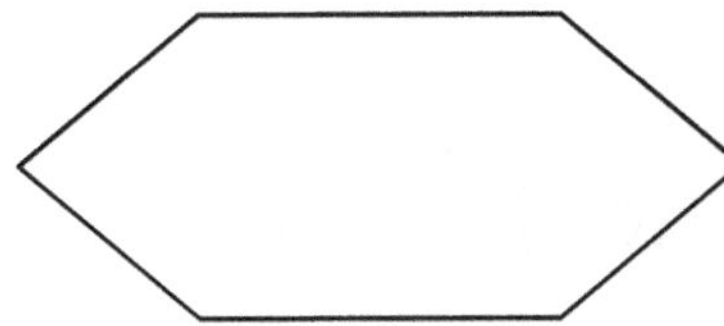

_ e _ _ _ on

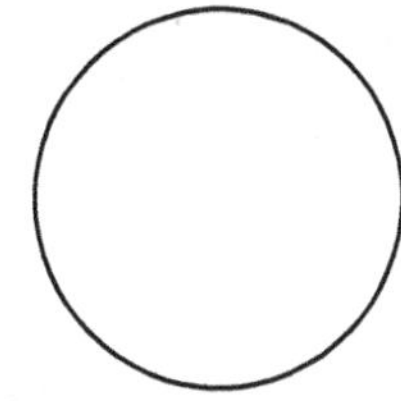

_ _ _ _ _ e

Make up your own shape.

Draw it here.

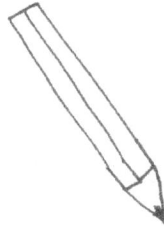

Make up a name for it

25
The Comic Maths Family

**Make some copies of the Comic Maths Bar Chart on the next page.**

Make a Grown-up's Comic Maths Tomato Bar Chart.

Ask 5 grown-ups.

Do you like tomatoes?

Do you like

______________?

# Comic Maths Bar Chart

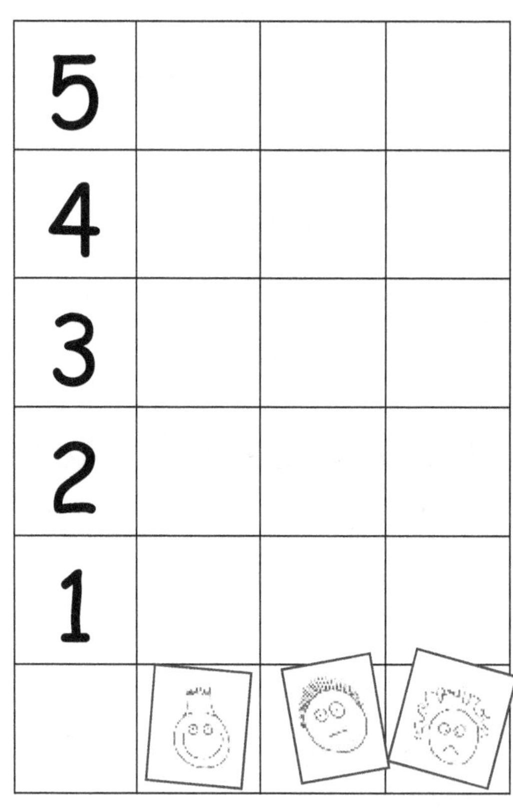


Draw the face

that shows what most people think.

Make a Comic Maths Children's Broccoli Bar Chart.
Ask 5 children.

Do you like Broccoli?


Make a Comic Maths Grown-up's Broccoli Bar Chart.
Ask 5 grown-ups.

Do you like Broccoli?


Make a Comic Maths Children's Parties Bar Chart.
Ask 5 children.

Do you like parties?


Make a Comic Maths Grown-up's Parties Bar Chart.
Ask 5 grown-ups.

Do you like parties?

## Background

Comic Maths has been created for children by reporting on children's own mathematical language, ideas and reasoning. I would guess that one half of this book has been written with children and the other half with reference to formal maths curricula.

## Organisation

Comic Maths is organized as a series of 25 short comics which spiral upwards in difficulty. There is a 'Big *Robert Says ...*' section containing miscellaneous exercises at the end of each turn of the spiral; and there are extension activities corresponding to each comic in 'Extra Sums for Greedy People'.

'Crazy *Baby*' pages aim to get us to gaze out of the widow and think crazy thoughts! Story-line pages aim to keep things a bit real and to lead the reader through the book.

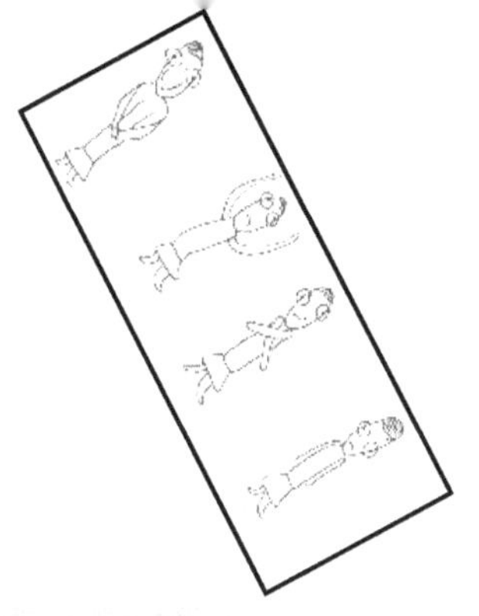

'Answers in The Back' gives answers to the questions set in each comic, the extension activities, and to the 'Crazy *Baby*' thoughts; but not to what 'Big Robert Says...' you have to do that!

## Mistakes

Some of Anne's pigtails are missing... but how many!? (See Answers)

The author has done his very best to cut out as many mistakes as possible and apologises for anything that he has missed.

(Apart from Anne's missing pigtails that is!)

## Pages you can photocopy

All pages marked:-

**COPY ME!**
© Brian Williamson 2009
Comic Maths

may be photocopied to provide more practice for one person or to support group learning, but may not be copied for commercial gain.

## Hooks

Comics start with a 'hook' that aims to interest the reader and start a discussion. In 'Bedtime' (Comic 8) the hook is the question: - when is yours? Hooks can be just something to look at or perhaps something that takes you by surprise! In Comic 1 it could be hedgehog. In Comic 2 it could be Sue holding a pen and in Comic 3 it could be the football.

# Teaching and learning

The learning of maths can happen in ways that nobody could predict ... how did they manage to divide before they could add, why do they recognise parallelograms but can't draw squares? How can they create their own play maths game, change one of the rules twice and still feel good about winning! Why don't they want to do sums out of a book but will be okay about playing a made-up pattern game with you?

Children surprising us grown-ups with their learning ideas shouldn't really be a surprise, should it? Maybe grown-ups should simply encourage, listen, sit back, observe, relax and enjoy!!

Do you think that one-to-one maths sessions could be like a game of ping pong?! They could go ... I write or draw this, wait, look, listen .... then you do that!! So, after a little thought ... I answer back by writing, drawing, saying or doing something .... and then wait patiently to see what happens! Maths, and maths books like this one, can grow out of a ping pong conversation between children and their grown-up helpers.

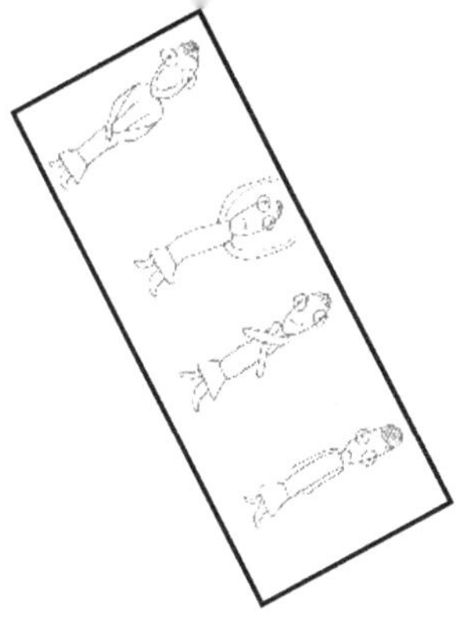

# Using this book

Here are 8 suggestions:-

Act it out! Make costumes for the Comic Maths characters and put on a Comic Maths Show. Each comic could be a short maths sketch. Act out the 'Hi' from the Comic Maths Family, Crazy Baby and Big Robert ... and let the story progress as Anne, John and Sue travel though the comic adventures, meeting Charlie the Monkey, Bad Girl Betty dancing, the Monster, Buzzy Bee, the Silly People, the Box of People, Granddad's sharing hands, Bill and his Everything Shop and more!

Use Comic Maths as a learning support resource. Look up those areas of the curriculum recently covered at school and see if Comic Maths can help.

Use Comic Maths as a primary home-schooling resource.

Read all the number-skill comics (1, 2, 3, 4, 5, 6, 11, 13, 14, 18, 19, 20 and 22) and then work through the comics that involve the application of number (7, 8, 9, 10, 12, 15, 16, 17, 21, 23, 24 and 25).

Go straight to a 'Big Robert says ....' section and make a start!

Show your young friend the exercises in 'Extra Sums for Greedy People!' observe their response and use this information to assess their leaning needs.

Go straight to the 'Comic Maths Colouring Book' to colour things in. Then visit the story-line pages that link the comics, colour them in as well and then find your way into a comic or two!

Just leave it around and see what happens!

Your best colouring. That's the answer!

Well Done!
You have made the next page of Comic 123.

CRAZY BABY!
thinks about 3

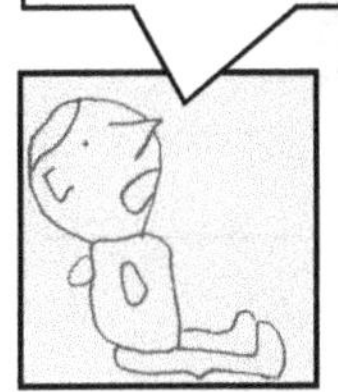

A word can be a number? Strange!
There can be one petal, one cloud or one hedgehog.
One of anything. Two of anything. Three of anything.
Help a grown-up to understand!

There are 6 animals
There are 10 aliens.
There are 10 of them.

There are 4 pieces.
There are 9 pieces
There are 16 pieces.
There are 25 pieces.

Your way is the answer!

CRAZY BABY!

Counts the aliens

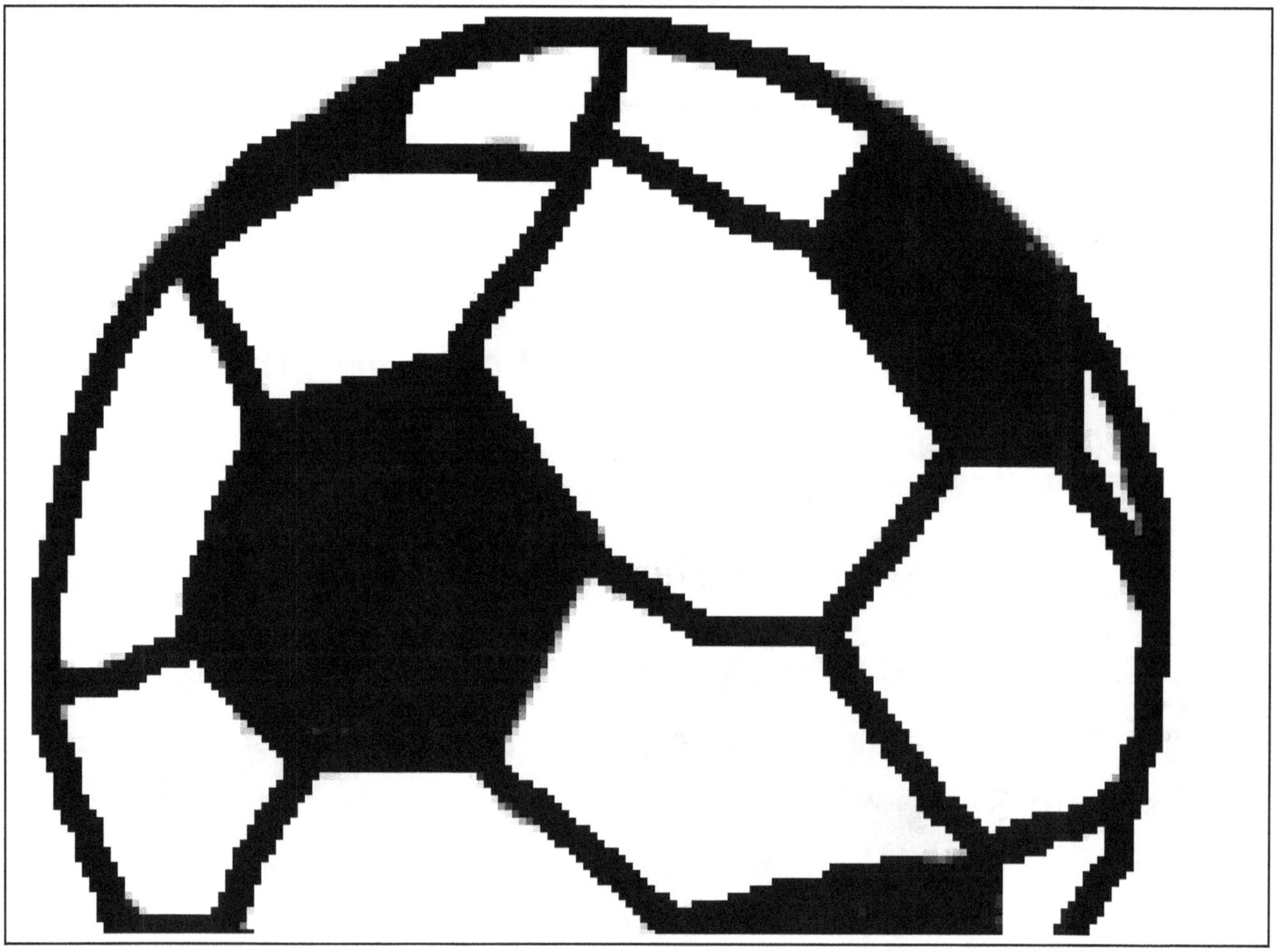

Draw 3, 4, 9 and 10 in the same way.

15

20

25

CRAZY BABY!
7 and 9 are like flowers

What do you think 8 is like?
8 could be like two planets touching,
a squashy alien, two plates, a funny flower ...

## Play Writing

4

### You try

This is fun if you like to draw and make noises at the same time! Try going round faster and faster, and making the noises louder and louder and then just STOP!!

Here is a number face using 0 0 1 3 5 and 7

The answer is one that curves round then flicks back.

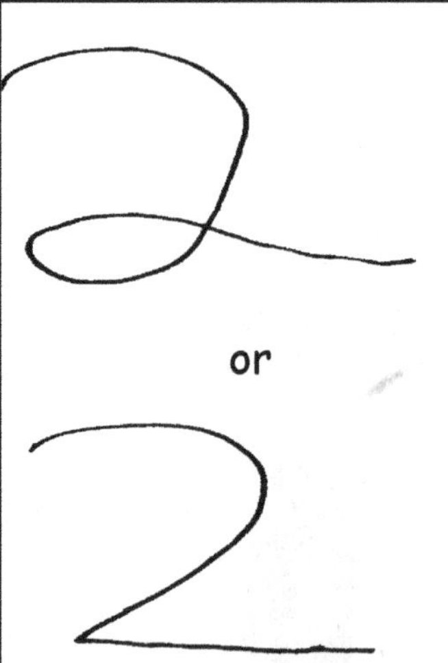
or

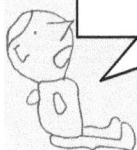

CRAZY BABY!
Likes a picture

Is he crazy?
Maybe Crazy Baby is just thinking 0 1 2 3 4 5 6 7 8 9 are the funny shapes we use to mean number.

Be Charlie.
Don't think. Don't count.
Just say a number!

You could say ...

LOOK
You have 100 noses on your face and you are wearing 0 pairs of trousers.

LOOK
There are 0 windows in that house and it has 1000 chimney pots.

**CRAZY BABY!**
Learns IS

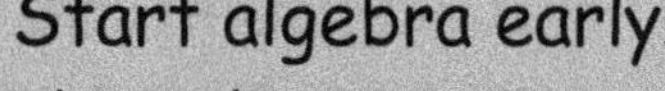

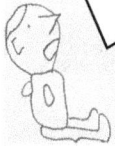

Start algebra early!
There have to be two sides to any equation.

Chair = Chair

$5 = 5$

$y = y$

$x^2 = 3x + 4$

6

# WHAT cOMES nEXT?????

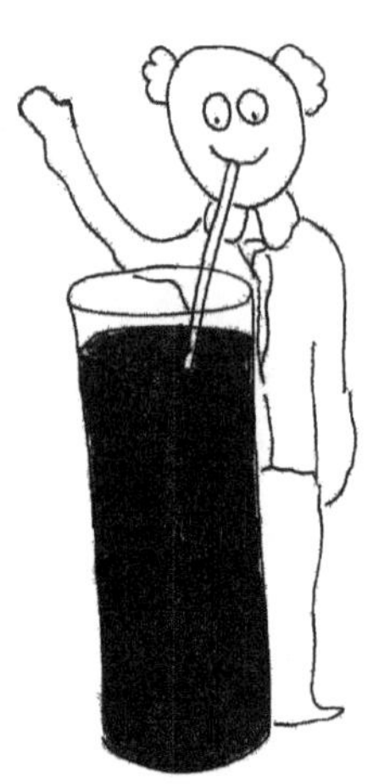

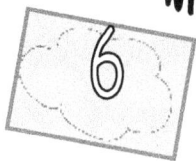

A B C D E F
A C E G I K
2 4 6 8 10 12
5 10 15 20 25 30
6 11 16 21 26 31
10 20 30 40 50 60
100 90 80 70 60 50
M T W T F S
(First letter of days of the week)
J F M A M J
(First letter of months of the year)
1 2 3 1 2 3 1 2

**CRAZY BABY!**
Makes a mess

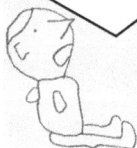

A mess can be fun.
Simple is good for maths.
Try both.
Is that the answer?

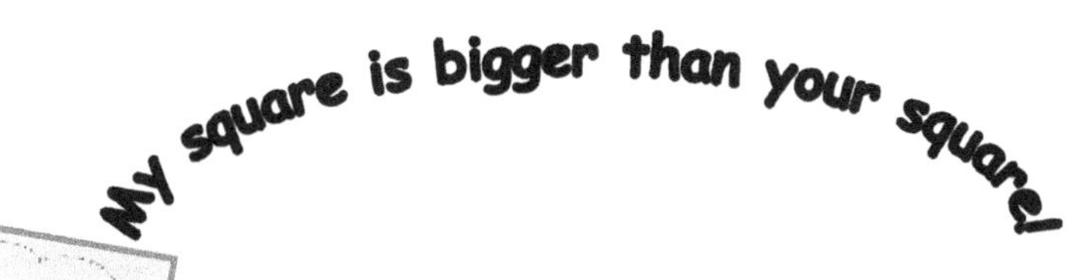
My square is bigger than your square!
7

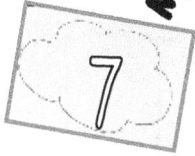

Colour in John.
Colour in Kilo.
Colour in Granddad.
Colour in Sue.

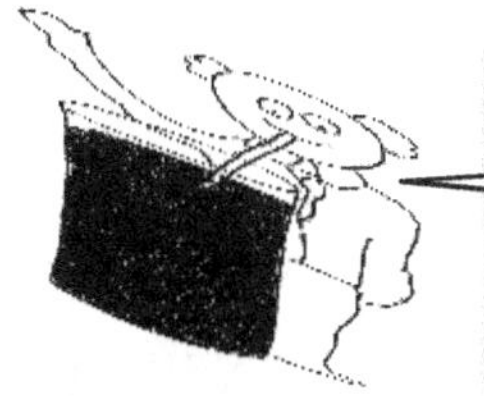

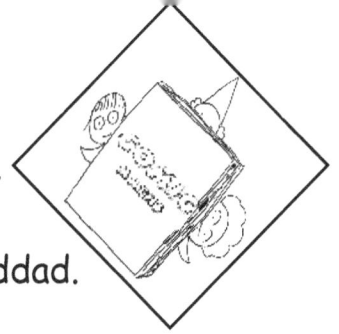

Have fun!   That's the answer!

**CRAZY BABY!**
Meets monster number

Lots of things need lots of room.
Counting lots of things needs a monster number.
Monster numbers need a lot of room.  Don't they?

What is the biggest number you know?
<u>54676766799999395593638683858684839658960864</u>
or something like this is the answer!

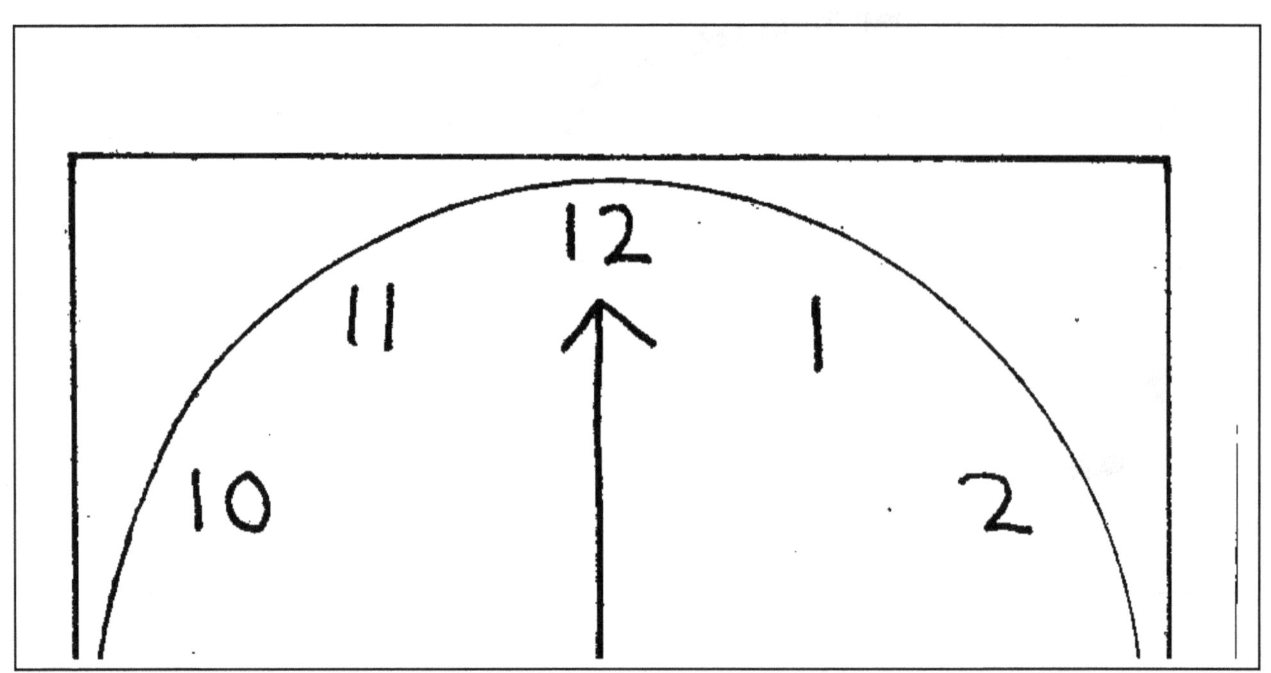

Your real bedtime!

Change John's day to make it as

**CRAZY** as you like ...

Any crazy times will do but take care drawing the hands on the clocks!

Don't be late asking the time!
That's the answer!

**CRAZY BABY!**
thinks it's always Sunday

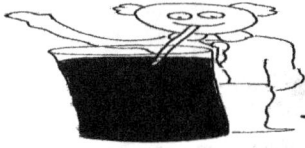

Why? It's because there are 7 days in a week. Have fun playing it's always Monday, it's always Tuesday, it's always Wednesday, it's always Thursday, it's always Friday and it's always Saturday!!

# CARDBOARD CASTLES

Draw the very best castle you can!
Use the words under, over, inside, behind and in front when you play.

You should win.
Cardboard boxes can't fight!

**CRAZY BABY!**
Meets a Shape family

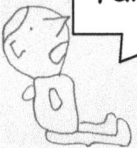

Do you know someone who looks like a triangle?

I can't think of anyone who looks like that!

# Silly People!!!

| Silly | 1 |
|---|---|
| Not Silly | 2 |
| Everyone | 3 |

| Silly | 2 |
|---|---|
| Not Silly | 3 |
| Everyone | 5 |

| Silly | 5 |
|---|---|
| Not Silly | 6 |
| Everyone | 11 |

It's OK if you don't agree with me. Maybe you thought different people were silly.

Have a good party!
That's the answer!

Space ship tens  Tree units

CRAZY BABY!
Plays tens and units

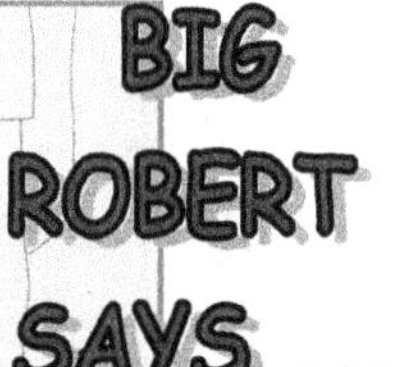

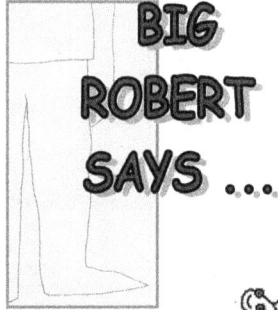

BIG ROBERT is the best

... at not telling anyone the answers!!

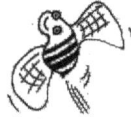

Colour in Charlie the monkey.

Colour in Kilo.

Colour in Milli

| Sue | Anne | Bill | Granddad |
|---|---|---|---|
| John | Anne's mum | Betty | Kilo |

| Anne | Bill | Granddad |
|---|---|---|
| Anne's mum | Betty | Kilo |

| Bill | Granddad |
|---|---|
| Betty | Kilo |

| Granddad |
|---|
| Kilo |

2 5 6 7 33 49 66 80

80 66 49 33 7 6 5 2

**CRAZY BABY!**

Jumps to his birthday

If your birthday was a lot of jumps away then very well done for doing all that jumping!!

## 12 John's Ice Creams

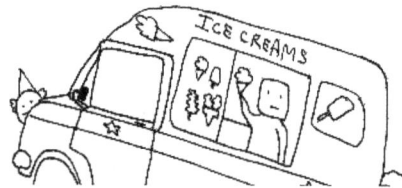

Anne has less than John. John has more than Sue.

Sue has the same as Anne. Anne has the same as Sue.

Sue has less than Betty. Betty has more than Sue.

Betty has more than Anne. Anne has less than Betty.

| Draw the pictures for this story. | | |
|---|---|---|
| Anything that means 8 | Anything that means +2 | Anything that means 10 |

Write the story for these pictures.

John has 2 ice creams.
He drops 1 ice cream.
John has 1 ice cream.

or

Has 2.
Drops 1.
Has 1.

Write the sum for this happy
sad happy ice cream story.

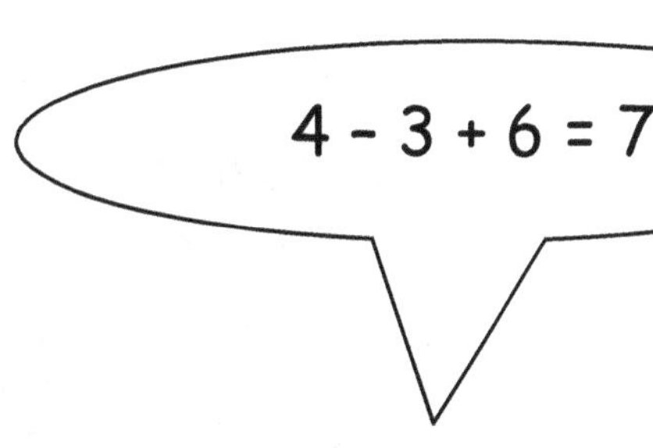


Write the story for this sum
8 - 8 + 3 - 3 + 10 - 4 - 3 + 2 - 1 - 4 = 0
It is going to be a long one!!

<u>Has 8</u>. <u>Drops 8</u>. <u>Given 3</u>. <u>Drops 3</u>. <u>Given 10</u>. <u>Drops 4</u>. <u>Drops 3</u>. <u>Given 2</u>. <u>Drops 1</u>. <u>Drops 4</u>. <u>Has 0</u>.
or the extended language version:-
John has 8 ice creams. He drops 8 ice creams. ...

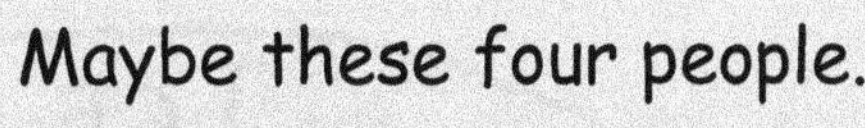

Maybe these four people.

| Sue | my sister | my dad | John |
|---|---|---|---|

Maybe these four things.

| head | hairs | ice creams | pencils |
|---|---|---|---|

3 + 5 = 8

My dad has 3 hairs on his head and he grew 5 more. Now he has 8 hairs!

6 + 12 - 7 = 11

John has 6 ice creams and Sue gave him 12 more. He drops 7. Now he has 11.

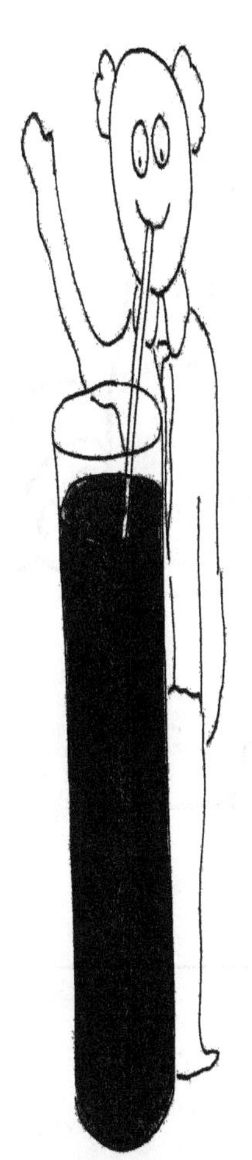

$1 - 1 + 3 + 20 - 6 = 17$

My sister gave me a pencil.

Then she took a pencil back.
Then she gave me 3 pencils.
Then she gave me 20 pencils.
Then she took 6 pencils back.
She is a **CRAZY** sister!!
I have 17 pencils now.

Listens to Betty's Story

# number
number

ICE CREAMS

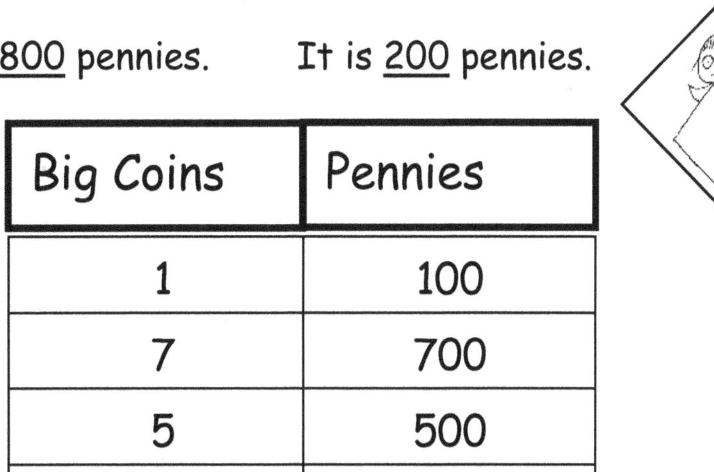

It is 800 pennies. It is 200 pennies.

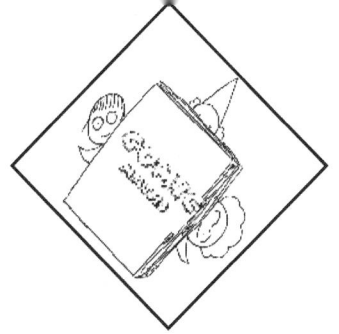

| Big Coins | Pennies |
|---|---|
| 1 | 100 |
| 7 | 700 |
| 5 | 500 |
| 11 | 1100 |
| 10 | 1000 |
| 6 | 600 |
| 9 | 900 |
| 12 | 1200 |
| 17 | 1700 |
| 22 | 2200 |

How many pennies in half a big coin? 50

| Big Coins | Pennies |
|---|---|
| $\frac{1}{2}$ | 50 |
| $1\frac{1}{2}$ | 150 |
| $2\frac{1}{2}$ | 250 |
| $3\frac{1}{2}$ | 350 |
| $9\frac{1}{2}$ | 950 |
| $6\frac{1}{2}$ | 650 |
| $8\frac{1}{2}$ | 850 |
| $12\frac{1}{2}$ | 1250 |
| $17\frac{1}{2}$ | 1750 |
| $22\frac{1}{2}$ | 2250 |

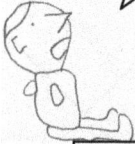

Counts past
THE HUNDREDS

98 99 100 101 102
198 199 200 201 202
298 299 300 301 302
398 399 400 401 402

# BAD GIRL BETTY

| | |
|---|---|
| 1 + 1 = 2 | 4 + 4 = 8 |
| 2 + 8 = 10 | 6 + 3 = 9 |
| 4 + 7 = 11 | 5 + 3 = 8 |
| 9 + 1 = 10 | 2 + 4 = 6 |
| 3 + 3 = 6 | 3 + 2 = 6 |
| 7 + 7 = 14 | 6 + 4 = 10 |
| 6 + 2 = 8 | 7 + 2 = 9 |
| 4 + 2 = 6 | 4 + 5 = 9 |
| 8 + 3 = 11 | 7 + 3 = 10 |
| 4 + 1 = 5 | 2 + 7 = 9 |

Do this sum really quickly while dancing! 6 + 5 = 11

Betty was a bad girl because ...?
Talk about this with a grown-up.

10 + 10 + 10 = 30
8 + 2 + 8 + 2 + 8 + 2 = 30
6 + 4 + 6 + 4 + 6 + 4 = 30
4 + 6 + 4 + 6 + 4 + 6 = 30
2 + 8 + 2 + 8 + 2 + 8 = 30
10 + 10 + 10 = 30 Nice pattern!

CRAZY BABY!
Goes wider
and longer

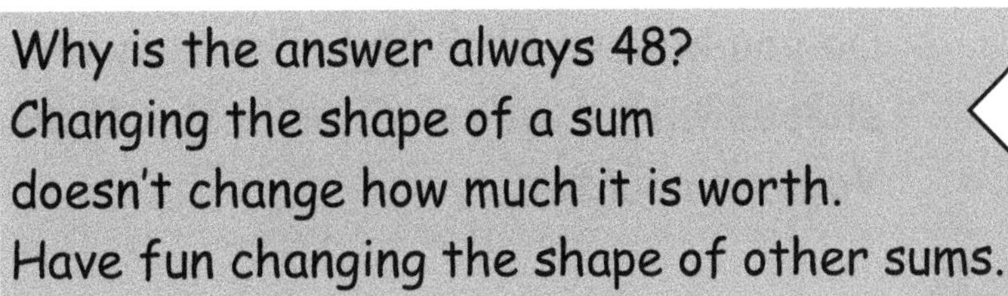

Why is the answer always 48?
Changing the shape of a sum
doesn't change how much it is worth.
Have fun changing the shape of other sums.

Tall Questions
The monster is 7 John's tall.
Granddad is 2 John's tall.

Heavy Questions
Kilo is lots and lots and lots Millis heavy.
Anne is 4 Millis heavy.

Drink Questions
Granddad's drink is 100 John drinks.
You know what size of drink would stop you being thirsty?

Flat Questions
Bill's shop window is 16 smiley face squares.
You know the area of the biggest window in your house?
You know the area of the smallest window in your house?

Here are some names I made up.
My made up name for a small thing is an elephant
My made up name for a big thing is a mouse
10 elephants = 1 mouse
but it could have been 10 sausages= 1 butterfly
or 10 houses = 1 pencil or something else!

Big Robert was the biggest. Why? We measured everyone to see who was the biggest. Big Robert got the biggest number so he won!

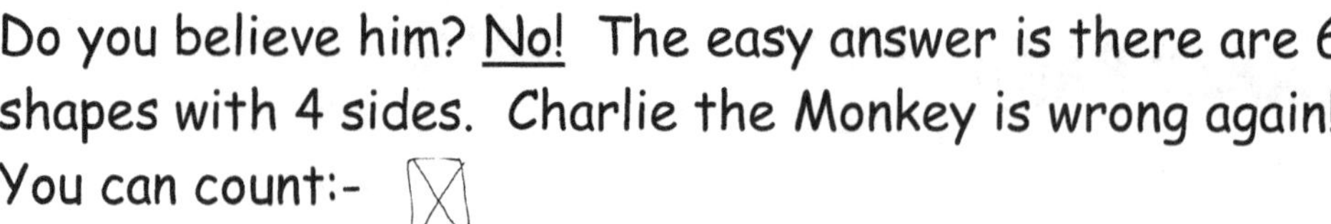

Do you believe him? <u>No!</u> The easy answer is there are 6 shapes with 4 sides. Charlie the Monkey is wrong again! You can count:-

ROUND bottom!

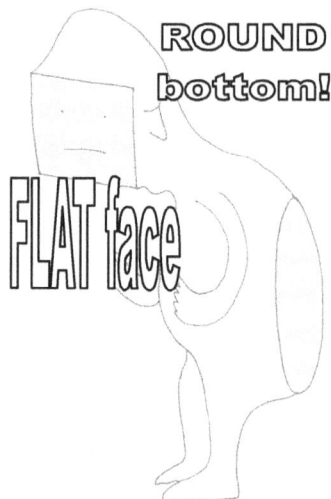

FLAT face

... but is this 1 shape with 4 sides or 4 shapes with 3 sides? Things like this can be good to talk about!!

Floors and walls have flat faces.
A glass you drink out of and a football have round bottoms.
Look around and see what you can see. Talk about it.

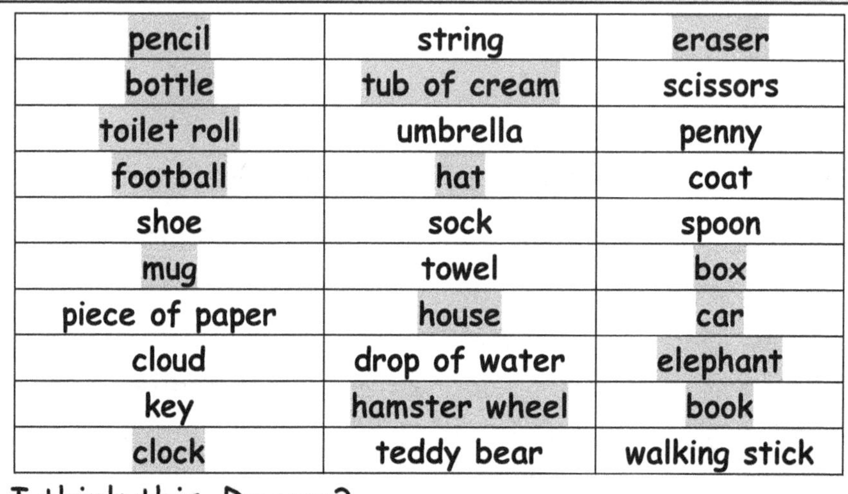

| | | |
|---|---|---|
| pencil | string | eraser |
| bottle | tub of cream | scissors |
| toilet roll | umbrella | penny |
| football | hat | coat |
| shoe | sock | spoon |
| mug | towel | box |
| piece of paper | house | car |
| cloud | drop of water | elephant |
| key | hamster wheel | book |
| clock | teddy bear | walking stick |

I think this. Do you?

| | | |
|---|---|---|
| pencil | string | eraser |
| bottle | tub of cream | scissors |
| toilet roll | umbrella | penny |
| football | hat | coat |
| shoe | sock | spoon |
| mug | towel | box |
| piece of paper | house | car |
| cloud | drop of water | elephant |
| key | hamster wheel | book |
| clock | teddy bear | walking stick |

I think this? Do you?

## CRAZY BABY!

Goes upside down

Do you like things upside down?
I hope you said yes!!
If a job doesn't work the right way up then try upside down, back to front or inside out .... some really good maths is done like this!

17

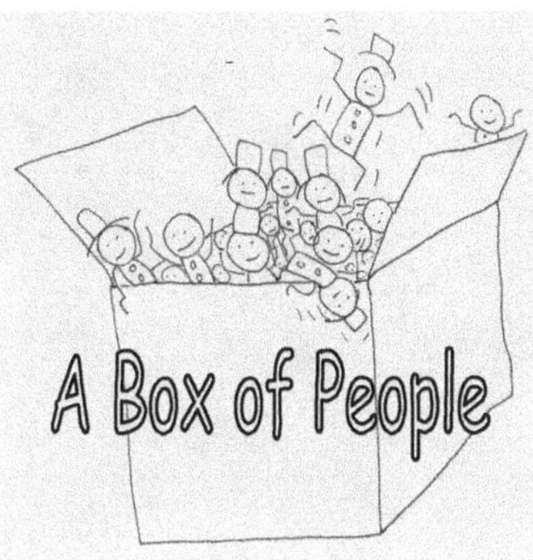


| Have a hat | 14 |
|---|---|
| Don't have a hat | 4 |

| 3 buttons | 10 |
|---|---|
| 2 buttons | 6 |
| 1 button | 2 |

| | 1 button | 2 buttons | 3 buttons |
|---|---|---|---|
| Hat | 2 | 3 | 9 |
| No hat | 0 | 3 | 1 |

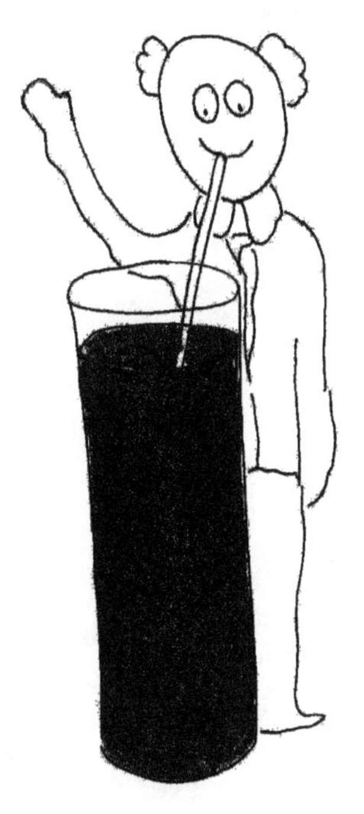

Asks about
100

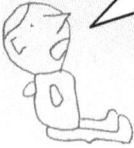

I hope you said

but if you said

then that's good too. Keep on playing!
You will wonder about it one day.

but I'm still NOT telling you the answers!!

40
20
20
70

<u>100</u>
200
100
200

**CRAZY BABY!**

Makes John think

What stretches your brain?
Anything that is really hard to understand.
Writing its name could be a first step to sorting this brain stretcher out!

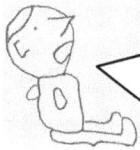

3 6 9 12 15 18 21 24 27 30 33 36

| | | |
|---|---|---|
| 1 x 1 = 1 | 1 x 2 = 2 | 1 x 3 = 3 |
| 2 x 1 = 2 | 2 x 2 = 4 | 2 x 3 = 6 |
| 3 x 1 = 3 | 3 x 2 = 6 | 3 x 3 = 9 |
| 4 x 1 = 4 | 4 x 2 = 8 | 4 x 3 = 12 |
| 5 x 1 = 5 | 5 x 2 = 10 | 5 x 3 = 15 |
| 6 x 1 = 6 | 6 x 2 = 12 | 6 x 3 = 18 |
| 7 x 1 = 7 | 7 x 2 = 14 | 7 x 3 = 21 |
| 8 x 1 = 8 | 8 x 2 = 16 | 8 x 3 = 24 |
| 9 x 1 = 9 | 9 x 2 = 18 | 9 x 3 = 27 |
| 10 x 1 = 10 | 10 x 2 = 20 | 10 x 3 = 30 |
| 11 x 1 = 11 | 11 x 2 = 22 | 11 x 3 = 33 |
| 12 x 1 = 12 | 12 x 2 = 24 | 12 x 3 = 36 |

| | | |
|---|---|---|
| 1 x 4 = 4 | 1 x 5 = 5 | 1 x 6 = 6 |
| 2 x 4 = 8 | 2 x 5 = 10 | 2 x 6 = 12 |
| 3 x 4 = 12 | 3 x 5 = 15 | 3 x 6 = 18 |
| 4 x 4 = 16 | 4 x 5 = 20 | 4 x 6 = 24 |
| 5 x 4 = 20 | 5 x 5 = 25 | 5 x 6 = 30 |
| 6 x 4 = 24 | 6 x 5 = 30 | 6 x 6 = 36 |
| 7 x 4 = 28 | 7 x 5 = 35 | 7 x 6 = 42 |
| 8 x 4 = 32 | 8 x 5 = 40 | 8 x 6 = 48 |
| 9 x 4 = 36 | 9 x 5 = 45 | 9 x 6 = 54 |
| 10 x 4 = 40 | 10 x 5 = 50 | 10 x 6 = 60 |
| 11 x 4 = 44 | 11 x 5 = 55 | 11 x 6 = 66 |
| 12 x 4 = 48 | 12 x 5 = 60 | 12 x 6 = 72 |

1 x 7 = 7
2 x 7 = 14
3 x 7 = 21
4 x 7 = 28
5 x 7 = 35
6 x 7 = 42
7 x 7 = 49
8 x 7 = 56
9 x 7 = 63
10 x 7= 70
11 x 7= 77
12 x 7= 84

1 x 8 = 8
2 x 8 = 16
3 x 8 = 24
4 x 8 = 32
5 x 8 = 40
6 x 8 = 48
7 x 8 = 56
8 x 8 = 64
9 x 8 = 72
10 x 8 = 80
11 x 8 = 88
12 x 8 = 96

1 x 9 = 9
2 x 9 = 18
3 x 9 = 27
4 x 9 = 36
5 x 9 = 45
6 x 9 = 54
7 x 9 = 63
8 x 9 = 72
9 x 9 = 81
10 x 9 = 90
11 x 9 = 99
12 x 9 = 108

1 x 10 = 10
2 x 10 = 20
3 x 10 = 30
4 x 10 = 40
5 x 10 = 50
6 x 10 = 60
7 x 10 = 70
8 x 10 = 80
9 x 10 = 90
10 x 10 = 100
11 x 10 = 110
12 x 10 = 120

1 x 11 = 11
2 x 11 = 22
3 x 11 = 33
4 x 11 = 44
5 x 11 = 55
6 x 11 = 66
7 x 11 = 77
8 x 11 = 88
9 x 11 = 99
10 x 11 = 110
11 x 11 = 121
12 x 11 = 132

1 x 12 = 12
2 x 12 = 24
3 x 12= 36
4 x 12 = 48
5 x 12 = 60
6 x 12 = 72
7 x 12 = 84
8 x 12 = 96
9 x 12 = 108
10 x 12 = 120
11 x 12 = 132
12 x 12 = 144

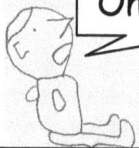

CRAZY BABY!
One times one

1 x 1 = 1

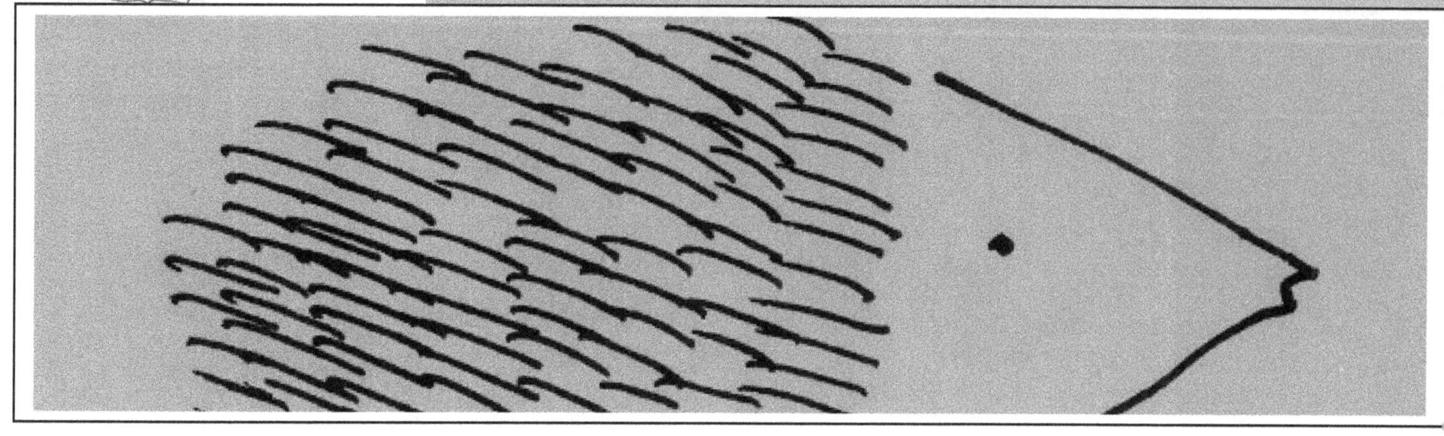

## Granddad's Sharing Hands

They have 1 each.
They have 2 each.
They have 3 each.
They have 4 each.

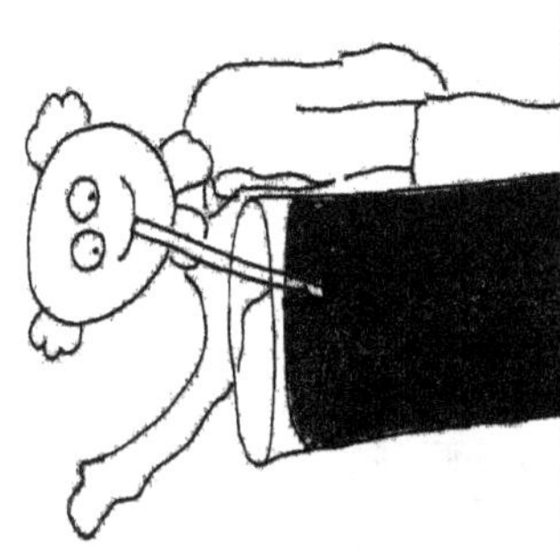

| | | |
|---|---|---|
| 6 between 2 | easy | $8 \div 2 = 4$ |
| 6 between 5 | hard | $12 \div 3 = 4$ |
| 8 between 3 | hard | $6 \div 6 = 1$ |
| $15 \div 5$ | easy | $12 \div 6 = 2$ |
| $21 \div 2$ | hard | $24 \div 6 = 4$ |
| | | $48 \div 6 = 8$ |

| | |
|---|---|
| $30 \div 2 = 15$ | $60 \div 1 = 60$ |
| $36 \div 4 = 9$ | $60 \div 2 = 30$ |
| $40 \div 4 = 10$ | $60 \div 3 = 20$ |
| $63 \div 7 = 9$ | $60 \div 4 = 15$ |
| $56 \div 8 = 7$ | $60 \div 5 = 12$ |
| $0 \div 8 = 0$ | $60 \div 6 = 10$ |

**CRAZY BABY!**
Shares nothing

$0 \div 10 = 0$

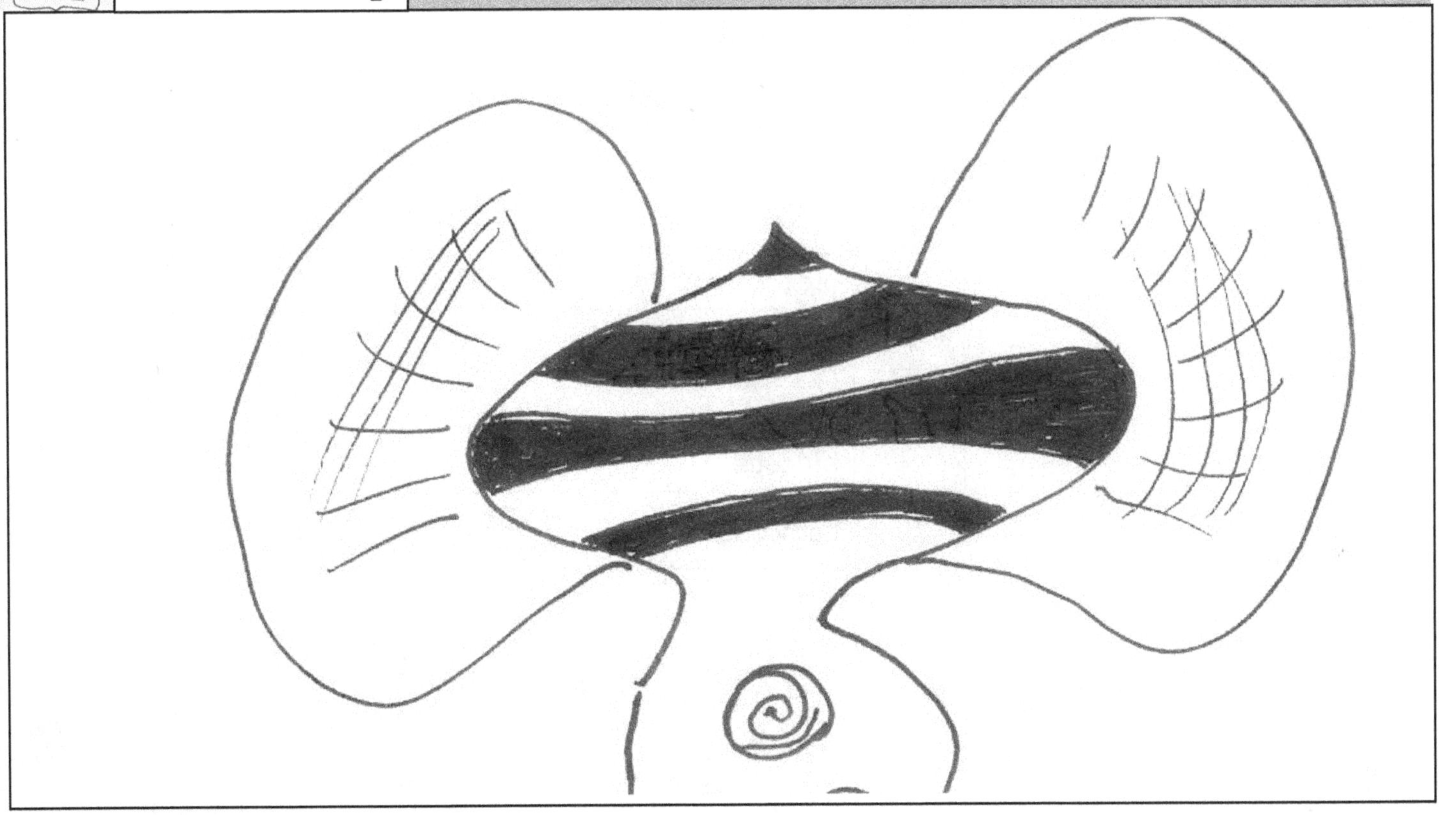

She should give Bill 100 pennies.
She should give Bill 100 pennies.
Charlie should give Bill 270 pennies.

3 things that cost 100 pennies altogether.
Birdcage, tin of paint and an apple.
There are others.

4 things that cost 100 pennies altogether.
Tin of paint, paint brush, banana and a set of pencils. There are others.

Hope you said yes!
I would buy a real submarine.

| Shopping List | | | |
|---|---|---|---|
| | | Pennies each | Pennies altogether |
| 1 | pea | 10 | 10 |
| 2 | carrots | 9 | 18 |
| 3 | hedgehogs | 8 | 24 |
| 4 | washing machines | 7 | 28 |
| 5 | footballs | 6 | 30 |
| 6 | pictures of Betty | 5 | 30 |
| 7 | dots | 4 | 28 |
| 8 | questions | 3 | 24 |
| 9 | hiccups | 2 | 18 |
| 10 | cobwebs | 1 | 10 |
| Costs this much altogether | | | 220 |

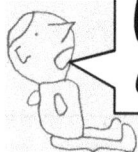

**CRAZY BABY!**
Goes shopping

**CRAZY BABY!** buys 55 things.

# Sue is five

and a half!!!

Nelly has $5\frac{1}{2}$ buns.
Gladys has $5\frac{1}{2}$ buns.
11 buns altogether.

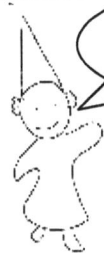

| | |
|---|---|
| $9\frac{1}{2} + \frac{1}{2} = 10$ | $\frac{1}{2} + \frac{1}{2} = 1$ |
| $8\frac{1}{2} + 1\frac{1}{2} = 10$ | $1\frac{1}{2} + 1\frac{1}{2} = 3$ |
| $7\frac{1}{2} + 2\frac{1}{2} = 10$ | $2\frac{1}{2} + 2\frac{1}{2} = 5$ |
| $6\frac{1}{2} + 3\frac{1}{2} = 10$ | $3\frac{1}{2} + 3\frac{1}{2} = 7$ |
| $5\frac{1}{2} + 4\frac{1}{2} = 10$ | $4\frac{1}{2} + 4\frac{1}{2} = 9$ |
| $\frac{1}{2} + \frac{1}{2} + \frac{1}{2} + \frac{1}{2} = 2$ | |
| $\frac{1}{2} + \frac{1}{2} + \frac{1}{2} + \frac{1}{2} + \frac{1}{2} + \frac{1}{2} = 3$ | |
| $\frac{1}{2} + \frac{1}{2} + \frac{1}{2} + \frac{1}{2} + \frac{1}{2} + \frac{1}{2} + \frac{1}{2} + \frac{1}{2} = 4$ | |
| $1\frac{1}{2} + 1\frac{1}{2} + 1\frac{1}{2} + 1\frac{1}{2} = 6$ | |
| $2\frac{1}{2} + 2\frac{1}{2} + 2\frac{1}{2} + 2\frac{1}{2} = 10$ | |
| $3\frac{1}{2} + 3\frac{1}{2} + 3\frac{1}{2} + 3\frac{1}{2} = 14$ | |
| $\frac{1}{2} + 1\frac{1}{2} + 2\frac{1}{2} + 3\frac{1}{2} + 4\frac{1}{2} + 5\frac{1}{2} = 18$ | |
| $10\frac{1}{2} - 1\frac{1}{2} + 2\frac{1}{2} - 3\frac{1}{2} + 4\frac{1}{2} - 5\frac{1}{2} = 7$ | |
| $\frac{1}{2} - \frac{1}{2} + \frac{1}{2} - \frac{1}{2} + \frac{1}{2} - \frac{1}{2} + \frac{1}{2} - \frac{1}{2} + \frac{1}{2} - \frac{1}{2} = 0$ | |

Halves a cherry cake

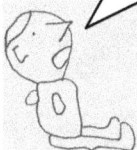

Yes! The cherry should be cut in half as well.

Colour in the pictures for:-

*The ice cream van is 6 meters long.*
*Betty weighs 10 stones.*
*The ice cream van weighs 1 ton.*
*John's drink is 1 litre.*
*John's leg is 60 cm long.*
*The monster is 7 John's high.*
*If 1000 millis get weighed they only weigh 1 gram.*
*Kilo runs 1000 meters and that is quite a long way.*

Find a carrot.
A measurement in cm or inches would be a very good answer.
A measurement in grams or ounces would be a very good answer.

A pint bucket will hold fewer apples than a gallon bucket.

Picture off the wall.
A measurement in cm or inches would be a very good answer. Long is bigger than wide.

Find a pullover.
Centimetre squares or inch squares would be a very good answer, but making squares of any size or even rectangles would be a good start! Big pullovers need lots of paper squares!

**CRAZY BABY!**
Say's "Alien is 2"

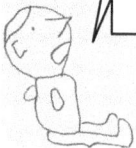

If ALIEN was shorter ...
how many houses tall would she be?
<u>1</u> house tall or <u>0</u> houses tall.

If ALIEN was heavier ....
how many tons would she weigh?
<u>3</u> tons heavy or more.

## Square

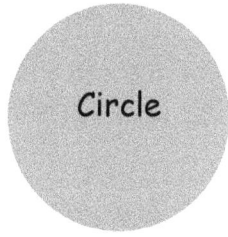

Circle

Square

Triangle

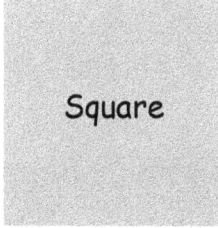

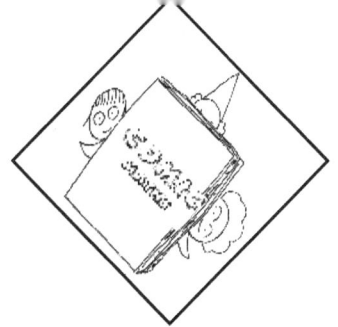

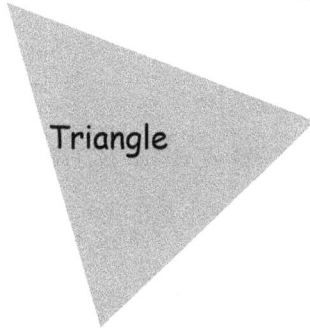

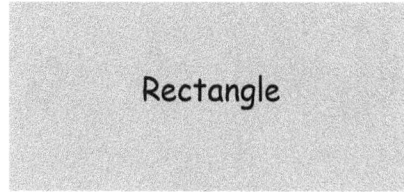

Rectangle

| |
|---|
| triangle |
| circle |
| rectangle |
| rectangle |
| circle |
| triangle |
| pentagon |
| square |
| hexagon |
| oval |
| pentagon |
| hexagon |
| circle |

Make up your own shape.
Any different closed shape will do but not a scribble!
You could call it any name that sounds like a shape's name.
'Circisquare' or 'sideagon' or just names like 'Sue' or 'Fred'.

CRAZY BABY!
Gets ...stung!!!!!

Buzzy Bee turns 7 times.

25

Your friends know the answers to these questions.

The Comic Maths Family

How many people think ice cream is?
Brilliant 5 people
OK 3 people
Horrible 2 people
And that's 10 people altogether.

## Comic Maths Bar Chart

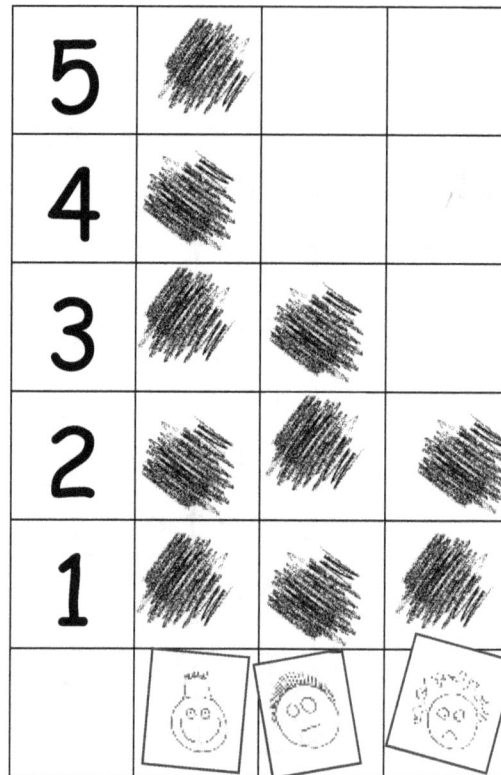

People

| | | | |
|---|---|---|---|
| 5 | | | |
| 4 | | | |
| 3 | | | |
| 2 | | | |
| 1 | | | |
| | | | |

Draw 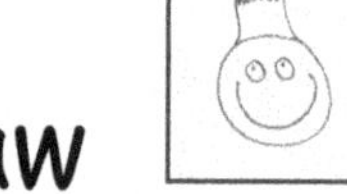

Your friends know the answers to these questions!

There are 14 pictures of me without pigtails.
28 of my pigtails are missing!!

Big Robert!

Big Robert!

Big Robert!

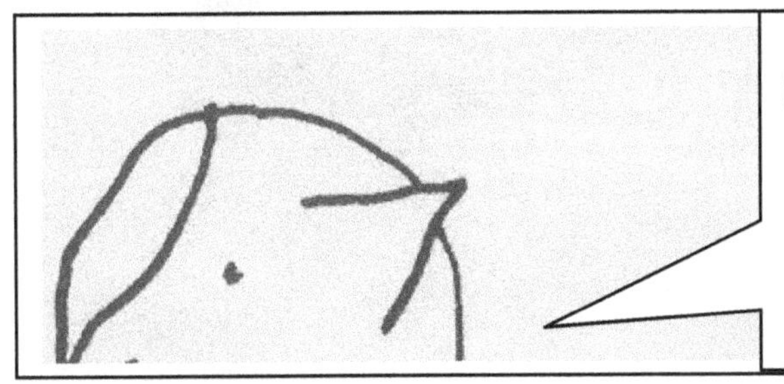


Don't worry! That's the answer

## A



## B

## C

## D



## E



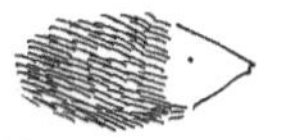

## L



## M



## N

## O



## P



## S



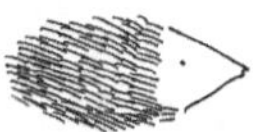

## T

www.ingramcontent.com/pod-product-compliance
Lightning Source LLC
Chambersburg PA
CBHW080323270326
41927CB00014B/3083

* 9 7 8 0 9 5 6 1 6 0 2 0 1 *